21/12/05

WATCHING WITH
THE SIMPSONS

Using our favorite Springfield family as a case study, *Watching with The Simpsons* examines the textual and social role of parody in offering critical commentary on other television programs and genres.

In this book, Jonathan Gray brings together textual theory, discussions of television and the public sphere, and ideas of parody and comedy. As a study, including primary audience research, it focuses on how *The Simpsons* has been able to talk back to three of television's key genres – the sitcom, ads, and the news – and on how it holds the potential to short-circuit these genres' meanings, power, and effects by provoking reinterpretations and offering more media literate recontextualizations.

Through examining television and media studies theory, the text of *The Simpsons*, and the show's audience, Gray attempts to fully situate the show's parodic humor within the lived realities of its audiences. In doing so, he further explores the possibilities for popular entertainment television – and particularly comedy – to discuss issues of political and social importance.

Jonathan Gray is Assistant Professor of Communication and Media Studies at Fordham University. His research and publications examine television and film textuality, audiences, and entertainment's contribution to the public sphere.

COMEDIA
Series Editor: David Morley

A GAME OF TWO HALVES
Football, Television and Globalisation
Cornel Sandvoss

HIDING IN THE LIGHT
On Images and Things
Dick Hebdige

HOME TERRITORIES
Media, Mobility and Identity
David Morley

IMPOSSIBLE BODIES
Femininity and Masculinity at the Movies
Chris Holmlund

THE KNOWN WORLD OF BROADCAST NEWS
Stanley Baran and Roger Wallis

MEDIA/THEORY
Thinking about Media and Communications
Shaun Moores

MIGRANCY, CULTURE, IDENTITY
Iain Chambers

THE PHOTOGRAPHIC IMAGE IN DIGITAL CULTURE
Edited by Martin Lister

THE PLACE OF MEDIA POWER
Pilgrims and Witnesses of the Media Age
Nick Couldry

THE POLITICS OF HERITAGE
The Legacies of 'Race'
Edited by Jo Littler and Roshi Naidoo

SPECTACULAR BODIES
Gender, Genre and the Action Cinema
Yvonne Tasker

STUART HALL
Critical Dialogues in Cultural Studies
Edited by Kuan-Hsing Chen and David Morley

TEACHING THE MEDIA
Len Masterman

WATCHING WITH
THE SIMPSONS

Television, parody, and
intertextuality

Jonathan Gray

R Routledge
Taylor & Francis Group

NEW YORK AND LONDON

First published 2006
by Routledge
270 Madison Avenue, New York, NY 10016

Simultaneously published in the UK
by Routledge
2 Park Square, Milton Park, Abingdon, Oxon, OX14 4RN

Routledge is an imprint of the Taylor & Francis Group

© 2006 Jonathan Gray

Typeset in Perpetua by
Keystroke, Jacaranda Lodge, Wolverhampton
Printed and bound in Great Britain by
The Cromwell Press, Trowbridge, Wiltshire

British Library Cataloguing in Publication Data
A catalogue record for this book is available from the British Library

Library of Congress Cataloging in Publication Data
Gray, Jonathan.
    Watching with the Simpsons : television, parody, and intertextuality /
Jonathan Gray.
        p. cm. — (Comedia)
    Includes bibliographical references and index.
1. Simpsons (Television program) 2. Intertextuality. 3. Parody. I. Title.
II. Series.
    PN1992.77.S58G73 2005
    791.45′72—dc22   2005014164

ISBN10: 0–415–36203–2   ISBN13: 9–78–0–415–36203–0 (hbk)
ISBN10: 0–415–36202–4   ISBN13: 9–78–0–415–36202–3 (pbk)

To my father, Ian MacFarlane Gray,
for encouraging me to laugh at the absurd

CONTENTS

CONTENTS

ACKNOWLEDGMENTS

The research for this book was generously funded by the Arts and Humanities Research Board of the United Kingdom, and so my first debts of gratitude go to the AHRB for ensuring that my only debts are ones of gratitude. I must also thank my interview subjects, who kindly gave their time and ideas to Part III. I apologize if I misconstrued any of your meaning.

Considerable inspiration, friendship, and/or support came from many people during the course of this project, but I would like to give particular thanks to John Alberti, Diane Alters, Joanna Briggs, Bertha Chin, Kate Coyer, Boris Ewenstein, André Favilla, Susan Hazan, James Lull, Angela McRobbie, Fernanda Maio, Chris Neidl, Bill Schwarz, Tyler Shores, and Gareth Stanton. Thanks, too, go to Roger Silverstone and Justin Lewis, to Routledge's readers, and to Rebecca Barden, for their assistance and recommendations regarding the strange alchemy of turning a PhD dissertation into a book. Will Brooker, Matt Hills, and Jean Retzinger also kindly read sections, and offered great advice; as did Nick Couldry, whose continued support and enthusiasm has often given me energy and encouragement when most needed. Where the book veers off course, this is no doubt due to me ignoring the sage comments of all these people.

For contributing to the very lifeblood of the book and its writer during the long research and writing process, though, special thanks are warmly extended to David Morley, my family, and Monica Grant. David Morley has been a great inquisitor, supervisor, editor, and friend, shepherding book and writer to publication. Meanwhile, Anne, Ian, and Matthew Gray (and Luc, Shadow, and Copper!) have provided continual love and comfort, and given me a respite away from my books. Finally, I cannot thank Monica Grant enough: nobody was subjected to more of my worries about the book than her, and yet nobody has helped me overcome them more than her. Her love and her rationalism made so much of this possible.

INTRODUCTION

T HE EPISODE OF *THE SIMPSONS* CALLED 'E-I-E-I-D'OH!' begins with the entire Simpsons family – Homer, Marge, Bart, Lisa, and Maggie – sitting in a movie theatre. As they wait for *The Poke of Zorro* to start, they watch an Allied soldier storm the beaches of Normandy and charge a German, skewering him with a bayonet. The German falls over dead, and the Allied soldier reaches into his adversary's breast pocket to reveal a can of 'Buzz' Cola. A peppy voiceover announces, 'Buzz Cola: the taste you'll kill for,' before the dead German sits up to add, 'Available in ze lobby.' Then, as the movie begins, we are treated to several scenes of a swash-buckling blockbuster replete with cheesy dialogue and stereotypical characters. Inspired by the lead character's penchant for dueling, Homer spends the next few days challenging random people to duels, until finally a Southern gentleman accepts, causing Homer to flee in fear with his family to a never-before-mentioned family farm. As the family arrive at the ramshackle home, Homer gleefully announces, 'This is our big chance: the Simpsons will be reborn as a bunch of gap-toothed bumpkins!' Oblivious to the decrepit scene around them, Bart cheerfully pipes in, 'I'll dig an outhouse!' and Lisa exclaims, 'I'll weed the floor!' For her part, Marge adds with considerable pep, 'I'll repress the rage I'm feeling!' From there, the story continues through multiple other hoops until finally the family is safe to return home, and the episode ends with the farm and dueling Southerner behind them.

But how are we to make sense of such an episode, and what about *The Simpsons*, for that matter, has made so many laugh? Following in the great tradition of *Monty*

Python, *The Simpsons* excels in offering the nonsensical, as the sheer incongruity of, for instance, resurrecting cola-selling Nazis or action adventure films starring both King Arthur and Zorro is certainly responsible for much of the humor. Beyond the lunacy, however, the humor embodied in many of these events, and a humor that pervades *The Simpsons*, is deeply parodic, relying on our knowledge of other genres and texts – here, *Saving Private Ryan* or other war films, cola ads, Zorro, Hollywood blockbusters, and family sitcoms – in order to complete the joke. When we laugh at such parody, we are laughing at those other genres and texts as much as we are laughing at *The Simpsons*. The cola ad, for instance, scorns the proclivity of ads to use any gimmick to grab attention, regardless of the ethics: as an indignant Lisa asks incredulously, 'Do they really think cheapening the memory of our veterans will sell soda?' *The Poke of Zorro* ridicules the outlandishness of Hollywood blockbuster fare, along with its blatant historical inaccuracies that unite the Man in the Iron Mask and ninjas in nineteenth century Mexico. Meanwhile, the sitcom genre is mocked at multiple turns, as the excessive cheerfulness of sitcom families is toyed with, the seething anger that one might imagine the sitcom mother to harbor is suggested, and the genre's remarkable ability to end exactly where it started is playfully highlighted. In other words, to watch and laugh at such humor, we are not only watching *The Simpsons*: we are watching with *The Simpsons* – watching ads, Hollywood blockbusters, sitcoms, and countless other genres, and making sense of, interpreting, and (re)decoding them as we view.

A great deal of this parody makes it into everyday talk. Long before *The Oxford English Dictionary* officially added Homer's 'd'Oh!' to the English language, many of the show's jokes, maxims, and parodic sketches were in the common vernacular. *The Simpsons'* frequently bite-sized instances of parody and satire often find their way into all manner of conversations, from discussions regarding the news, nuclear power, or child-rearing, to police work, religion, and the treatment of elderly people. If we recount the Buzz Cola ad, or any other *Simpsons* parody, to a friend, once again we and our friend are watching with *The Simpsons*, laughing at and playing with discourses of genre, and indirectly discussing *and criticizing* other media forms. This process of indirect viewing, and hence the mechanics of parody, are the topic of this book, as I will argue that parody has great power and potential to write back to and even write over other texts and genres, to contextualize and recontextualize other media offerings, and thus to teach and engender a media literacy of sorts.

From textuality to intertextuality

To say this is to radically redefine textuality and the nature of how it works, and thus, in essence, this is a book about intertextuality. Particularly today, we find ourselves in an environment saturated with all manner of texts: there are texts in books, at bus stops, on football pitches, on the road side, on t-shirts, even shaved into people's heads, and there is the constant textuality available on television or the Internet. If anything, then, the stakes involved in understanding the nature, ontology, and phenomenology of textuality, and in ascertaining how texts network power, identity, effects and meaning, are only increasing. Often, though, the attempt to understand the text has taken the form of examining it as a singular, autonomous entity, and as a sealed packet of meaning. Another tradition of research has examined the interrelation between this packet of meaning and its audiences, seeing how an audience interacts with its contents after opening the packet. However, texts do not just interact with audiences: they interact with other texts, and as Johan Fornäs (1995, 2000) argues, an exciting and relatively new area of study for media scholars exists in examining the 'passages' and 'mediations' between texts. The singular text, by itself and studied in a vacuum, cannot truly help us, for 'the text itself' is an abstract, yet ultimately non-existent entity, wished into creation by analysts. The text can only ever exist through, inside, and across other texts, and through its readers, and in this book I will actualize this observation into a workable theory of textual meaning, power, effects, and activity. In short, I will chart precisely how we can 'watch' one text while seemingly watching another.

I will focus on one aspect and trajectory of intertextuality, namely what I call critical intertextuality. First, though, a certain amount of conceptual clarification of 'intertextuality' is needed. After all, intertextuality has become an increasingly popular buzzword, popping up in many indexes, tables of contents, and titles. To some, it is a mere synonym for deconstruction and/or post-structuralism (see Mai 1991), while to others it is another word for influence and allusion (see Iampolski 1998; Riffaterre 1990). Likewise, evaluations of it range from Bakhtin (1981, 1986) and Kristeva's (1980a, 1980b) excited appraisal of intertextuality as perpetual and liberating dialogue, to many critics of postmodernism, to whom it represents cultural 'exhaustion' (Sharrett 2002) and recycling, where 'everything is juxtaposable to everything else because nothing matters' (Gitlin 1988: 36). In some contexts, intertextuality refers to the infinitely open space of textual interaction (Barthes 1990; Collins 1992; Fiske 1989a), and in other contexts it simply means 'all texts considered.' Intertextuality, it seems, is powerfully chameleonic.

Particularly frustrating for an in-depth understanding of intertextuality, though, is the frequency with which — as buzzword — it is treated in a rushed and superficial manner. As Ellen Van Wolde (1989: 43) notes, many critics 'stretch their legs at the station of intertextuality but the question remains of how seriously they use their time to get acquainted with what this station has to offer.' In these pages, I will do more than stretch my legs, as I will suggest the degree to which the concept of intertextuality augments many media and television studies conceptions of textuality. For now, let me propose the working definition of intertextuality as 'the fundamental and inescapable interdependence of all textual meaning upon the structures of meaning proposed by other texts.' Issues of genre, aesthetics, identity, textual power, ideology, and audience reception all come together at the station of intertextuality, and I will be particularly concerned to see how this process works with televisual texts. Moreover, as opposed to focusing on the general system of intertextuality, I will examine how the above-listed issues are focused by texts with intertextual *intent*, by texts that aim themselves at other texts and genres, and that want us to read them through other texts or genres. As such, I will be focusing on televisual parody.

Parody and critical intertextuality

Hannah Arendt has stated that 'The greatest enemy of authority is contempt, and the surest way to undermine it is laughter' (quoted in Hull 2000: 64), and I will study the powers of parody to talk back to more authoritative texts and genres, to recontextualize and pollute their meaning-construction processes, and to offer other, 'improper,' and yet more media literate and savvy interpretations. In short, I will study parody as a critical form of intertextuality, and its talent at invading other texts and at criticizing them from within. As Laurent Jenny notes of inter-textuality, parody is 'a definitive rejection of the full stop' (1982: 60), a technique that disallows the comfortable closure of a single decoding and that demands further decoding, both of the already-read and of the yet-to-be-read. It is a form that speaks of form, that both reveals the hidden tricks and assumptions of its target genre(s), and, as Bakhtin observes:

> rips the word away from its object, disunifies the two, shows that a given straightforward generic word [. . .] is one-sided, bounded, incapable of exhausting the object; the process of parodying forces us to experience those sides of the object that are not otherwise included in a given genre.
>
> (Bakhtin 1981: 55)

As such, it seeks both to teach and to correct.

A governing dialectic in media and cultural studies in recent years has been the tension between the ideologically 'bad' media text and the potentially astute and resistive 'good' reader. However, here I will examine the role of critical inter-textuality in confusing this binary. Parody may be one of the most taken-for-granted and least-respected art forms, but it is also one of the oldest and potentially most powerful. Thus, in providing a more complex picture of the textual landscape whereby texts contest each other's meanings, I will show how parody works as an intertextual force to reevaluate, ridicule, and teach other genres. This process involves the reader of parody, both as individual and as member of an interpretive community, and so a theory of critical intertextuality allows not only for texts and texts, but also for texts and readers to interact in altogether more interesting and various ways than media scholarship has often proposed. Thus, a theory of critical intertextuality and parody stands to redefine for us the key figures of text, reader, and textual experience. Similarly, while many books and articles track what 'the media' say about race, class, gender, law, or many other issues, too little has been written on what the media say about the media, or on how various media texts comment upon the mechanics of other media texts and institutions (for a notable exception, see Couldry 2000, 2003). Ultimately, what are at stake are more detailed pictures of textual power, of the media's mediation of the media, and of the role of our world's seemingly infinite (inter)textuality.

This interest in textual interaction may seem wonderfully 'postmodern' (or awfully so, depending upon the reader's tastes). Indeed, intertextuality has often been talked of as an inherently postmodern strategy, and *The Simpsons* in particular has frequently been seen as inimical of postmodernism. However, intertextuality is endemic to all textuality, not just contemporary textuality, and thus I will avoid postmodernism as a frame in this book, largely because it can be distracting to a study of both intertextuality and parody. While intertextuality was born as a term around the same time as postmodernism, and hence is often seen as belonging to the same theoretical cohort, its presence throughout world literature makes it a considerably older process. Likewise, while *The Simpsons* relishes its self-referentiality and frequently engages in pastiche, my interest here lies in its parody – its critical intertextuality – and in those moments when it moves beyond mere postmodern play so as to criticize. Arch-theorist of postmodernism, Fredric Jameson (1984), famously pronounced the death of parody in a postmodern era, seeing it replaced by uncritical pastiche, but I will argue that parody is alive and thriving. *The Simpsons* provides us with numerous examples of postmodern pastiche – setting baby Maggie's escape from daycare to the music from *The Great Escape*, for instance – but it also offers significant parody, argument, and intertextual commentary. Post-Jameson, postmodern parody carries the stigma of being impotent and toothless, and so I find it more helpful to talk of parody and of intertextuality without the adjectival shackles of 'postmodern' slung around them, focusing instead on parody's potency and on its teeth.

The Simpsons and/as parody

Why focus on *The Simpsons*? Primarily, I turn to *The Simpsons* since it is global television's most prodigious and most well-known example of parody. For sheer density of parody, few others match it, as the average episode brings together multiple types of parody. Over its 350-plus episode career, the show has mocked most genres, and constantly returns, and hence adds to, its parodic critique of the sitcom, ads, and the news in particular. *The Simpsons* is watched by an estimated 60 million viewers weekly in 70 countries (Pinsky 2001: 2), and at the present time, after it first began as a full-fledged half-hour show on the Fox Network in January 1990, it is still part of a common cultural language. Turner's comment that, 'if there is a common cultural currency, it's got Homer Simpson's picture on it' (2004: 10) might smack of hyperbole, but the text is still widely talked about, as friends, colleagues, and strangers swap *Simpsons* jokes and parody, even among non-viewers all over the world. The show's parody is expansive, and is also, therefore, likely to be familiar at some level to most readers.

For those readers less schooled in the world of *The Simpsons*, the animated program follows the lives of Homer and Marge Simpson, their children Bart, Lisa, and Maggie, and the entire town of Springfield, USA (state debatable). Created by Matt Groening, of subversive cartoon *Life in Hell* fame, *The Simpsons* began as a series of animated shorts on *The Tracey Ullman Show* on April 19, 1987. Growing in popularity, the family were given their own Christmas special on December 17, 1989, and thereafter were given a full show. As I write, they are still with us, production personnel are now talking of continuing the run until at least 2009, and reruns will undoubtedly keep them on television long past that date. Since 1990, the show has shot to success. Debuting with a 12.4 Nielsens rating and a 26 per cent share, the program remains Fox Television's most successful premier to date. While rarely in the Nielsens top 10 any longer, the program is often in the top 25, and frequently tops its timeslot among the coveted 18–34 year olds demographic (Bonné 2003). Over 180 affiliates carry the show in the USA; over 250 stations air its immensely successful reruns in the USA and Canada (Pinsky 2001: 2), bringing its estimated syndication revenues to over $1 billion; and it has experienced similar success worldwide. In the United Kingdom, in 2002, Channel 4 wrestled broadcast rights away from BBC Two by agreeing to pay a reported £700,000 per episode (as opposed to BBC Two's old price of £100,000 per episode); the program regularly places highly in the BARB ratings; and it accounts for nearly one-fifth of Sky One's viewership and a substantial portion of its advertising revenue (Cassy and Brown 2003). Australia's love for the program led to a highly successful 16-day, round-the-clock marathon on Foxtel in 2000, and similar tales and figures from around the world testify to its popularity.

Beyond dollars and ratings points, though, the show has, as Turner (2004: 25) notes, tapped popular cultural 'resonance.' *Time* dubbed *The Simpsons* the best program of the twentieth century (cited in Owen 2000: 64), Homer Simpson has his own star on Hollywood Boulevard, and a 1999 Roper Starch Worldwide survey found that 91 per cent of American 10–17 year olds, and 84 per cent of adults could identify the Simpson family members (Pinsky 2001: 3). It is also one of television history's most highly respected texts, having received a Peabody Award, numerous Emmys, and considerable academic attention in the form of university courses (such as a hugely successful class at University of California, Berkeley), multiple essays (Alters 2003; Cantor 1999; Glynn 1996; J. Gray 2005c; Henry 1994; Hull 2000; Parisi 1993; Weinstein 1998), and a growing legion of books (Alberti 2004; Irwin *et al.* 2001; Pinsky 2001; Turner 2004). The show is a favorite pedagogical tool (see Hobbs 1998; Scanlan and Feinberg 2000), and receives considerable respect from many otherwise detractors of popular culture. While President George Bush Sr was vocal in his dislike of the show, calling for 'a nation closer to the Waltons than to the Simpsons,' British Prime Minister Tony Blair claims to be a fan, the Archbishop of Canterbury Rowan Williams has said the program is 'on the side of the angels' (BBC 2004), and the show's never-ending line of Hollywood celebrity and public figure guest stars (including Blair) is itself a clear sign of the program's hit status.

More than just popular, *The Simpsons* was in many ways an iconic show of the 1990s, and of a new style of parodic television. In her study of *Dallas*, Ang talked of that program as a modern myth and as a symbol of a particular age of television (Ang 1985: 1–2), and the same may be said of *The Simpsons*. Parody and irreverent humor are certainly no strangers to television, but *The Simpsons* seems to have ushered in a new era of ironically distanced and distancing humor, and of the *expectation* of such humor. Many of today's better parodies owe a debt to *The Simpsons*. Moreover, a great deal of its popularity is centered precisely on the fact that it is a parody, and is irreverent. When one finds *Simpsons* chips in England, for instance, bearing the show's debased corporate sellout, Krusty the Clown, his 'stamp of approval' (one that, in the show, adorns malfunctioning goods and disease-ridden candy), and a speech bubble announcing, 'I heartily endorse this event or product,' it becomes obvious that part of what *The Simpsons* is selling, part of its *raison d'être*, is parody. Consequently, a central reason behind my choice of *The Simpsons* as case study is that it is in some ways a front-runner for other televisual parodies and for the parodic humor that, from *South Park* to *The Daily Show with Jon Stewart*, is so prevalent in today's televisual lineup. It could claim such status, though, only if the program spoke to an audience who wanted its style of humor, and who responded to it. Therefore, *The Simpsons'* success can be seen as indicative of a parodic sensibility and a widespread desire for the criticism and ridicule upon which the program's humor frequently relies.

While *The Simpsons* is a show about a family, it is also a show about television. As the opening credit sequence ends, the Simpsons crowd around the television, and the final credits appear in the center of an animated television box, signaling that we as viewers are watching television with the Simpsons and with *The Simpsons*. Whereas few other television shows depict their characters watching television,[1] the Simpsons are frequently in front of the tube, the program regularly shows us what they are watching, and much of the dialogue follows their reactions to television. So much of the show and its characters' lives revolves around the television. Matt Groening has said that he uses the show to wake people up 'to some of the ways we're being manipulated and exploited' by modern American culture (quoted in Pinsky 2001: 133), and the manipulations of television are particularly central to the program, for as Groening has also said, *The Simpsons* is 'about watching television' (quoted in Pinsky 2001: 147). As I will examine in Part II, *The Simpsons* relentlessly ridicules and mocks the aesthetics, structure, and logic of the traditional American family sitcom, ads and promotional culture, and the news. The show 'deconstructs and informs the media soup of which it is a part' (Rushkoff 2004: 296) by intently focusing its critical eye on exactly how television speaks and how we listen.

The business of parody

However, *The Simpsons* is also big business, and if it is critical of commercial television, it is also one of commercial television's favorite children. With its ratings and popularity come lots of money for its creators and for Fox and parent company News Corporation. The show has contributed well over one billion dollars' worth of revenue to Fox in direct proceeds alone (Chocano 2001). Indirectly, *The Simpsons* is widely credited with getting Fox Television onto its feet as America's fourth network in the early 1990s, and in giving the network an identity, and a reputation for the new, ultra-cool, and hip. As Fox Television co-president Gary Newman told *Daily Variety* in 2000:

> *The Simpsons* was the guiding light that kept us motivated and believing that our division would grow. What may never happen again is another show that comes along and has the overall importance to a particular company like *The Simpsons* has had for [Fox parent] News Corp.
>
> (quoted in Chocano 2001)

With the central position in media studies demonology that Rupert Murdoch occupies, we must therefore acknowledge *The Simpsons'* complicity in allowing this fearful figure to rise from the dark. Much academic theory on fandom and cult television posits the beloved text as somehow outside the mainstream (see Hills 2002), but as Brooker notes of the parallel exception of the *Star Wars* films, *The Simpsons* 'inspires the devotion of a cult, yet is far too big, too successful, too current, to fit that term's usual definition' (Brooker 2002: xv). Consequently, as well-written and popular a parody as it is, it is simultaneously a powerful limb of an even more powerful capitalist giant. Meanwhile, its economic role extends to the plethora of merchandise that has sprung from its loins. Hundreds of *Simpsons* products exist worldwide, from bowling balls to asthma inhalers, car floor mats to computer games. *Simpsons* merchandise sales totaled $750 million by the end of 1990 alone (Turner 2004: 25) and t-shirt sales are estimated to bring in $20 million each year (Bonné 2003), leading Peter Byrne, Fox's Executive Vice-President of Licensing and Merchandising, to observe that the show is 'without a doubt the biggest licensing entity that Fox has had, full stop' (Bonné 2003). Over 500 companies worldwide are licensed to use the *Simpsons* name, 96 per cent renew their licenses (Bonné 2003), and *Simpsons* characters can be found in the advertising world plugging everything from Mastercard to Burger King.

While to some readers, it may seem as though I am stacking the deck by discussing such a successful, well-written, and in some ways unique show, with a following matched by few others, as a case study of parody in action, the essential point is that *The Simpsons* also brings television parody's central dilemma into tight focus: economic complicity. As much as the show criticizes commercial television, and particularly as much as it gouges at ads and promotional culture, its success serves as fuel for the system, and its merchandising and advertising wing has made *The Simpsons* into exactly the type of brand that the show regularly derides. Consequently, by examining *The Simpsons'* navigation of the dark waters of complicity, and, further, by examining how audiences respond to this apparently blatant hypocrisy, we can study how parody avoids becoming a key supporter for that which it mocks, and we can better interrogate the nature of the complex relationship between intertextual attacker and target. Overall, though, here I study parody's *potential*. Thus, the *Simpsons* case study is illustrative of central issues – such as complicity and the role and powers of humor – that face most parody. I use *The Simpsons* not to give a definitive account of the program, but to show parody in action, and to discuss its abilities, its obstacles, and what it can tell us about contemporary television.

Contextualizing *The Simpsons*

Given *The Simpsons'* iconic status and infusion into popular culture around the world, one could study the program from any number of angles and still only scratch the surface of its cultural resonance. However, this book makes no promise to offer a complete picture; rather, it focuses on *The Simpsons* as a means of illustrating the peculiar powers of televisual parody, and, hence, the importance of an intertextual mode of textual and sociological analysis. The focus is on how *The Simpsons* talks to and about other texts and genres, and, as such, elements of the program that some readers regard as of great value may be underplayed. Other scholars could meaningfully examine *The Simpsons* from a political economic standpoint; as ushering in a certain moment in the history of animation; as auteur television; as hub of one of television history's most heavily merchandised texts; as postmodern mélange and pastiche; and/or as commentator on American society. While this study will touch upon all of these modes, it will not, for instance, engage in a production analysis seeking to show how such a text was able to emerge; nor will it detail animation history pre- or post-*Simpsons* (see Stabile and Harrison 2003; Wells 1998); discuss Matt Groening's personal vision for the program at length (see Chocano 2001; Doherty 1999); track the armies of *Simpsons* spinoff products that populate stores worldwide; enter into the program's pastiche hall of mirrors; or chart the program's views on religion (see Pinsky 2001), politics, or the American education system. I will also not be charting nuanced differences in reception between different countries, as fascinating as such study would be. Consequently, when I write of 'television,' I refer to an American commercial system of *delivery*, with the proviso that the sites, and hence contexts, of *reception* of that system are multiple and diverse (although, much international television content and regulation is increasingly mimicking this system anyway: see Hesmondhalgh 2002).

Why focus on the program's parodic intertextuality, though? When a text is as popular and as talked about as *The Simpsons*, there is a great risk that analysis will focus largely upon how it is an exception to the supposed rule of bland televisual normality. While *The Simpsons* has certainly proven to be unique, it operates not in a vacuum, but in a textual network of other programs. Moreover, much of its humor is deeply transitive, pointing outside the borders of *The Simpsons* to all manner of other genres, texts, and discourses. To laugh at these jokes is frequently to read those other genres, texts, and discourses as much as it is to read *The Simpsons*. *The Simpsons* talks about other texts, and if its jokes 'leak' out of the program – if we activate them in everyday discussion, if they force a reevaluation of other texts, or if we recall them when watching other texts – then it becomes important for us to study how and with what effect this parody attacks other textual forms and formats: we can no longer focus on *The Simpsons* alone. Textual studies have a long history of analyzing texts one-by-one, carefully respecting their boundaries, but when a text itself shows little care for these boundaries, neither must the textual analyst.

Ultimately, though, *The Simpsons* is by no means alone in moving beyond its borders. I have chosen to focus on it due to its popularity and to the sheer density of its intertextual commentary, but television is home to a surprisingly large number of parodies. All of these American and English shows, for instance – some better, some worse – are by some criteria either parodies or frequently adopt a parodic mode: *Monty Python's Flying Circus* (see Thompson 1982), *Saturday Night Live, Second City TV, Not the Nine O'Clock News, Spitting Image* (see Meinhof and Smith 2000), *The Muppet Show, Police Squad, Moonlighting, Quantum Leap, The Dave Letterman Show, Pee Wee's Playhouse* (see Caldwell 1995), *TV Nation, Married . . . with Children, The Tom Green Show, The Day Today, Kids in the Hall, Roseanne* (see Rowe 1994), *South Park,*

King of the Hill, Brasseye, Northern Exposure, The Larry Sanders Show, Ally McBeal, Have I Got News For You, The Conan O'Brien Show, MAD TV, Buffy the Vampire Slayer (see Wilcox and Lavery 2002), *Angel, The Awful Truth, Malcolm in the Middle, Da Ali G Show, Family Guy, The Sopranos* (see Lavery 2002), *V Graham Norton, Mr Show, The Office, The Daily Show with Jon Stewart, My Big Fat Obnoxious Fiancé, My Big Fat Obnoxious Boss, The Graham Norton Effect, Reno 911, Director's Commentary, Scrubs, Average Joe, TV Go Home, The Joe Schmo Show,* and *Drawn Together.* Doubtlessly, this list has missed many, and although it includes numerous shows no longer in production, many can still be found in syndication, on DVD, and/or bolstering a cable channel's prime-time schedule. And, of course, to these we could add the many parodic advertisements, movies, and music aired on television, as well as those moments when other programs wax parodic, a practice on the rise (see Lury 2001).

The fool at work

When done well, the parody plays fool to its generic king. Fools were common in medieval courts (Welsford 1935; Willeford 1969), and can be found in various forms internationally (Handelman 1998). When the king or other authority figure speaks and proclaims, then in his shadow, the fool counters. And because the fool is amusing and likely to make us laugh, we stay and listen. The fool's speech mocks the king's and highlights its errors, comfortable assumptions and rhetoric, and in doing so becomes the rogue (parodic) member of the royal (generic) family. As Bakhtin states of the 'merry rogue':

> Opposed to the language of priests and monks, kings and seigneurs, knights and wealthy urban types, scholars and jurists – to the languages of all who hold power and who are well set up in life – there is the language of the merry rogue, wherever necessary parodically re-processing any pathos but always in such a way as to rob it of its power to harm, 'distance it from the mouth' as it were, by means of a smile or a deception, mock its falsity and thus turn what was a lie into gay deception. Falsehood is illuminated by ironic consciousness and in the mouth of the happy rogue parodies itself.
>
> (Bakhtin 1981: 401–2)

In contrasting its own more playful, self-conscious language with the seemingly natural, taken-for-granted language of the king, and in commenting specifically on the king's statements, the fool can chip away at the king's authority and circulate counter hegemonic discourses that challenge the form and content of the king's authority. For their part, kings often hired fools to act as safety valves – to allow, but in doing so, to *contain* rebellion – but this is a dangerous gamble on a king's part, for we can never determine in advance if the semiotic challenge to authority will be controlled, or will escape control.

So too, then, with parody: parody can become a genre's other, responding to it, revising it, and drawing attention to its rhetoric, its constructedness, and to the audience's role in allowing this construction to work with such stealth. To wholly equate parody with the fool risks romanticizing its work, but it nevertheless proves an operational metaphor with which we can understand parody's relationship to its targets. After all, while Bakhtin writes of parodies 'destroy[ing] the thick walls that ha[ve] imprisoned consciousness' (1981: 60), and while I agree that parodies throw the balance of power into flux, their powers are more reformative than destructive or revolutionary. Indeed, many writers' discomfort with parody stems from this 'paradox of parody,' as Linda Hutcheon calls it (1985: 75), that parody is 'simultaneously conservative and subversive, simultaneously supportive and destructive of the status quo' (J. Palmer 1987: 12). The parody conducts its business on authority's ground, making raids on power and using specific genres' powers against themselves. Parody sets about the task of teaching media literacy in the very site where generic artifice must be challenged, and thus where viewers will have use for media literacy.

Of course, different parodies will work with their abilities to varying degrees of success, and many – perhaps most – will be weak and/or inconsequential. Moreover, since parody involves fool play, not foul play, it is never wholly antagonistic, and it can at times be either loving and reverential, or perceived as such. In this book, then, I will speak largely of *potential*, of parody's potential to mock, make us laugh, and teach all at once, and at no point do I claim to be sure of either *The Simpsons*' or any other parody's actual success with any or all specific audience members. Meanwhile, while the fool parallel is still relevant to today's parody and parodists, the 'court' has changed, and so this book examines the contemporary televisual fool and the contemporary televisual court, so as to ask what role parody plays in today's televisual lineup.

Studying television, parody, and intertextuality

A few prefacing remarks are required on the show's multiple levels and on my own position as analyst. To begin with, *The Simpsons* is not just parody. If viewers laugh, often these laughs will be not just at its parody, but also at its irony, at slapstick, at wordplay, at screwball or zany elements, and/or at its more grotesque moments. Thus, I do not at all wish to efface, for instance, Homer's 'Mmmm . . . donuts!' or Bart's mooning authority figures. I do, however, wish to focus on the parody within, and therefore will give these other elements short play. It should also be acknowledged that, as Dan Harries notes in his study of film parody, 'my own viewing (infused with the constant pausing and rewinding of the videotape) is one inscribed with possibly knowing the genre, the target and the parody in too much detail' (Harries 2000: 101). While I would not consider myself a manic fan of *The Simpsons*, this project has made one of me by default, and thus my own analysis perhaps risks focusing overmuch on minute details. To counter this, I have tried to keep analysis simple, and not engage in much deep close reading (I have not watched with Derrida and Lacan by my side). Moreover, although in Part II, I try to chart the variety of *The Simpsons*' parodic commentary, and thus quote from many episodes, in doing so, I am by no means suggesting that we regard all these quotations and scenes as a coherent and unified argument. An 'average' *Simpsons* viewer would be exposed to only some of this parody, and so analysis must therefore focus on 'bits,' rather than on a complete *oeuvre*.

I am using *The Simpsons* as case study, so as to tell three interrelated tales: of intertextuality, of parody, and of television. Thus, behind the illustrated examples of *The Simpsons* in action lie theories and arguments of the nature of intertextual practice, of the power of comedy and parody, and of the complexity of contemporary television and television studies. As such, the book argues for the necessity of more intertextual study, and attempts to show how rich and bountiful such study can prove; for a renewed appreciation of parody, and of its and comedy's peculiar yet often awesome powers; and of television's oft-underappreciated complexities, and of the medium's potential for parody and criticality. This is not three books in one, though, for I want to argue for the powerful interrelations between intertextuality, parody, and television. After all, parody is a form of intertextuality, and, as will be argued, all television is intertextual to some degree. Of course, one could question my ability to use one text for an intertextual study, and yet the focus is on this text's intertextual travels to and from other genres. Similarly, one might question how this text could be seen as in any way representative of parody or television. Following Gitlin's (1994) pessimism regarding good television, we could just see *The Simpsons* as a notable exception that proves the 'rules' of televisual standardization. Indeed, if *The Simpsons* were not exceptional, I would have little reason to write a book on it.

However, exceptions do not just prove rules: they create them. A judge who rules against prior rulings creates precedent, and so too with *The Simpsons*: if it has been an exception to the 'rules' of parody and/or television, its remarkable and sustained success creates precedent, and suggests deep rifts of either faulty logic or internal problems within those 'rules.' *The Simpsons* is not just a blip on television history's map — it is one of the longest running, most beloved, and recognized shows. Thus, as Gitlin himself outlines in arguing that television is a 'recombinant' medium, where one innovator goes, countless others will *and can* follow. *The Simpsons*, for instance, created room for *South Park*, *Family Guy*, *King of the Hill*, *Malcolm in the Middle*, and several other outstanding television parodies. Instead of seeing *The Simpsons* as wholly unique and irregular, then, I argue that its success shows lines of intertextual, parodic, and televisual practice that exist and that can be followed by others.

Structure

Part I starts by setting the backdrop for parody's inner mechanics, establishing how intertextuality works. Chapter 1 examines how others in literary, film, media, and television studies have used intertextuality, but I then propose my own model of intertextual practice. Part II follows this model and presents three case studies of parody in *The Simpsons*. First, focusing on the program's attack on the American traditional family sitcom, Chapter 2 examines how genre is, at root, a form of intertextuality that brings multiple texts together in a dialogue that can ultimately destabilize any of these texts' meaning-making processes by parody. Thus, the chapter studies how parody undercuts generic strategies, codings, and logic so as to surreptitiously add further meanings and reform a genre through ridiculing it. In Chapter 3, I turn to *The Simpsons'* parodic ridicule of advertising and promotional culture, in order to illustrate how parody works with televisual form. Television is often spoken of as a realm of perpetual commodification, consumption, promotion, and hypercommercialism, yet in Chapter 3, I examine the medium's fundamental porosity, and hence vulnerability to parodic attack, and to strategic anti-consumerist raids. As with all texts, ads and any of television's hypercommecialized messages can be made sense of only in their full intertextual setting, and so I examine what parody might contribute to our decoding of ads and of the televisual environment. Building on previous discussion, Chapter 4 then argues that parody is a vital contributor to and even moderator of the public sphere, one that teaches media form and content from within the media. Focusing on how *The Simpsons* parodically attacks the news, the chapter takes aim at some of the binaries that television studies too easily rests upon at times, such as serious exposition and 'mere entertainment,' inculcation and education, public-spirited information and bread-and-circuses spectacle, and high and low culture, so as to argue for parody's and comedy's powers as media literacy educators of sorts.

However, neither parody nor intertextuality can work through text alone, and so Part III examines *The Simpsons'* parody as a lived and socialized sensibility, and explores its workings within interpretive communities, before closing with a discussion of how its audiences make sense of and value it. As such, Chapters 5 and 6 look at intertextuality's journeys through talk, examining the intertext beyond the text; intertextuality's actualization in the lived realities of audiences and, by extension, television's role in everyday life; and the contributions to meaning and value that occur at the level of consumption. Part III represents qualitative audience research conducted with 35 viewers. With a sample of such a size, it would be ludicrous to suggest these responses are 'representative' (if *The Simpsons* could even be said to have 'representative' viewing responses). Thus, I consult them not to provide 'proof' of my assertions, but rather to open a window to the consumption – through interpretive communities – of *The Simpsons* and its parody, and to televisual (inter)textuality as sociological and discursive practice. I also hold off discussion of many of the criticisms of parody and comedy until Part III, as my audience research subjects often addressed these directly. Finally, I conclude the book with some observations on parody beyond *The Simpsons*.

Part I

READING THROUGH INTERTEXTUALITY

Chapter 1

INTERTEXTUALITY AND THE STUDY OF TEXTS

B EHIND PARODY, MOTORING ITS COMEDY AND SEMIOTICS at a basic, fundamental level, is intertextuality. Thus, any attempt to explain the theoretical,
comic, or political powers of *The Simpsons* specifically, or of parody more generally,
must be preceded by adequate theorization of how intertextuality works. Before
closely examining *The Simpsons* and its parody, as I will in Part II, then, we must first
establish *how* one text can comment on and talk to another. Hence, this chapter will
detail what intertextuality is, how texts interact, and why television and media
studies scholarship could benefit from more use of an intertextual mode of practice.

The divine text in textual studies history

However, given that academia has added intertextuality to its vocabulary and critical
repertoire only since the early 1970s, any discussion of television and intertextuality must itself be preceded by a brief archaeology of academic understanding of
the text, so as to figure out why intertextuality has arrived so late in textual studies
history. After all, as Foucauldian discourse theory informs us, the ways in which
we delimit or conceive of a field feed back into how we study it and into what data
or 'knowledge' the field will produce (Foucault 1972). Textual studies have a long
history of festishizing the text as a solitary, pristinely autonomous object, and this
notion of textuality has exerted considerable pressure particularly on literary and

film studies, but also on media and television studies. Even now, intertextuality is often invoked in a merely hit-and-run manner, without its full ramifications for televisual form and phenomenology of reception being carefully considered. As is evident in the use of literary studies terminology of 'texts' and 'readers' to describe anything from blue jeans to television programs, media and television studies are in many ways outgrowths of literary studies, with the latter's mental framings often still in place. The primacy of the text, and many scholars' presumptions that it *could* be studied alone, reveals a dense history of overly text-centric analysis that any intertextual theory must move beyond.

So what has the text historically meant to literary studies? Wordsworth and Coleridge's 1798 publication of *Lyrical Ballads* represents a landmark in literary studies and poetics' conceptions of text, author, and reader, and hence a useful starting point. In the book's preface (Wordsworth 1991), and in subsequent apologias for poetry by Coleridge (1991) and Shelley (1991), the English Romantics posited poetry as a thing divine. '[E]ndowed with a more lively sensibility, more enthusiasm and tenderness [and . . .] a more comprehensive soul' (Wordsworth 1991: 264), the poet was figured as a conduit for divine inspiration and 'the spontaneous overflow of powerful feeling' (1991: 260), or as a wind harp over which divine inspiration played (see Shelley 1991: 260). The Romantics thus denied any influence from previous writers and asserted the text's utter uniqueness. Meanwhile, the text's supposedly inherent boundaries were asserted by cutting off all connection to the reader. Theorists from Plato and Aristotle onward have frequently assumed reader response and refused readers any ability to construct meaning themselves, but the Romantics removed the reader altogether. To Wordsworth, the poet did not write to be read, and as such, the reader became irrelevant. Instead, fetishized as the locus of genius and enlightenment, the text and its creator pair of God and Author were the alpha and omega of textuality.

This view of poetry as pure benevolence carried through the Victorian era largely unchanged (see, for instance, M. Arnold 1978), and crystallized into discipline with the founding of literature departments across the United Kingdom and United States. Guiding this institutionalization of the study of texts were Leavis (1962) and I. A. Richards' (1978) 'practical criticism' in England, and Brooks (1949) and Ransom's (1979) 'new criticism' in the United States. Following proclamations of the text's central contribution to a discourse of Kantian enlightenment, the intent behind studying the text became to extract its meaning, authority, and wisdom, as if some rare ore. Practical and new criticisms developed a theory of 'close reading,' whereby texts were to be studied in and of themselves, as if in a vacuum. Richards' (1978) famous experiments with students at Cambridge represent the apex of this belief in the unitary text, as students were presented with poems with no background information or author's names and asked to analyze them. Having supposedly placed extra-textual contaminants to the side, Richards believed that his students could best understand individual texts by burrowing deep 'into' them, and by engaging solely with what was 'there.' As might be expected, Richards' students often produced vastly different readings of the 'same' text. His conclusion, though, was that better training was needed: students needed to be taught how to read a text properly, and the critic-professor would fulfill this task. In effect, the critic-professor was elevated to priest of textuality, as mediator between the power of the text and the inexperience of the reader.

Richards' theory is rife with contradictions; most notable, though, is his notion that the critic-professor could hold an Archimedean vantage point over the text when his theory espoused that each textual structure and mode of enunciation is unique and self-contained. Paradoxically, then, Richards' theory of close reading rules out the possibility of having obtained tools of reading from any other text: such tools would be extra-textual contaminants. Surely, Richards would defend his professorship and high priesthood of literature on the grounds that he had substantially more *experience* of reading than did his students, but experience and the ethos of close reading are incommensurable. Richards aimed to provide his students with a toolbox for reading texts, but that toolbox is filled with structures and tropes *from other texts*. Even a simple sentence requires a reading history to understand, and so the only way to square the circle of privileged readers and unique texts is to make compromises on one or other of these concepts.

Nevertheless, the theory remained and solidified into standard textual/analytical practice. As will be discussed, much literary and media theory from the 1970s onwards has challenged these beliefs, but many departments, universities, and particularly schools have resisted such theory, and thus the shadow of close reading and of the divine text remain with us, forming 'common sense' understandings of textuality for many.

The text and the world: four models of intertextuality

Intertextual theory truly arrived with the French *Tel Quel* school of theorists in the 1960s and 1970s, the word 'intertextuality' having been coined by Julia Kristeva (1980a, 1980b). Kristeva and Barthes (1990) developed the theory for literary studies, but its transference to media and television studies was slow in coming. Arguably, media and cultural studies' first major (if only implicit) step toward a theory of intertextuality came with Stuart Hall's (1980) encoding/decoding model and intervention, and subsequent work into decoding by what Alasuutari (1999) has dubbed the 'first generation' of reception analysts (see Ang 1985; Buckingham 1987; A. Gray 1987; Hobson 1987; J. Lewis 1986; Morley 1980, 1986; Radway 1987). Central to this generation of work was the idea that meaning comes not only 'from the text' or from its creator/'encoder,' but also from its reader/'decoder.'

Taken together, first generation work provides compelling evidence to suggest that an individual reader's positioning within societal structures and groupings, and his or her context of reception, frequently inflects what meanings that reader will 'find' in the text. Radway's study of romance book readers, for instance, left her with the conclusion that, while a close reading would suggest conservative, patriarchal content, the ways in which her subjects interacted with the books suggested an opposition to patriarchy (1987: 209–10). As this and other work documented, text and context bleed into each other, becoming intermingled: the text is (of) the world, while the world is (made of) texts.

Here, intertextuality is born in media and cultural studies, for while none of these early commentators drew the direct connection themselves, their findings point naturally to intertextuality if we only interrogate what 'context' and 'the world' or our positioning within it entails. As numerous critics have argued, our world is in large part a textual one. We are, as Abercrombie and Longhurst (1998) and Bird (2003) document, audiences all the time, forever consuming more texts than we could even be aware of. Much of what we learn of the world we learn from texts, leading some commentators to question if a world beyond the text still exists (see Baudrillard 1983a, 1983b; Debord 1995). Almost everything in the world, from our sense of self (Abercrombie and Longhurst 1998: 106; Hartley 1999), ontological security (Silverstone 1994), and lifestyle (Chaney 2001; Lull 2001), to what we conceive of as our nation and our relationship to it (Cardiff and Scannell 1987; Dayan and Katz 1994; Morley 2000), our family (Morley 1992; Silverstone 1994), or even our intimate relations and feelings (Galician 2003) is in part pieced together from the texts that flow through our 'mediascapes' (Appadurai 1995). And when we talk to one another, much of that talk is of the media, and not only the topics but the vocabulary and grammar. Working with several studies of conversation, Allen (1982) has estimated that, on average, a third of our talk is about the media, and more so with strangers. What, too, of our sadness, happiness, anger, mirth, and lust? How much of these and other emotions (and the people to whom they are attached) are played out in texts (see J. Gray 2005a; Grossberg 1992; Harrington and Bielby 1996; Hills 2002)? Ultimately, everyday life is in many ways a series of texts, and when the first generation of reception researchers found text and world bleeding into each other, by implication they found texts bleeding into each other. They may not have intended to open the Pandora's Box of intertextuality, but they certainly did.

Of course, though, to say texts interact with texts is overly vague, and critics have offered several models of what sort of interactions occur. Crudely, we can distinguish between four predominant models, and if we liken intertextuality to teamwork, we can talk of a hierarchical model, a working together model, a divided responsibility model, and a fully interactive model. In the first model, intertextuality is restricted to influence. Speaking of *The Simpsons*, for instance, we could observe the numerous instances in each episode when the show draws upon and references popular film, television, or art and literature. Under such a model, the single text now belongs to a network, becoming as literary theorist Harold Bloom has noted in his discussion of influence, 'only part of a meaning; it is itself a synecdoche for a larger whole including other texts' (Bloom 1975: 106; see also Bloom 1973). The close reader's supposedly impervious textual borders begin to lose their sealant under this theory, and it becomes possible to talk of how one's reading of one text may directly affect one's reading of another. Influence, though, is itself but a part of, and a synecdoche to, intertextuality, as intertextuality in its fullness is significantly richer in possibilities for textual interaction. Although influence theory situates texts within a network, it posits this network as strictly vertical, allowing for meaning to go in only one direction, one of chronology from *The Iliad* to the present day. Influence theory also fails to allow for the possibility that texts might work together (or in spite of each other), rather than endlessly feed into one another. According to influence theory, Kubrick or Hitchcock, say, can talk to and inflect *The Simpsons*, but the reverse is impossible, nor can *The Simpsons* talk to its peers. Influence theory's picture of textuality is also relatively lifeless, largely disinterested in the readers who might travel through such intertextual networks. As such, while it explodes the myth of the solitary text, it also denies the reader agency, and the text or author the ability to talk back, and hence the scope of its intertextual vision is strictly limited.

A second model of intertextuality envisions each text as a team member engaged in the same task as all other members, and the object of study becomes their combined work. Two clear examples of this model can be seen in work on the role of the media in articulating and/or creating nationality, and in cultivation analysis of long-term media effects. In the former, each text is seen to offer an image of the nation, and our individual notions of national identity will therefore be in part an aggregate of texts A, B, C, etc. These texts may well take on differential value (some team members work better than others), but each text is seen as fulfilling the same role within the 'team' (see J. Richards 1997; Street 1997). Similarly, cultivation analysis (see Gerbner et al. 1994; Shanahan and Morgan 1999; Signorielli and Morgan 1990) charts long-term media effects by looking not at, say, violence in one text, but at violence as a general *theme* in television, strung out over multiple texts as team members. Again, the interest is in the texts as aggregate, and in their combined effort.

The third model, by contrast, divides different responsibilities or roles between different team members. Under this model, the media are seen as fulfilling multiple functions, with each text or genre of texts concentrating on a different function. A particularly stimulating example of this model can be found in Marie Gillespie's *Television, Ethnicity and Cultural Change* (1995). Gillespie's data, based on ethnographic work among Punjabi teenagers in the London suburb of Southall, suggest a model whereby, for instance, ads are used as modern myths of cultural citizenship and aspiration, television news is used to develop national citizenship, and imported Indian videos are used to maintain links to cultural heritage. Each genre, in other words, is routinely employed by its users for a different task. Another example of this model can be found in Joke Hermes' (1995) work on women's magazines, in which she concludes that not all media texts are consumed equally by users, with different texts serving different functions (women's magazines being 'putdownable' and an 'inbetween activity'). Both Gillespie and Hermes suggest that, in order to understand any text, critics must place it in the context of its user's or reader's overall media consumption and ask what role it is being asked to perform.

All three of these models have produced interesting and valuable insights into the nature and role of texts, showing how a significant amount of textual meaning and value is created *across* multiple texts, at the level of intertextuality. However, I would like to look beyond them to a fourth model that involves a more complex interaction between texts, seeing texts working on each other's ground, setting up shop in each other's offices and working through and sometimes against one another's work. To do so, we turn to intertextuality's genesis as term, and to its theoretical forefather, Mikhail Bakhtin. Bakhtinian theory was introduced to the *Tel Quel* theorists most prominently by Julia Kristeva, and Kristeva cites Bakhtin as source for many of her ideas on textuality, dialogism, doubling, and polyglossia. When Kristeva penned the term 'intertextuality,' it was while writing of Bakhtin. Bakhtin and fellow theorists Volosinov and Medvedev's vision of intertextuality is an extremely dense, rich, and at times complex one, whose full ramifications have yet to be fully acknowledged and appreciated.[1]

Bakhtin's textuality takes root in a post-Saussurean, dialogic theory of linguistics. Saussure famously distinguished between *parole*, as any spoken or written utterance, and langue, the system of language, and his *Course in General Linguistics* (1983) sets an understanding of *langue* as the ultimate goal for linguistics and semiology, further positing that *langue* can be studied quite independently of *parole*. Bakhtin disagrees, centering his own linguistics on what he calls the 'real unit' of communication, the utterance (Bakhtin 1986: 71). Hence, where, as Tony Bennett (1979: 74–5) notes, Saussure's *langue* was magic carpet-like, with no explanation offered of how it is propelled, Bakhtin proposes dialogism as this propeller. Saussurean linguistics was quite content to use the sentence as basic unit of language and to study it in a vacuum, but Bakhtin argues that nobody 'is the first speaker, the one who disturbs the eternal silence of the universe' (1986: 69). Rather, every utterance begins as a response to something else, and ends, prepared or otherwise, as something to be responded to. All communication, in other words, is 'but one link in a continuous chain of speech performance' (Volosinov 1973: 72), for 'The word wants to be heard, understood, responded to, and again to respond to the response, and so forth, *ad infinitum*' (Bakhtin 1986: 127). As opposed to the 'abstraction' (Volosinov

1973: 77) required by Saussurean structuralist linguistics and which has, as Volosinov points out, 'always taken as its point of departure the finished monologic utterance – the ancient written monument, considering it the ultimate realium' (1973: 77), the Bakhtin circle propose a 'concrete' (Volosinov 1973: 77) system sensitive to context, and, as a result, sensitive to the true nature of meaning-construction.

With such a system, understanding an utterance involves placing it into a context of other utterances. 'The text lives,' Bakhtin writes, 'only by coming into contact with another text (with context). Only at the point of this contact between texts does a light flash, illuminating both the posterior and anterior, joining a given text to a dialogue' (1986: 162). By itself, and isolated in a bubble, as new and practical criticisms tried to do with the text, the utterance is completely meaningless, for we only know how to make sense of it through having read and experienced other utterances. To understand, in Volosinov's terms, 'means to refer a particular inner sign to a unity consisting of other inner signs, to perceive it in the context of a particular psyche' (1973: 35), where the particular sign is the text at hand, and the unity of other signs is the accumulation of already-experienced events and texts.[2] '[I]n the process of introspection, we engage our experience into a context made up of other signs we understand. A sign can be illuminated only with the help of another sign' (Volosinov 1973: 36). Thus, where to Saussure *langue* could be studied separately, and where it acted as a 'sort of contract signed by the members of a community' (1983: 14), language to the Bakhtin circle is not simply handed down as contract with a 'Sign on Dotted Line' inscription, nor can it be stabilized. Instead, 'it endures as a continuous process of becoming' (Volosinov 1973: 81). Effectively, every utterance reaches us lifeless with thousands of protruding wires. For that utterance to make sense, for it to come alive, we must hook it up to active wires already-possessed. And those already-possessed wires will in turn have formed as a result of previous meaning-making activities.[3]

One of media studies' finer examinations of intertextuality, significantly informed by Bakhtin, is Bennett and Woollacott's (1987) *Bond and Beyond*. Bennett and Woollacott (1987: 7) boldly state that '"the text itself" is an inconceivable object', for the text 'is never "there" except in forms in which it is also and always other than "just itself," always-already humming with reading possibilities which derive from outside its covers' (1987: 90–1). Taking the case of James Bond, they explain that most readers viewing or reading a Bond text have already encountered this character elsewhere, from merchandising, ads, and texts within the Bond franchise. From reading these texts, then, most readers will have some concept of what a Bond film or book is likely to entail: it will tell a tale of international espionage, involving larger-than-life megalomaniac villains from corrupt Communist nations or less-developed countries, trips to exotic locations, debonair womanizing, a black-tie gambling scene, and an elaborate display of gadgets, stunts, and phallic imagery. One could expect good fun and lots of action, but should not hope for intense social realism. Thus, before reading the Bond text at hand, readers have already had constructed for them a set of expectations, desires, assumptions, and meanings for the text, and it is only through and among these meanings that this 'new' text will come to make sense. Effectively, 'inter-textuality' prepares us for the text,[4] and prepares the text for us, so that any resulting meaning, power, or effects that 'the text' may be seen to possess are in part a function of the already-read. As such, Bennett and Woollacott argue, 'the case of Bond throws into high relief the radical insufficiency of those forms of cultural analysis which, in purporting to study texts "in themselves," do radical violence to the real nature of the social existence and functioning of texts' (1987: 6). Reading, to Bennett and Woollacott, becomes a process by which the 'inter-textually organised reader meets the inter-textually organised text' (1987: 56), and the text 'itself' becomes not 'the place where the business of culture is conducted,' but rather the site 'around which the pre-eminently social affair of the struggle for the production of meaning' occurs (1987: 59–60).

Where influence theory sees a limited, unidirectional network of texts, Bakhtinian intertextual theory sees a textual universe of criss-crossing wires, and focuses on 'the life of texts' (Bakhtin 1986: 114). Texts are always talking to each other, this theory suggests, and any new text as utterance will find its meaning only by adding its voice to the already-existent dialogue. Yet since the individual reader will come to understand a text only by 'listening' to this dialogue, and since, therefore, we can comprehend one text only by using others, Bakhtinian linguistics and textual dialogism suggest a profound fluidity of textual boundaries. No longer is poetic language divinely inspired, a direct bolt from above that hits first writer then reader; instead, it is determinedly of this world and, more importantly, of this world's texts. Moreover, as Bennett (1979) points out, dialogism is a perpetually open process, so that any single text 'is liable to constant shifts and displacements as new forms of writing transform and reorganise the entire system of relationships between texts' (1979: 59). Dialogue, to Bakhtin, is endemic to textuality and to fiction.[5]

Intertextual theory provocatively asks us to what degree a text as entity can exist outside of itself as physical object, and live *through* other texts. Bennett and Woollacott (1987), for instance, observe that popular heroes or characters can become matrixing principles or 'dormant signifiers,' awoken by, but preceding, the individual text. Parallel work on Batman in the collected essays in Pearson and Uricchio's (1991) *The Many Lives of the Batman* and on Judge Dredd by Barker and Brooks (1998) points to a similar conclusion (see also T. Miller 1997). And popular heroes are not alone, for as John Fiske (1989b) finds of Madonna, and Barker and Brooks (1998) find of Sylvester Stallone, performers/stars also exist intertextually, as do whole stories through remakes (Chin and Gray 2001), and, as I will soon discuss, genres. Writing on Batman in the superhero's 1989 filmic reincarnation, Bennett states that the 'early Gothic Batman, the Cold War Batman of the 1950s and his 1960s parodic successor: these are all *there*, like so many sedimented layers of plot, narrative, and characterization which the text works with – or against' (Bennett 1991: ix emphasis added), but, of course, Bennett's *there* and his sedimentary layers are not actually *in* the text as location. Instead, as Fiske (1989a: 66) writes of intertexts, they are 'ghost texts,' but these ghosts come from the reader, and from other texts the reader has encountered. Resilient in refusing death, any text that we read can potentially live on forever – ageless as Bond and Batman have proven to be – to 'haunt' future texts. Ultimately, texts stay with us, alive in our memories.

To Kristeva, the literary text is a 'productivity' (1980a: 36), and 'an intersection of textual surfaces' (1980a: 65). As such, she observes, Bakhtin's dialogic theory problematizes the very notion of the text. If one could now make such seemingly paradoxical statements as 'the text [. . .] is a permutation of texts' (1980a: 36), clearly 'text' had become too slippery a word to handle. With this in mind, she coined the term 'intertextuality' to describe the inherent nature of textuality as 'transposition of one sign system into another, such that the new signifying system may be produced with different "signifying material" and thus does not have to occur entirely within language' (1980b: 59–60). As is evident in her talk of *inter*textuality and *trans*position, to Kristeva, the text's constitutive state is one of motion, with meaning sliding along the dual axes of subject-addressee and text-context (1980a: 66). Kristeva's text redistributes language in a 'destructive-constructive' manner (1980a: 36) – destructive because it disallows a singularity of meaning, but constructive because it allows a polyphonic text to emerge.

Mounting a frontal assault on Aristotelian logic, Kristeva writes of intertextuality as offering a text the chance to mean multiple things at once, so that the text may propose one meaning for itself, while each intertext may add others. Kristeva intended intertextuality as a means of answering her own call for a 'literary semiotics [that] must be developed on the basis of a *poetic logic* where the concept of the *power of the continuum* would embody the 0–2 interval, a continuity where 0 denotes and 1 is implicitly transgressed' (1980a: 70, original emphasis). To Kristeva, the 1 of 'God, Law, Definition' (1980a: 70) is inherently dogmatic, demanding a single meaning, whereas the play and power of the intertextually provided 2, 3, etc. offer the possibility of multiple meanings. Kristeva dubs this system of 2, 3, etc. as 'ambivalence,' celebrating it as a central artistic quality of poetic language and as one of literature's inherent appeals. Along with Bakhtin, Kristeva develops what Clark and Holquist call 'a metaphysics of the loophole' (1984: 247), whereby there is never just one determinate meaning to a text.

As John Frow has argued, texts 'are not structures of presence but traces and tracings of otherness. They are shaped by the repetition and transformation of other textual structures' (1990: 45). The text is always in flux, being created by other texts and in turn creating other texts. Furthermore, an important component of this textual system is temporal, not just spatial. Textuality occurs and reoccurs. Thus, while spatial metaphors are more common in discussing the text, they can only be accurate if we incorporate a temporal component, whereby a text is regarded as both a *field of action* in which languages and other texts come together in dialogue, and as simultaneously moving through other textual spaces, jostling with others.

Genre and intertextuality

If, as Bennett and Woollacott have suggested, though, we meet the text 'always-already humming with reading possibilities' (1987: 90–1), then genre is responsible for a great deal of that noise, and hence for a great deal of textual becoming. Genre is the grammar of a text, and as such, it is largely internalized. Just as a language's native speakers will rarely if ever pause to notice gerunds or adverbial clauses (let alone be able to explicitly state the rules for their usage), so too does genre come 'naturally.' As Ryan and Kellner (1988: 78) suggest, 'Genres depend on receptive audiences who are willing to grant credibility to the conventions of the genre to the extent that those conventions become invisible. Once that is accomplished, the generic illusion can assume the characteristic of verisimilitude.' Each genre has its own 'common sense' rules that, by and large, we internalize and use to make sense of future texts. When we express eagerness to watch the next Bond film, or quickly change the channel to avoid the latest Madonna video, we prove a proficiency with the generic codes of the Bond film and the Madonna brand of pop music respectively, a proficiency for which intertextuality is directly responsible.

Genres are important grammatical tools to us precisely because they serve both a menu function and a digestive function. Or, to use Neale's (1980: 19) definition, genres are 'systems of orientations, expectations and conventions that circulate between industry, text and subject.' In a world of seemingly infinite texts, genres help us to taste-test and select what to watch. Once we have selected, and are listening, watching, or reading, genre codes serve as shorthand to tell us what is going on. There is never a genre-less moment, for to step outside genre is to step into a chaotic semiosis in which shopping lists and great novels are read alike. As Neale writes of film genres, they

> do not consist solely of films. They consist also of specific systems of expectation and hypothesis which spectators bring with them to the cinema and which interact with films themselves during the course of the viewing process [. . .] They offer a way of working out the significance of what is

happening on the screen: a way of working out why particular actions are taking place, why the characters are dressed the way they are, why they look, speak and behave the way they do, and so on.

(Neale 2000: 31)

Every genre has its 'regime of verisimilitude' (Neale 2000: 32) – people sing problems away in musicals, but fight them away in action films, for instance – and it is partly by knowing these regimes that we are able to navigate ourselves through a cinema multiplex, an evening in front of the television, a trip to the library, or a session on the Internet.

Much early genre theory, however, looked on these regimes and on generic codes as set in stone.[6] Particularly in film studies, where genre theory has received its most attention, genre has frequently been viewed as it relates to Hollywood formulas, with 'genre film' a synonym for Hollywood conveyor-belt schlock, proof positive of Adorno and Horkheimer's thesis of the standardization of cultural forms in late capitalism (Adorno 1991). It has been considered largely as a tool whereby producers ensure a stability of meaning and profit in their studios' output by keeping genre conventions in perennial, and hence reliable, stasis. As such, much genre criticism has been, as Mittell notes, 'less interested in how genres are *actually* defined in cultural practice than in identifying the abstract theoretical "essence" of a genre in idealized form' (Mittell 2004: 4, original emphasis). However, Altman (1999), Neale (2000), and Mittell (2004) have pushed to refocus a more fluid and more cultural definition of genre, with readers as the focal point.[7]

This push begins with the observation that there is no point in time at which we are each handed, in 12-point Times New Roman, a nice list of genres, cross-referenced by title, cast, director, and including a concordance of genre definitions. Rather, genres are cultural categories, as Mittell insists, 'constituted by media practices and subject to ongoing change and redefinition' (2004: 1). Genres may appear to be basic, unmoving categories that function '*as if* they emerged from intrinsic textual features, seemingly flowing from that which they categorize' (Mittell 2004: 10, original emphasis), and their utility as taxonomic labels may convince us they are in some way permanent. However, as Altman and Mittell illustrate with film and television genres respectively, a close analysis of genres over time shows considerable movement. Mittell, for instance, studies the generic evolution of the quiz show from the dominant conception that such programs would offer legitimized intellectual competition, to a later interest in giveaway programs with the 'everyman' contestant, to the more contemporary marriage of these dominants in shows such as *Wheel of Fortune*. Genres, Feuer (1987: 118) notes, 'are made, not born,' but they can also be remade. As labels, they are only as good as they are culturally useful to specific groups at specific times, and thus by definition they must remain 'contingent and transitory, shifting over time and taking on new definitions, meanings, and values within differing contexts' (Mittell 2004: 17). Within any given period of time, Mittell cedes, 'generic terms are still sufficiently salient that most people would agree on a similar working definition for any genre' (2004: 17). Feuer (1987) observes that genres act on the triple axes of aesthetics, ritual, and ideology, and thus descriptions of genres can focus on markedly different aspects of a genre, and may privilege different *elements*, but many of the same basic elements are often detected within a given time period. Over time, though, these elements, and hence the genre itself, are often characterized not by stasis but by flux. Consequently, Mittell argues persuasively that genre analysis must be a *cultural* genre analysis, looking not for generic essences, but instead at the processes of categorization, and at what cultural and media practices and interests are behind them.

Genre literacy

Mittell's insistence that scholars examine the cultural experience of genres represents an important intervention in genre theory, calling for greater examination of how media practices such as distribution and promotion, textual criticism, new historical contexts, industrial needs and, of course, texts themselves all feed into the (re)construction of genre, and into our notions of how any given genre works. At the level of the individual viewer, though, this means that a significant amount of genre understanding is intertextual by nature, based on the individual's viewing experiences and history. If texts and audiences are surrounded by multiple discourses of what a text or genre means, with genres operating across multiple cultural realms, for us to piece together an understanding of genre, and to work out contexts and groupings into which we as readers should place any given text, we rely on our intertextual competence. We only know of genres what we have experienced or been told of them. Much of this 'instruction' comes from outside of genre texts themselves, and so, as Mittell insists, we must avoid a genre study that focuses only on texts; but at the same time, every text that speaks and is listened to has something to tell us. Whether we are conscious of the process or not (as is most likely), we will group any given text with other texts of what we feel to be its sort. We then carry with us this category in its entirety as a 'memorial metatext' (Jean-Louis Leutrat, cited in Neale 1980: 51) to be activated at a future point when we find ourselves faced with another text that may fit this category. Each genre is, at any given point in time, made up of a certain semantics and syntax (Altman 1999: 89), and our understanding of that grammar will partly determine our genre literacy to sort and comprehend further texts.

I use the term 'literacy' loosely here, for genre literacies or competencies can be variable, and we need not adopt a firm system of evaluative hierarchies for varying literacies, as we would, say, with English language literacy. More or less 'correct' readings may well exist; on the whole, however, the relative value of these literacies is at this point unimportant. As Mittell explains, multiple competing genre definitions often exist, such that 'genres are commonly sites of cultural struggles and dissent rather than clearly established consensus and regularity' (2004: 46), so differential competencies and literacies can exist without the need for the analyst to designate one or the other as 'right' or 'wrong.' Key, though, is that these literacies are often intertextually constructed. As Brunsdon (1981) notes of soap operas, for example, many male viewers in particular lack the lived and intertextual histories of the genre's many female fans, hence lacking many of the emotional-textual resources with which the genre's fans make sense of it. Here, then, different competencies exist, which generate different reading strategies and different cultural relations to the genre. Meanwhile, British or American soap watchers are likely to conceive of the soap opera and its mechanics slightly differently based upon their differing intertextual histories – where the American soap tends to be populated by the rich leisure classes, British soaps mainly follow the lives of the working class.

Just as genres are in flux, however, so too are genre literacies and competencies. Not only do genre and expectation partially control our understanding of a text upon entrance, but that text can partially control our understanding of the genre upon exit. Each new text we encounter carries with it the potential to expand, or otherwise modify, our knowledge of its genre's semantics and syntax. Genres, notes Cohen (1986: 204), 'are open categories. Each member alters the genre by adding, contradicting, or changing constituents.' Just as grammar changes over time, then, as each new utterance or accumulation of utterances can disrupt the system, so too with genre, as each new text can reconstitute the system. Moreover, while literacy works in a largely internalized way, it also has a conscious, public side, for literacy (or even the lack thereof) serves also as a form of 'popular cultural capital' (Fiske 1992: 34). While, as Fiske explains, this form of cultural capital carries with it no inherent link to *economic* capital, as does Bourdieu's (1984) cultural capital, it is nevertheless something to be traded and performed publicly. For many audiences, being a 'knowing audience' is a sought-after position (see Barker and Brooks 1998). Certainly, genre literacies often serve as pass cards into many contemporary communities: know too little about any given genre and one will find oneself excluded from numerous groups or conversations. As 'discursive clusters' (Mittell 2004), genres serve multiple social, cultural, and discursive roles, as do varying levels of literacy. As Barker (2000: 57) suggests, a display of competency even provides the source of enjoyment for a fair deal of our media consumption. Buckingham (1987), for instance, documents that part of the fun for young fans watching English soap *EastEnders* is to predict what will happen next, to foresee upcoming plot turns, and hence to test and to prove their generic literacies.

Whenever we share these predictions, 'debrief,' or discuss (whether humorously or pseudo-intelligently) generic rules, we participate in a co-learning of genre literacy. Therefore, while intertextual theory often suggests an intensely individual process, through the carrier wave of discussion, the learning of genre literacy is an intrinsically *social* process. Much of our media consumption occurs with others and/or is subsequently reactivated in conversations, and so it is rare that our genre literacies stay personal. Rather, genre understanding and delimitation happen through interpretive communities (Fish 1980a; Lindlof 1988; Lindlof et al. 1998), and most if not all texts or genres become 'pieces of collective property, ownable through talk' (Barker and Brooks 1998: 54), and 'the property of varied and productive publics' (T. Miller 1997: 5).[8] We may even belong to contradictory interpretive communities, and hence work with *multiple* literacies, criticizing a genre with one group, for instance, and indulging in it with another group. Genre literacy, and by extension any form of intertextuality, is networked and channeled through interpretive communities. This fact not only means that the study of genres should inherently be socio-cultural, but also severely limits the possibilities for the supreme relativism and open-endedness that an intertextual literacy theory may at first suggest. Such a view of the text, though, is clearly at odds with much established theory in media and cultural studies, and with the field's default models of textuality. Therefore, to pose an intertextual mode of practice is to write back against such models, and to revise them to better account for the reality of textual and audience activity.

Reading through: a phenomenological model of reading

Arguably the still-predominant model of textuality in media and cultural studies is that of Hall's (1980) encoding/decoding model. Admittedly, most who write of it offer modifications (see, for instance, Corner 1980; J. Lewis 1983; Morley 1992), but its common-sense simplicity has assured it the position of base model for much work. I too believe the model still has much to offer us, but propose that it suffers from two critical errors. First, it requires an elaboration upon the decoder's societal positioning as including the wealth of accumulated *textual* experience and knowledge that I wrote of earlier. It is not just our race, class, gender, or age that talk to texts — texts too talk to texts. Second, Hall incorrectly describes decoding as a 'determinate' moment (1980: 129), and in doing so, he plots this moment on a chart, and thus spatializes what is an inherently temporal process. Texts do not just take place: they also take time. As Kress (2000: 132) points out, intertextuality as a word exists only 'to patch up a problem caused by starting with the wrong theory [of textuality] in the first place' and this 'wrong theory' is one that sees text as location or moment, rather than as becoming or process.

To begin with, all but the briefest works require time to decode. Thus interpretation or decoding is not just something we do after finishing the work: it is a process that we go through *as we read*. Expounding upon his 'affective stylistics,' Fish explains that:

> in an utterance of any length, there is a point at which the reader has taken in only the first word, and then the second, and then the third, and so on, and the report of what happens to the reader is always a report of what has happened *to that point*.
>
> (Fish 1980b: 74, original emphasis)

While reading, we make suppositions that are later proven correct or incorrect (or are left as enigmas), as we engage in a constant give-and-take 'game' of meaning-making with the text (Lotman 1977: 288). As critics, though, we too often forget this, our analytical moment of interpretation so far removed from the various moments of reading that we can forget the process of reading (Fish 1980a: 5–6). But, Fish argues, such 'stepping back is what an analysis in terms of doings and happenings does not allow' (1980b: 79). Rather than step back, we should step *through* to remind ourselves how a text came into being for us.

If we view decoding as a process of 'reading through,' we realize that we read through, not only in the sense of moving temporally and spatially *through* a text, but also in the sense of reading *via* other texts. As we try to make sense of a text, we activate our (intertextual) genre literacies all the time. Other texts are always there with us as we work our way through a text. Indeed, Klinger (1989) helpfully illustrates this point by analyzing 'digressions at the cinema,' those comments spoken aloud while watching a film. Many of these, she notes, take a highly intertextual form, as quotations from other films are blurted out, or as parallel scenes or characters from other texts are discussed. Or, as Jackson (2001) notes, a similar process can be witnessed by reading scribbled-in marginalia in books, which often compare and contrast the work at hand with others. Such 'digressions' may well be performances, rather than strictly interpretation aids – a fact that Klinger overlooks – and her word choice suggests they are interferences more than they actually become part of the text. Nevertheless, as she argues, they show the degree to which, as we watch, we engage in what Umberto Eco (1979) calls 'inferential walks' to other texts. And once we accept that other texts are constantly traveled to, or brought to and with us, as we read other texts, we are led to the conclusion that texts do not truly end when we reach the work's physical end. No end, of course, also means no 'determinate moment' of decoding . . . which returns us to the question of what *is* a text.

To answer this, I borrow Wolfgang Iser's (1978, 1980) notion of a textual 'gestalt.' Employing a phenomenological approach to reading, similar to Fish's affective stylistics, Iser wrote of how the text continuously changes as we read it, and as each successive sentence or paragraph revises, clarifies, or obscures the already-read. To describe this text as becoming and as experience, Iser wrote of the text as gestalt. 'We do not grasp [the text] like an empirical object,' he argues, 'nor do we comprehend it like a predicative fact; it owes its presence in our minds to our own reactions, and it is these that make us animate the meaning of the text as reality' over time (Iser 1978: 129), so that, 'we actually participate in the text, and this means that we are caught up in the very thing we are producing. This is why we often have the impression, as we read, that we are living another life' (1978: 127). Henry Jenkins (1992) observes a similar process at work in television texts, whereby we must constantly construct them, adding information from new episodes, or even objecting to material from other episodes when it does not match up against our gestalt, or, as Jenkins calls it, our 'metatext.' However, to Iser, once our direct and *physical* reading of the work is over, the gestalt left with us becomes the finished text. As Jenkins (1992) notes, though, while the text is indeed a gestalt, like Fiske's ghost texts of intertextuality, the 'other life' of the text/gestalt/ metatext continues beyond its physical reading. As ghost, what it wants of us, or, more to the point, what we want of it, is to continue using it.

But interaction is multidirectional. Not only can we reactivate texts to help us understand other texts, but also their gestalt will always be open to reconstitution and reinterpretation itself. Recently, for example, I reread Tolkien's *Lord of the Rings* trilogy, and in doing so, reactivated my *Lord of the Rings* movie gestalt to make sense of the books, but simultaneously the books caused a reappraisal of the films and much of their contents. In reading Tolkien, then, I was also reading the films once more. As Morgan writes, this suggests that as critics we should shift our attention 'to the *verbing* of media experience instead of the *noun* of text' (Morgan 1998: 128, original emphasis). Moreover, this is a process that, memory willing, continues potentially forever, for as Bakhtin (1986: 170) noted, 'Nothing is absolutely dead: every meaning will have its homecoming festival.' Annette Kuhn's work with elderly 'enduring fans' of 1930s films shows that, even six decades later, some interviewees were still finding fresh meanings for their favorite texts, for as 'the text is appropriated and used by enduring fans, further layers of inter-textual and extra-textual memory-meaning continuously accrue' (Kuhn 1999: 145). True to what the Bakhtin circle argued, textual gestalts remain in conversation, and with this dialogue, the text's work goes on: 'ceaseless semiosis' (Kress 2000: 135). The text continues and reading continues.

I propose, therefore, that we talk not of encoding/decoding, but of encoding/ redecoding and of reading through. Both reading and the text are a continual journey *through*, a continuance of motion, and while there might be determinate moments, there are always potentially more determinate moments to come. Consequently, I write of 'reading through' to highlight the refusal of reading or of the text to stand still. This model conceives of reading as forever a temporal process and sees any space that a text occupies as potentially a space of motion and inter-action, the 'space as process' model for which writers such as Massey (1994) and Clifford (1992) have argued. And, while I have written of this as intertextuality, by using the word I imply no difference from textuality, for the latter *is* the former. As Kress obstinately states in objecting to the use of the word 'intertextuality,' 'both the unrelatedness and connections of texts are unremarkable: they are what is normal, and no special term needs to be invented to name the situation' (2000: 135), and I propose a reading through model to signify this normality.

A particularly interesting and encouraging essay that charts a form of reading through in action is John Ellis' (1999) 'Television as Working-Through'. Here, Ellis looks at television as a 'vast mechanism for processing the raw data of news reality into more narrativised, explained forms' (1999: 55) and works with the psychoanalytical notion of 'working-through,' 'a process whereby material is not so much processed into a finished product as continually worried over until it is exhausted' (1999: 55). Ellis suggests that the news presents us with important information and ideas, but they require time and work to come to terms with, and thus soaps, documentaries, talk shows and sports programs all tend to pick up these topics (these news *texts*) and work toward rounding them off and fleshing them out in a more satisfactory manner. To Ellis, then, news texts are *read through* other texts (and, thus, other texts read through news texts), with worry or concern as motor.

Clearly, though, there is more that can be done with this model than Ellis alone does, or than I will be doing – or could hope to do – in this book. After all, a lot revolves around the *potential* of texts to be kept alive, and this model requires work on issues as disparate as: how redecodings might be initiated, or halted; which texts or types of texts are particularly long lasting and why; which texts are prone to frequent decodings (is it only the news?) and why; which *people* are more or less likely to redecode; what strength a redecoding has relative to initial decodings; and so forth. Given the importance of texts and textuality, such work could help us to better understand our textual environment. As I have suggested with many of the studies quoted in this chapter (see also Bird 2003; Radway 1988), fortunately there is already a fair amount of work other than Ellis' that fits within this model, or that can be read as fitting it. As such, I do not wish to suggest that this model is a sparkling new one; rather, my aim is to enunciate what to date has only been implied by critiques of established textual theory and wisdom.

Supportive and critical intertextualities

However, to use such a model, we must establish its parameters, and its control functions. If intertextuality has frequently been under-utilized, and if it commonly appears in media theory as a throwaway reference to the chaotic world of textual interrelations, this is because much intertextual theory leads us to the frustrating dead end of over-individualistic, random textual networking. Bakhtin, Kristeva, and Barthes impressively theorized a point of entry to the confusing world of intertextuality, but insufficiently mapped out its landscape. By under-appreciating the role of the reader in particular, they offer a picture of reading that renders the act a purely personal process, never producing consistency between readers, and governed solely by the chaos of differential reading histories. As Culler (1981: 11) has noted, such a theory sets 'before us perspectives of unmasterable series, lost origins, endless horizons,' as any text can potentially connect with any other text, leaving the analyst trying to unravel a mess of tangled wires; as he argues, then, in order to work with the concept of intertextuality, we must focus it. Intertextuality's history with media studies has been too closely aligned with that of postmodern theory, and thus is often seen as an open, unlimited intertextuality of play, refutation, resistance, and elusiveness, a process that perennially repels the analyst from getting a grip on the text (see particularly Collins 1992; Fiske 1989a, 1989c). Intertextuality may indeed act at times as a chaotic force, but there is considerable order within it too, and if we are to see it as anything more than a small-print footnote to postmodernism, we must examine how it can be controlled, limited, or even programmed.

One of the more obvious instances of intertextual control, or at least of the *attempt* to control intertextuality, is at the level of what we could call the *supportive intertextuality* of 'paratexts.' Gerard Genette (1997) coined the term *paratext* as a subset of intertextuality to refer to those elements of or surrounding a text whose sole aim is to inflect particular readings of that text. Writing of books, Genette further distinguishes between *peritexts*, as paratexts materially appended to the text – titles, contents pages, prefaces, covers and the general 'look' of an edition – and *epitexts* as paratexts 'outside' the text – interviews with the writer, ads for publication or reviews. Genette describes the paratext as a form of 'airlock' between reader and textual world, one 'that helps the reader pass without too much respiratory difficulty from one world to the other' (1997: 48). In actuality, though, the paratext does not stand between reader and text as much as it infringes upon the text, and invades its meaning-making process. Furthermore, where the image of an airlock may suggest no natural connection between text and paratext, we must add the proviso that the two become virtually inseparable, with the experience of one wrapped up in the experience of the other. And in a media world flooded with synergy, cross-marketing, and endless advertisements and promotions, producers' epitextual airlocks in particular are everywhere, aiming to acclimatize us to texts in certain ways.

Much has been written of such epitexts – or, as they are variously known, 'narrative images' (Ellis 1993) or 'commercial intertexts' (Meehan 1991) – particularly of cinematic epitexts, as the 'Coming To A Theatre Near You' trailers, 'spoilers,' and gossip all start instructing us on how best to situate an upcoming film. In the words of Ellis, 'The sale of tickets depends upon the public knowledge of the cinematic experience. The expectation of a particular kind of entertainment, with a particular social role, is one crucial factor in the kind of commodity that cinema offers' (1993: 29–30), and thus cinematic paratexts have the job of delivering such public knowledge, of offering such expectations and of getting to us before the movie does. One need only consider how often we look at movie posters and think to ourselves 'Wow, that looks awful/great' to realize the power of the paratext. Television is, of course, similarly wallpapered with paratexts: most ad breaks contain at least one preview of upcoming shows; from July to October, the airwaves are alive with 'Fall Previews' and hype; and many shows are dedicated to discussing other television (*Entertainment Tonight*, *Celebrity Justice*, latenight talk shows, The E! Network, etc.). Many networks even invade their own programs with pop-up text ads at the bottom of the screen mid-show.

Indeed, as Genette observes, a 'text without a paratext does not exist and never has existed' (1997: 3). Thus, paratext-less television viewing is made nearly impossible by our knowledge of network branding and genre programming, and of what sort of shows are plugged into certain time slots in the schedule. However, if texts without paratexts are impossible, the same is far from true of the reverse. Our 'Wow, that looks awful/great' can easily become, 'Wow, that *is* awful/great,' as we all regularly pre-judge texts based solely or largely upon our exposure to their paratexts. To some degree, then, we actually consume some texts through paratexts and supportive intertexts, the text itself becoming expendable. As many of these paratexts are controlled and produced by the text's authors or producers, this allows them ample opportunity, using networks of intertextuality, to construct meanings for their texts outside of the texts themselves. Authors or producers can attempt to hem in certain readings, to keep readers away from others and, overall, to authorize and legitimate their own favored reading strategies (see J. Gray 2005b).

However, if paratexts and intertexts can be used by producers to direct readers to certain readings, they can also be used by others to attack a text, to subvert its preferred meanings and to propose unofficial and unsanctioned readings. This is the territory of *critical intertextuality*. Looking at paratexts, for instance, we could note the power of censorious reviews to wholly undercut a text. Infamously, for example, the Ayatollah Khomeini's fatwa on the head of Salman Rushdie acted as a decree/'review' of *The Satanic Verses* that led to thousands feeling so deeply insulted by the unread text that they wanted its writer executed. Kevin Glynn (2000: 122), meanwhile, finds a considerably more playful critical intertextuality to be rife in tabloid news programs, as all manner of popular music is played alongside news stories in order to suggest particular readings. Texts are always open to re-reading and re-decoding, and while the industry saturates the public sphere with intertexts so as to establish and hopefully maintain their preferred interpretations, television in particular (as will be argued further in Chapter 3) allows for all manner of critical intertexts to upset those readings.

Intertextuality and discursive power

The rest of this book will examine parody as a heightened and particularly effective form of critical intertextuality. First, however, it must be made clear that intertextuality is not 'just' about meaning and interpretation, for intertextuality networks power as much as it does meaning. Certainly, an interest in power, if not central, at least swims under the surface of much of the theory that I have discussed. To re-energize our discussion of intertextuality with a discussion of power and politics, though, I will now raise this interest to the surface, by examining where intertextuality fits in with the discussions of linguistic capital and discursive power initiated by Pierre Bourdieu and Michel Foucault. Like the Bakhtin circle, Bourdieu saw grave problems with traditional linguistics, which, he believed, had failed to study power, treating language 'as object of contemplation rather than as instrument of action and power' (Bourdieu 1991: 37). Similarly, Foucault was greatly interested in studying how discourses as sites of power take root in language. Whereas, until now, I have focused on how texts talk to one another, much of this assumes a textual environment in which all texts are equal, and in which texts can draw freely from the same language pool. Bourdieu's contribution to linguistics, though, was to discount the fine delusion of 'linguistic communism which haunts all linguistic theory' (1991: 43). As opposed to the Comte-ian belief in language as treasure-trove for all, Bourdieu described language as containing many 'keep out' signs, and as demarcating speaking territory and forums for discussion according to economic and social capital.

In his 'Order of Discourse,' Foucault (1981) attempted to catalogue the forces that perpetuate discourses of power, and looked to the exclusion of speakers as a key operative force in the maintenance of dominant powers and institutions. Foucault notes a

> rarefaction [. . .] of speaking subjects; none shall enter the order of discourse if he does not satisfy certain requirements or if he is not, from the outset, qualified to do so. To be more precise: not all regions of discourse are equally open and penetrable.
>
> (Foucault 1981: 61–2)

In short, language is spoken and listened to with differential authority and respect according to the speaker's societal position and power. Utterances, writes Bourdieu, 'are not only (save in exceptional circumstances) signs to be understood and deciphered; they are also *signs of wealth*, intended to be evaluated and appreciated, and *signs of authority*, intended to be believed and obeyed' (1991: 66, original emphasis). In Bourdieu's (1984) *Distinction*, he describes how economic capital is transformed into cultural capital, and both he and Foucault see a similar process at work in the creation of linguistic capital. Linguistic competence, they observe, determines who can speak, where, when, and with how much clout, and such 'competence' is inextricably tied to capital and class. Wherever there is language, there is exclusion, there are privileged speakers, and there is the perpetuation and nourishment of existing relations of domination and power. Texts, as such, are not only units of meaning, but also units of power.

The ramifications of this politicized view of language for my work here are many. On one level, Bourdieu and Foucault insist that we cannot merely treat all texts as equal, for if we are to understand the actual intricacies and functioning of intertextuality, we will need to be aware of differential power. On yet another level, Bourdieu and Foucault pose the important challenge to intertextuality of whether it in any way cuts through or circumvents discourses of power, competence, and exclusion. It may be, after all, that certain intertextual interactions are governed by their texts' discursive power, hence automatically precluding certain meanings from coming to the fore. Or, as Foucault writes, 'Although every text possesses countless points of intersection with other texts, these connections situate a work within existing networks of power, simultaneously creating and disciplining the text's ability to signify' (quoted in Clayton and Rothstein 1991: 27).

However, intertextuality poses its own challenge to Bourdieu and Foucault, for if each text is a unit of power, intertextuality holds a key to increasing, reinforcing, or reducing that power. Certainly, to all of intertextuality's 'parent' figures – the Bakhtin circle, Kristeva, and Barthes – intertextuality represented a liberating force. To the Bakhtin circle, dialogue was never just a linguistic process; rather, it was an ethos, or in Hirschkop's (1999) words, 'an aesthetic for democracy.' Bakhtin regarded monologism in all forms as inherently inferior to dialogism, and he saw meanings as requiring the constant testing that only contestation, affirmation, or negotiation by other meanings provide. Similarly, to Kristeva and Barthes, intertextuality offered a way around the flawed and oppressive humanist constructs of God, Law, Truth, and Definition. Crosman (1980: 157) astutely observes that behind the argument by textual purists such as E. D. Hirsch or the new and practical critics that texts have a determinate meaning is the essentially political argument that they *should* have only one meaning, that God, Law, Truth, and Definition should exist. Intertextuality, though, potentially denies any text or group of texts solitary power, and thus intertextuality at heart is a political theory whose reach, importance, and relevance stretches beyond the search for textual meaning. As Aldon Nielsen notes poetically of intertextuality, 'the mystic writing pad is never erased, but it is always overwritten' (1994: 25), and so intertextuality can ensure that texts and textual meanings will stick to other texts, like a rumor, rewriting finished stories and told histories, placing them under a new light. If our textual world is populated by intertextual ghosts, this is a system that allows for texts to haunt, target, and beleaguer others, and hence for counter-discursive struggles for both meaning and textual power.

Part II

WATCHING WITH
THE SIMPSONS

Chapter 2

DOMESTICOM PARODY, GENRE, AND CRITICAL INTERTEXTUALITY

TELEVISION CRITICAL INTERTEXTUALITY CAN TAKE MANY FORMS, ranging from television criticism and reviews, to ads or previews that compare and contrast one program to another, to the popular and academic press' growing catalogue of television studies. The role and relative success of these texts in criticizing and/or attacking others has gone largely understudied, but given that popular television criticism is nowhere near as well developed, robust, or seriously utilized as literary, film, and art criticism; given the predominantly superficial hit-and-run nature of ad/preview 'criticism'; and given that the audience for academic work on television is diminutive proportional to the television audience itself, these forms rarely amount to a popularly *available* and *prevalent* critique. Rather, critical intertextuality's crown form exists in parody. With a long and venerable history, parody has proven popular throughout the course of art and literature in multiple societies. As Bakhtin writes, 'there never was a single strictly straightforward genre, no single type of direct discourse – artistic, rhetorical, philosophical, religious, ordinary everyday – that did not have its own parodying and travestying double, its own comic-ironic *contre-partie*' (1981: 53). From the 'fourth drama' or satyr play of Greek theatre, to Alexander Pope's 'Rape of the Lock,' to its modern televisual form, parody's ability to intertextually toy with the grammar of genre has assured its continued relevance and popularity over the ages. It has also seen it remain a powerful tool for revealing the absurdities within specific genres, and for teaching and testing genre literacy. Parody attaches itself to generic discourses and either playfully or scornfully attacks them, aiming to destabilize the common sense of genre, and intertextually chip away at already-read and yet-to-be-read texts.

This chapter will elaborate upon the inner workings of genre evolution by which parody comes to critique and talk back to past constructions of a genre, and by which it potentially destabilizes the ideological grounding of a genre. To illustrate this process, the chapter will later focus on *The Simpsons* as parodic critique of the pre-1990s American family sitcom and its fuzzy-happy depiction of the American Dream of home, family, suburb, and nation. The Simpson family's home at 742 Evergreen Terrace, Springfield is in many ways a parodic and mischievously dystopian recasting of the warm, embryonic homes and environments of American television history's famous sitcom families such as the Cosbys, Seevers, Cunninghams, Cleavers, and Nelsons, and of the utopian space of *Father Knows Best*'s Springfield, after which the Simpsons' town is named.

Parody and genre

As Neale and Krutnik observe, 'Parody has its own techniques and methods, but no particular form or structure' (1990: 19), and as such is more of a style than a genre itself. While genres have their own semantics and syntax (Altman 1999), parodies are only truly related to each other by a comic, lampooning style. Harries defines parody as:

> the process of recontextualizing a target or source text through the transformation of its textual (and contextual) elements, thus creating a *new* text. This conversion – through the resulting oscillation between similarity to and difference from the target – creates a level of ironic incongruity with an inevitable satiric impulse.
>
> (Harries 2000: 6, original emphasis)

If we add a proviso that the source text is often a *genre* of texts, parody is more an intertextual and generic *process* than it is its own stand alone genre. Parody always needs a 'host' genre and works by invoking other generic grammars, and thus by setting up shop on another genre's (or several genres') ground. As Bakhtin explains:

> in parody, two languages are crossed with each other, as well as two styles, two linguistic points of view, and in the final analysis two speaking subjects. It is true that only one of these languages (the one that is parodied) is present in its own right; the other is present invisibly, as an actualizing background for creating and perceiving.
>
> (Bakhtin 1981: 76)

Or, as McLuhan (1971: 170) notes, parody is 'Putting one space inside another space.' In order that an audience be aware of what genre or text is being referenced, parody must quote or borrow wholesale, and thus we have a case of 'ghost' textuality, with one text or genre (the parody) invisibly, yet hopefully still sensed by its audience, on top of and coexisting with the other (the parodied).

However, if parody exists on another's ground, it is not always an ideal guest. Parody can be tributary and loving, serving as homage and flattery, but it can also take the ground in order to transgress and subvert. Following Foucault, Stallybrass and White (1986: 196) note that any given space correlates to a certain power matrix, but add that, 'precisely because discursive domains are hierarchically arranged, metaphorical displacements from one domain to another can never be purely arbitrary,' nor ideologically meaningless. Parody's act of stepping onto another text's or genre's space thus threatens to destabilize that space and, with it, that text's or genre's power. Here we may think of de Certeau's (1984) and Jenkins' (1992) metaphor of the poacher, the outside force that steps onto land that is not its own and uses it as it wishes. The 'land,' or text/genre, that has been trespassed on can be turned into a resource for its deconstruction, as parody makes fun of the way in which a genre works. This is criticism from within, 'artistic jujitsu,' as Stam (1989: 228) calls it, that turns a genre's force against itself. As Jenny (1982) observes of parody, its basic mode is frequently one of criticism, and yet it realizes that the target text's or genre's ground cannot be destroyed outright. Therefore:

> Since it is impossible to forget or neutralize the [target] discourse, one might as well subvert its ideological poles; or reify it, make it the object of a metalanguage. Then the possibility of a *new* parole will open up, growing out of the cracks of the old discourse, rooted in them. In spite of themselves these old discourses will drive all the force they have gained as stereotypes into the *parole* which contradicts them, they will energize it.
>
> (Jenny 1982: 59, original emphasis)

This process and style are fundamentally intertextual and, thus, critical intertextuality can become a key matrixing principle of genre (re)construction.

Much of the sense we make of any text relies upon our genre literacy, and upon our overall understanding of its generic grammar. Many media, industry, and audience practices inform our literacy, both individually and as part of a group or culture. However, as many genre studies have pointed out, producers often try to keep a firm grip on genre, and hence much of the world of intertextuality is filled with supportive intertexts such as ads, previews, and making-of specials that allow producers the opportunity to control what would otherwise entail the wild semiosis of genre. Similarly, television production often works in preset grooves. Producers must, of course, provide something new to distinguish their product, and so as

Altman (1999) and Caughie (1991) convincingly argue, producers positively *aim* to change genres over time. But it is also in producers' best interests to tread carefully and respect the boundaries that other texts have already set. After all, by hemming in a genre, they can attempt to limit an audience's possible reactions through partially setting the context for viewing. If producers control their textual output to limit the dynamism of genres, as hard as the task may be, they can then measure their audience's expectations with more confidence (and a producer's confidence in measurement is an advertiser's confidence in doing business). As Feuer observes, 'From the television industry's point of view, unlimited originality of programming would be a disaster because it could not assure the delivery of the weekly audience' (1987: 119). Gitlin's (1994) seminal study of prime time television amply documents the industry's fear of innovation, and certainly, a glance through this week's *TV Guide* offers the prospect of the starkly similar *CSI*, *CSI: Miami*, *CSI: New York*, *Law and Order*, *Law and Order: Special Victims Unit*, *Law and Order: Criminal Intent*, *Cold Case*, *Without a Trace*, *Navy NCIS*, and *JAG*.

However, in a crowd of programs inclined toward standardization, perhaps only a few rogue texts are needed to destabilize if not generic conformity then at least the invisibility of a genre's grammar. Genre literacy, as such, not only may act as a powerful tool for conformity to be maintained, but also provides two integral conditions for a critical intertextuality: it is a system that can be disrupted and reconstituted by one text, allowing one text to affect many, and given the prevalence of media discussion today, it is a system that allows for communities to form around such rogue texts, communities that can act to reinforce, further disseminate, or even amplify such texts' disruptive force. This chapter will examine the workings of the first condition, whereas I will return to the role of interpretive communities in Part III.

Genre tampering

If we conceive of genre literacy as being formed by a melting pot of the already-read, this is a system that allows for strategic tampering with the melting pot. Individual texts can be added to the mélange in the hope that they will work *against* established notions of a genre, teach us (of) that genre, and inspire a knowing literacy, changing the taste, color and texture of this melting pot. Intertextuality is everywhere, but the system can be employed to allow for *critical* intertextuality. Through parody, transgressive texts can work to disarm and dismantle the hegemonic status quo, defining the genre through ironic contrast, and provoking a new, counter-hegemonic understanding of that genre. Writing of deconstruction, Derrida talks of the need for structure to be '*methodically* threatened in order to be comprehended more clearly' (1978: 6, original emphasis), and certainly, as Schatz notes, as a genre's conventions are eventually 'parodied and subverted, it: parency gradually gives way to *opacity*: we no longer look *through* the form [. . .], rather we look at the *form itself*' (Schatz 1981: 38, original emphasis). As parodic attack mechanism, *The Simpsons* acts as an American family sitcom, yet knocks away at its walls from inside, hence rendering the genre opaque.

Parody is often confused with satire or with pastiche, but neither of these forms shares parody's interest in a genre's form and conventions. Parody can be satiric, but pure satire bypasses concerns of form and aims straight at content, whereas pastiche alludes to form and/or content, but with no critical comment on either. By contrast, parody's jokes are at the expense of genre conventions, for as Tavia Shlonsky remarks, 'the method of parody is to disrealize the norms which the original tries to realize, that is to say, to reduce what is of normative status in the original to a convention or a mere device' (quoted in Rose 1993: 83). To laugh at parody is to acknowledge comprehension of those conventions under attack, and hence is also an acknowledgment of a genre's artificiality. Consequently, the parody's act of working on its target's ground, and through its target's own voice, is particularly effective, for the criticism is appended to the host genre parasitically. Stam (1989: 201) notes that parody's laughter is a 'corrosive' one, for once the target's comfortable external garb has been removed to reveal the mechanization within, it may prove hard to take the genre at face value again. Moreover, because parody takes the form of its target genre, effectively the target is made to do this to itself. The parodic text adds itself to our genre understanding, and works toward corroding away that which has been allowed to work undetected in the genre. This process by no means kills a genre, and some parody may provoke a new appreciation for genre, but it brings the genre's techniques to the surface, calling for, and frequently conducting, their analysis.

Ultimately, though, because it is up to the audience to make the connection between referenced texts/genre and text-at-hand, and thus to comprehend the joke and criticism, parody's crowning touch is that the 'audience is, in effect, transformed into the site of critical commentary' (Ott and Walter 2000: 436). Parody is a teacher, but its method is Socratic, encouraging the audience to make the final and decisive link between criticism and target, rather than merely proselytizing on genre. It constantly risks failure, miscomprehension, or simply being overlooked. If and when successful, though, parody can encourage the further step of activating a renewed understanding of text or genre to apply to previously-read or yet-to-be-read texts, so that the parodic effect will step beyond the text-at-hand to other texts, as a truly corrosive, yet truly helpful instructor of genre literacy. Parody can potentially shift our frame of reference, suggesting a new, more critically aware frame for viewing other textualities, enabling the parody to travel to other texts, to stay with us.

It is helpful to look at the effect of parody in terms of Giddens' (1990) and

Silverstone's (1999) discussion of the primacy of trust in everyday life and in our encounters with the media. As Giddens (1990: 21) explains, modernity is characterized by a plethora of 'disembedded' abstract systems, systems in which work and delivery are separated from each other across time and space, and in which social relations have been lifted out of local contexts of interaction, existing instead along indefinite spans of time-space. These systems rely on faceless commitments and thus on trust: we are forced to trust in others' good intentions and on the smooth running of everything around us. We trust, Giddens proposes, due largely to the system's moments of 'reembedding,' of consolidating trust with 'facework' at the 'access points' of system-visibility. Thus, for instance, a bank reembeds our trust with the facework of professional, well-groomed tellers, and clean and organized branches. However, reembedding must continue *ad infinitum*, for as Silverstone (1999: 119) notes, 'trust has to be continually worked at.' Genres, too, work by trust, for as long as they deliver enjoyable or informative information, we have no reason to distrust them – their 'facework' is successful. That said, parody is a tool of disembedding. By thrusting our faces up close to and by mocking the machinery of genre, parody can engender distrust and hence short-circuit a genre's reembedding and 'facework.'

Domesticom and anti-domesticom

The Simpsons' parody in particular is fundamentally expansive, taking in all manner of discourses and genres, and serving as a purveyor of distrust of televisual form. When interviewed, *Simpsons* creator Matt Groening and other key personnel, such as Al Jean, Jim Brooks, and George Meyer, are often quick to posit their goal and 'message' for the show as precisely one of distrust. *The Simpsons*' message, says Groening, for example, is that 'your moral authorities don't always have your best interest in mind' (Pinsky 2001: 134), or as Meyer echoes, the show's purpose is 'to get people to re-examine their world, and specifically, the authority figures in their world' (Turner 2004: 56). Elsewhere, Groening has been more explicit in linking this goal to television; as he told *Mother Jones*:

> For me, it's not enough to be aware that most television is bad and stupid and pernicious. I think, 'What can I do about it?' [. . .] I feel a bit like a fish trying to analyze its own acquarium water, but what I want to do is point out the way TV is unconsciously structured to keep us all distracted [. . . and] what I'm trying to do – in the guise of light entertainment, if that's possible – is nudge people, jostle them a little, wake them up to some of the ways in which we're being manipulated and exploited.
>
> (Doherty 1999)

In its many seasons, *The Simpsons* has parodically attacked seemingly all major televisual and cinematic genres, from cop shows to talk shows, kids' television to art house, and I will return to its extended parody of ads in Chapter 3, and of the news in Chapter 4. However, all of these parodic outings have been mounted from within the overarching framework of a sitcom parody. As 'the Antichrist of television sit-coms,' as John Carman calls it (quoted in Mittell 2001: 20), *The Simpsons* cannibalizes its own generic grammar and ideology often with brutally astute accuracy. More specifically, *The Simpsons* takes aim at the American family sitcom, or 'domesticom' as Marc (1989) calls it, particularly as it existed in its more glowingly optimistic and artificial, utopian versions most prevalent in the 1950s, 1960s, and 1980s, and before *The Simpsons*, *Roseanne*, *Married . . . with Children*, and *South Park*. Offering continual primers on domesticom form, *The Simpsons* criticizes the domesticom's over-easy answers to issues such as child-rearing, the growth of suburbia, familial communication, and the myth of the American Dream, and it chips away at the genre's mode of address.

The task of first defining the domesticom is made more difficult by media, communications, and cultural studies' frequent act of ignoring comedy. While work on the news, ads, or television violence sits more comfortably in the center of the field, as Attallah (1984: 223) notes, 'As a rule, one does not talk about situation comedy.' In spite of the genre's decades-old vice grip on prime time ratings,[1] and while comedy accounts for 38 per cent of American primetime programming, with comparable figures worldwide (*The Economist* 2002: 15), work on the sitcom has rarely made it into the mainstream. Save for occasional references by Morley (1986), Spigel (1992), and Hartley (1999), and reception research into *The Cosby Show* by Jhally and Lewis (1992) and black sitcoms by Means Coleman (2000), sitcom work can often be found only in occasional essays,[2] and little-known treatments such as a British Film Institute (BFI 1982) dossier on sitcom, and books by Grote (1983), Jones (1992), Marc (1989), Morreale (2003), Staiger (2000), and E. Taylor (1989). This relative exclusion is all the more peculiar given these works' well-illustrated assertion that the American family sitcom has served as a prime huckster selling the American Dream and its related notions of family, home, and suburb. While some genres' ideologies require more detailed close reading to ascertain, the American family sitcom's voice has been resolutely clear, as have its popularity and, hence, the potential impact of its voice. However, while many in academia were overlooking the domesticom, *The Simpsons* began its parodic play.

As its title suggests, the sitcom is a comedy *situated* in one or two main locations, with each episode conforming to a constant *situation* between a set group of characters. Everyone's individual or group exposure to a genre can lead to differences in emphasis upon any genre 'definition,' but the sitcom has been one of the more penned-in fictional genres, due largely to time constraints. Most fictional forms on television have 45 minutes or more per episode, and with more time comes more space for development, and thus more room for difference. By contrast, the sitcom writer and producer are faced with 22 minutes of program time and so must hold more variables constant in order that the viewer will need little time to acclimatize, and will instead get on with enjoying the show. As such, the family sitcom has not changed overmuch. Remarkable consistency exists between, say, *Father Knows Best*, *Diff'rent Strokes*, and *Full House*, consistency that allows a fairly uniform definition.

While the workplace sitcom (e.g. *MASH* or *The Office*) is another subgenre of the sitcom, and while some sitcoms are set in leisure sites (*Cheers*, most famously), the home has proven a particularly popular setting, especially the family home. A full list would be huge, but we may think of such notables as *I Love Lucy*, *Father Knows Best*, *Leave it to Beaver*, *The Andy Griffith Show*, *The Beverly Hillbillies*, *Bewitched*, *The Brady Bunch*, *Happy Days*, *Diff'rent Strokes*, *Family Ties*, *The Cosby Show*, *Growing Pains*, *Full House*, *Who's the Boss?*, and *The Fresh Prince of Bel Air*. Within the sitcom, action rarely if ever overflows – save for 'special episodes' – and so the sitcom typically 'resets' itself with each episode: characters and group dynamics go back to ground zero, and new topics are introduced. Consequently, central figures and character relationships are usually stock characters and relationships, peripheral walk-on characters (who may have only a line or two to establish character) are even more typed, and development is extremely rare, saved for no more than one or two episodes a season. Particularly given the pressures of often non-chronological syndication, consistency is the name of the sitcom game – after all, any given episode must be able to follow any other episode (see Nelson 1990) – and its humor is a reliable one: the precocious little child will take the authority figures to task each week, the parents will put everything right, and so on.

Sitcoms constantly 'reset' themselves, living in, as Eaton (1978: 74) notes, an 'existential circle' in which nothing really changes, and every episode starts more or less where the last one started; and *The Simpsons* frequently plays with this sitcom clock, and with the amnesia of sitcom memory. The family members often forget important events in their 'history,' so that, for instance, Homer has no recall of having heart surgery ('Bart Carny'), and Mr Burns is forever asking his assistant Mr Smithers who Homer is, even though, as Smithers once adds (in a line that simultaneously parodies the degree to which peripheral characters' lives are put on ice 'off stage'), 'All the recent events of your life have revolved around him in some way' ('Homer the Smithers'). Similarly, in 'Saddlesore Galactica,' when the family contemplates getting a horse – a feat already accomplished in an earlier episode – the show's nerdy fan stand-in, Comic Book Guy, interjects, 'Excuse me, I believe this family already had a horse, and the expense forced Homer to work at the Quik-E-Mart, with hilarious consequences.' Later in the same episode, Bart expresses fear that his mother is developing a gambling problem – again, the topic of an earlier episode – at which point Comic Book Guy mysteriously appears again, warning, 'Hey, I'm watching you.'

Notably, in all of the above instances, the action continues as normal, as sitcom memory (or lack thereof) is pointed out but comically not acted upon. Thus, where Grote (1983: 67) notes that sitcom episodes 'live in a kind of time-warp without any reference to the other episodes,' producing a situation whereby everything 'remains inviolate and undisturbed, no matter what transitory events may occur' (1983: 59), *The Simpsons* comically reflects upon this. Likewise, the program makes fun of the sitcom's conflation of real time and occasional predilection for time jumps. In 'Eight Misbehavin',' for instance, in order to fit a character's pregnancy into one episode, we skip nine months. Marking this for the audience, the show cuts to the family talking. Homer remarks, 'Man, the last nine months sure were crazy,' to which Bart replies, 'I'll say. I learnt the true meaning of Columbus Day,' Marge adds, 'I enjoyed a brief but memorable stint as Sideshow Marge,' Lisa states, 'I became the most popular girl in school, but blew it by being conceited,' and lastly Bart claims also to have learnt 'the true meaning of Winter.' Here, we are treated to a parody not only of how awkwardly time jumps are proposed, but also of how ultimately irrelevant any sitcom time is — nothing really changes, after all — and finally, of the sort of plots that traditionally fill sitcom time.

The Simpsons is also particularly persistent in highlighting the pressures that a 22 minute time limit puts on a sitcom, that, when combined with the desire for a happy, circular ending, sees the average sitcom rush to tie everything up in the last minute. Often such endings sacrifice logic and ask for considerable suspension of disbelief, and a favorite *Simpsons* strategy is to take such illogicality to absurd extremes. For instance, at the end of 'Trash of the Titans,' with the town's ecosystem destroyed, the citizens opt for 'Plan B,' whereby the entire town is moved five miles down the road. Meanwhile, in 'The Principal and the Pauper,' after Principal Skinner has been revealed as an impostor, then reinstated so as to provide closure and end everything as it began, Judge Snider decrees:

> By the authority of the city of Springfield, I hereby confer upon you the name of Seymour Skinner, as well as his past, present, future, and mother. And, I further decree that everything will be just like it was before all this happened, and no one will ever mention it again, under penalty of torture.

He delivers this last line to the viewer, acknowledging the necessary complicity of the audience in taking each episode as a new one. Sitcoms habitually rely on *deus ex machina* for endings, and *The Simpsons* goes out of its way to point this out, to leave them dangling embarrassingly from the theater ceiling.

Family and fairytales

In the sitcom's chicken and egg story, either the desperate need to close on a happy note causes such rushed, over-tidy endings, and/or the desperate need to close without having disturbed anything necessarily leads to happy, moralized endings. However, while many of *The Simpsons'* endings highlight the artificiality of sitcom time and memory, so too do many endings toy with the traditional happy, moralized ending. Or, rather, it is common for *The Simpsons* to provide a saccharine sweet ending, and then severely undercut it. For instance, in a Christmas episode (traditionally a 'feelgood' episode for sitcoms) in which the family lose everything, Marge offers the tired wisdom that, 'in a way, having nothing reminds us how lucky we really are [. . .] We still have each other, and isn't that the best gift of all?' and thus we have our sweet ending . . . except Lisa then interjects, 'But we would've had each other anyway,' and Bart adds, 'Yeah, plus lots of cool stuff,' hence undermining the saccharine ending, and simultaneously responding to an overused Christmas episode moral ('Miracle on Evergreen Terrace'). Meanwhile, in 'Dancin' Homer,' Homer narrates the tale of his brief stint as a major league baseball mascot, a stint that is, of course, over by the episode's end. But the family supports Homer, and he ends by exclaiming, 'What a family! My wife and kids stood by me.' Lest *The Simpsons* allow a traditional sitcom end, though, he tacks on, 'On the way home, I realized how little that meant to me.'

Family sitcoms are supposed to remind us constantly of the strength of family to overcome all problems, but Homer's story ends (tongue-in-cheek) with a moral of the family's ineffectivity. In many respects, then, we might consider the American family sitcom as a form of modern fairytale, and *The Simpsons* as its parodic echo. In *Morphology of the Folktale*, Vladimir Propp (1992) studies the folk or fairytale as a form containing a remarkably constant sequence of dramatic functions, and it is easy to apply these functions wholesale to most typical domesticom plots. Consider, for example, this generic sitcom plot offered by Jones:

> Domestic harmony is threatened when a character develops a desire that runs counter to the group's welfare, or misundertands a situation because of poor communication, or contacts a disruptive outside element. The voice of the group – usually the voice of the father or equivalent chief executive – tries to restore harmony but fails. The dissenter grabs at an easy, often unilateral solution. The solution fails and the dissenter must surrender to the group for rescue. The problem turns out to be not very serious after all, once everyone remembers to communicate and surrender his or her selfish goals. The wisdom of the group and its executive is proved. Everyone, including the dissenter, is happier than at the outset.
>
> (Jones 1992: 4)

This plotline reads like Propp's list of functions (see 1990: 26–63), with a family member absenting him or herself from home (function 1), violating an interdiction (2, 3), succumbing to deception or villainy (4–7), harm caused to the family (8) or a feeling of familial lack (8a), misfortune or lack made known (9), attempt at counteraction (10), the 'testing' of the hero (12, 25, 26), an attempt to use the help of a donor (13–15), villainy defeated and problem liquidated (18, 19), and resolution (26), with, no doubt, many of the other functions appearing along the way. There is quite a primordial, moralistic simplicity to the domesticom.

If the above defines the *form* of family sitcom, though, it has also taken on a particular ideological role over time. While I have, to the present, predominantly written of genres as about aesthetic conventions, genres are by no means 'merely' aesthetic. Rather, genres 'are situated within larger systems of power and, thus, often come "fully loaded" with political implications' (Mittell 2004: 27). If we take some of the more salient definitions of genre, and remove the word 'genre' from them, they even begin to sound like definitions of ideology. Consider, for instance, Neale's formulations that genres are 'systems of orientations, expectations and conventions that circulate between industry, text or subject' (Neale 1980: 19), or, rather, 'not systems: they are processes of systematisation' (1980: 51), 'regimes of verisimilitude' that 'entail rules, norms and laws' (Neale 2000: 32). Genres establish, as Altman (1999) points out, a set grammar that positions the world and its players, assigning specific roles to each and delimiting in advance what it is possible to do or think within that worldview. All of a genre's aesthetic or textual components individually and/or in aggregate involve positing the world in a certain way, and thus they are all to some degree ideological. Ryan and Kellner (1988: 77) look to genres as that which 'hold the world in place, establishing and enforcing a sense of propriety, of proper boundaries which demarcate appropriate thought, feeling, and behavior, and which provide frames, codes, and signs for constructing a shared social reality.' Ideology, they note – and particularly hegemonic ideology – easily houses itself within genre.

The domesticom has served stalwart duty as a mouthpiece for a contemporary fairytale of patriarchal, middle-class, consumerist suburban morality and for the myth of the American Dream. The genre grew with television, surviving and thriving from early on, and spearheading the prime time schedule in one guise or another since the 1950s. Of utmost importance to its success is that it mastered the ability to address, as Marc (1989: 44) calls it, 'the prissiest common denominator.' Residing in prime time, it realized that a considerable portion of its audience would be made up of families, and, as such, from the 1950s on, 'The aim was to be attractive but not at any cost. Cuteness, blandness, emptiness, and boredom were all acceptable alternatives to exciting the puritan beast that lay buried beneath the go-go surface of a postwar America' (Marc 1989: 44). The domesticom is all about 'good, clean family entertainment.' Themes must be 'appropriate' for families, and the action and situation must be understandable, operating in a safe world that all can relate to and appreciate . . . at least, ideally for its producers. The American family sitcom, then, was fashioned: by networks assuming families at home wanting happy, value-affirming entertainment suitable for the kids; by producers wanting an effective delivery system for ads that pay the bills; and, arguably, by the postwar nation trying to (re)sell the American Dream to itself (see Jones 1992; Marc 1989). It is thus no surprise that, ideologically, the family sitcom leans toward expounding the virtues of the nuclear family, consumerism, and the American middle-class suburban dream.

To begin with, in the domesticom, we have a product in which the family as audience is presented with the family as characters,[3] 'the living room within the living room' (Marc 1989: 127). As Lull (1990), Morley (1986, 1992, 2000), Silverstone (1994), and Spigel (1992) note, the television itself is already a profoundly domestic and domesticating technology, with home and hearth as both 'product and precondition' (Morley 1992: 203),[4] but the sitcom is the medium's nuclear family trump card in this respect. Even in the 1950s, nuclear families were by no means 'normal' in any statistical sense (Carter 1995: 186), but television, with the family sitcom at the forefront, has somehow managed to convince us that they are so. As Hartley argues:

> Family or domestic sitcoms were perhaps the bedrock of broadcast television. They were what you grew up on, gently and amusingly teaching two important skills: how to watch television (media literacy); and how to live in families with tolerant mutual accommodation, talking not fighting (life skills).
>
> (Hartley 2001: 66)

At prime time, that time of the day when many a family is supposedly brought together, the family sitcom enters the home and offers images of what form familial relations might take, of what constitutes 'father' or 'husband,' 'mother' or 'wife' (see Haralovich 1988), 'sibling' or 'child,' and, importantly, 'family' and 'home.' Then, tomorrow or next week, the same images return, and when one changes channels to another sitcom, more images are offered, often remarkably similar in nature. And by episode end, all is reconciled, hence stressing the comfort and continuance of familyhood.

American family sitcoms frequently take the nuclear family for granted, and in doing so, suggest to viewers the fundamental normality of this image of family. Admittedly, many family sitcoms feature non-nuclear families, but most still yearn for 'nuclearity,' and frequently provide surrogates to make up the nucleus – witness *Who's the Boss?*, in which housekeeper Tony stands in for husband and father, until he fully adopts the role by marrying Angela – and/or bemoan the loss of the missing member – witness *Full House*, in which the dead mother is eulogized on an almost weekly basis. Jones (1992), Marc (1989), and E. Taylor (1989) all document how the 1970s marked a period in which the family sitcom appeared to be either dying or changing, as *All in the Family* in particular disrupted the blissful serenity of sitcom suburbia, as *Mary Tyler Moore* introduced the notion of (limited) character development (see Feuer 1987: 128), and as both *Mary Tyler Moore* and *MASH* challenged network heads' faith in the home as proper (read popular) setting for sitcoms. Nevertheless, in the 1976–7 season, *All in the Family*'s string of five straight seasons at the top of the Nielsens ratings was ended by the nostalgic and peppy family sitcom throwback, *Happy Days* (Brooks and Marsh 1999: 1252). American television experienced the 'aggressive reinstatement' of the nuclear family (E. Taylor 1989: 164), and with shows like *Family Ties*, *The Cosby Show*, and *Growing Pains* soon following in *Happy Days*' footsteps, and taking over the Nielsens, neoconservative 'family values' once more had the stage.[5]

Anti-fairytale

However, if ideology can peg itself to genre, trying to ride along with it inconspicuously, any act of revealing and externalizing a genre's grammar and inner workings stands to reveal and externalize the ideological partner. As aspects of the genre are hence rendered absurd, one of two possibilities presents itself: either the ideology will therefore be pulled into the parodic critique, similarly ridiculed, and rendered problematic, or at least the ideology's host loses its rich soil for unproblematic ideological growth, and part of the connection between ideology and genre is broken. As Ryan and Kellner explain of teaching genre and ideology:

> once the generic conventions are foregrounded, the genre can no longer operate successfully as a purveyor of ideology. The conventions become unstable and variable; [. . .] and the generic signifiers themselves increasingly become signifieds, the referents [. . .] rather than the active agents of [. . .] practice, a matter of content rather than a vital form.
>
> (Ryan and Kellner 1988: 78)

Parody, then, aims to make genre's formal and ideological work considerably harder, for it can serve as a powerful foregrounding element, potentially making us more genre literate and more attuned to look at the ideological content that resides within the form itself.

Mittell notes that the act of mixing two genres 'creates a site of heightened genre discourse' (2004: 156), whereby 'the conventions of both genres are made manifest and explicit, heightening genre assumptions and undercutting their illusion of naturalism through juxtaposition' (2004: 157). He sees this process at work in *The*

Simpsons, caused by its mix of cartoon and sitcom, but of course, parody itself mixes genres, strategically bumping up against its target genre so as to shine light on its conventions. *The Simpsons* is, as such, particularly genre conscious, and it offers its viewers a similar consciousness. To date, the show has provided 16 full years and counting of sitcom parody. It now follows more surrealistic, less sitcom-based plotlines, but this is perhaps because it has already exhausted almost all of the stock family sitcom plots, some several times over. Many of its episodes take a stock plot and proceed to deconstruct it from inside, so that all of the following have been lampooned: the good child has gone bad; the parents' marriage has hit a rut; we have had several road trip episodes; one of the kids has been forced by his mother to befriend an 'uncool' kid; the household has had to cope with the mother going away; there have been conflicts with in-laws; long lost relatives have reappeared; we have had flashback episodes; the kids have been forced into sports by the parents; student elections have taken place; the family has had to deal with troublesome pets; the kids have associated themselves with bad crowds; and strangers have come to stay with the family. Constant, though, in *The Simpsons'* use of all these stock plots have been the parodic modifications that the series inflicts upon them. Endings are undercut, and, similarly, characters are often transposed, plot components are exaggerated, and irreverent or rude content is added to what are supposed to be tame storylines.

To take one episode and its multiple parodic modifications as an example, 'Lisa's Sax' opens with a particularly pointed attack at sitcom nostalgia, as Homer and Marge sit at a piano together singing 'Those Were the Days.' The couple at the piano, song title, and tune will be recognized by some viewers as having been taken from *All in the Family*, and thus the episode immediately attaches itself to that show's own critique of the happy American Dream. Whether the reference is noticed or not, though, *The Simpsons* then takes the critique further, for as they sing, the 'camera' pans through Springfield. At first, the view is of a nice, idyllic town, but we then see a tire fire raging. The camera cuts to Evergreen Terrace, and while at first we see lovely suburban houses, the camera settles on the Simpsons' house, run-down and dirty with an old mattress in the overgrown front yard. A rare voiceover intones, '*The Simpsons* is filmed in front of a live studio audience,' and, at that, Homer enters the living room drinking beer and greets Bart with Archie Bunker's famous, 'Hey there, meathead!' Whether the audience is aware or not of the *All in the Family* subtext, the show thus opens by contrasting the saccharine nostalgia of affluent, suburban, happy family life with the reality of a grotty town and home, housing a beer-drinking father who is rude to his children. This is definitely not the Cosbys' world.

The episode then continues as a semi-flashback episode in which Homer and Marge tell the story of Lisa's first saxophone, following Bart's destruction of said instrument. Throughout, sitcom norms of family behavior are violated, as particularly Homer is shown to be a drastically incompetent father. He blindly allows baby Maggie to play with an electric drill, and his great fatherly attempt to make Lisa feel better when her sax is ruined consists of offering to destroy something Bart loves. When Bart objects, he retorts, 'Don't worry: if that bothers *you*, I'll destroy something Maggie loves' (causing Maggie to hug her drill protectively). Bart and Lisa are shown (justifiably) to have little respect for their father; the family cannot afford to put Lisa in a gifted school; Homer tries to feed Maggie beer; and at one point Marge explodes, 'Sometimes I feel so smothered by this family, I just wanna scream till my lungs explode!' As in every episode of *The Simpsons*, all manner of family sitcom rules are contravened, and as in so many other episodes, *The Simpsons* invites us over and over again to laugh at these rules.

For sheer density and frequency of jokes, nothing on *The Simpsons* receives as much parody and ridicule as the sitcom and its surrounding apparatus, and key among that surrounding apparatus is the sugar-coated sitcom version of the nuclear family, familial roles, and relations. Indeed, it is worth returning to Propp to discuss the *functions* of different sitcom characters, especially since the traditional American family sitcom holds much in common with the folk tale. Propp (1990: 79) observes that of the many (set) functions in a tale, certain ones always tend to join together in 'spheres' that correspond to specific 'performers' or roles. Therefore, for instance, the 'hero' is responsible for counteraction, victory, and punishment; the 'donor' for testing or interrogating the hero, and provision of a helpful agent; the 'helper' for guidance, liquidation of lack, rescue, solution, and transfiguration, whereby the hero is given a new appearance; and the 'villain' for evil-doing, struggle, and pursuit/chase (1990: 79–80). Drawing the connection to the sitcom world, the hero is often the child (and, as with the folk tale, action begins when s/he leaves home and violates some form of implicit or explicit interdiction), the donor and helper are the parents and/or older siblings, and the villain is inevitably a person or force from outside of the home. As such, within the standard 22 minutes of sitcom time, the hero will face and overcome the villainy due largely to the implicit or explicit help and advice of the parental donors/helpers, nearly always in a manner that moralizes the wisdom of the advice or help, and that reaffirms the strength of the nuclear family unit in overcoming all obstacles. In a notable divergence from Propp's folk tale, though, as Grote (1983: 72) observes, whereas folk tale heroes improve or better their worlds, sitcom heroes and helpers keep things as they were/are.

However, that was Propp, this is Springfield, and character roles are radically redistributed in *The Simpsons*. Beginning with Homer, as sitcom father, he should be our upstanding role model. Instead, he is a gluttonous, lazy oaf who puts butter in his coffee, and whose aspiration in life is to be a 'pin monkey' at the local bowling alley. His fatherly advice to Bart and Lisa consists of such maxims as, 'always blame it on the guy who doesn't speak English,' he rewards them for not apologizing, and complains about taking his kids out on Saturday. Meanwhile, as completely incompetent nuclear safety manager at the power plant (he needs to write 'Red = Meltdown' on his arm), he is a danger to his community, he regularly throttles his 10-year-old son, loves revenge, and when dragged to church, sleeps or brings a bucket of fried chicken. In short, helper or donor he is not. Homer regularly stands in the way of his children's progression, even adopting the role of villain at times, thus inverting the role of the typical sitcom dad. At other times, though, he switches roles with the children, and takes on the role of hero. Part of Homer's immense comic appeal is his infant-like conception of the world, which just as often sees him as the struggling hero, and places Bart and Lisa in the roles of donor and helper. Homer frequently gets over-excited, runs out of the house screaming, 'Ice cream man! Ice cream man!' when his children make dinging noises, and in an amusing parodic sequence in 'Take My Wife, Sleaze,' complete with *Wonder Years*-style soundtrack, it is he who is taught to ride a (motor) bike by son Bart. Sitcom fathers have often been goofy, but ultimately have remarkably little to learn, and few if any voyages of discovery to embark on, but Homer is forever needing to learn.

In the role of teacher most frequently is Lisa. Many sitcoms have a precocious child, but Lisa is beyond precocious. She is nearly always aware of what is going on around her, not just in terms of actions, but also in terms of sociological and ecological significance. Lisa is a repository of any knowledge *The Simpsons'* writers may have picked up, and in countless instances, it is she who makes things right, who makes key familial decisions, who dispenses 'parental' advice and help. Indeed, while Bart has attracted the most popular attention as rebellious kid, particularly in his pariah days of the early 1990s (see Glynn 1996; Parisi 1993), it is Lisa who represents a more distinct challenge to neoconservative 'family values,' for it is she who, as 8-year-old *girl*, in many ways keeps the family and even the community together and keeps everything running smoothly.[6]

This role is shared with Marge, who in this respect holds true to her traditional sitcom function of donor/helper. Certainly, Marge holds more in common with June Cleaver and Clair Huxtable than Homer does with Ward or Cliff: apron and oven-mitts on, Marge is the near-perfect sitcom mother. That said, *The Simpsons* often writes cracks into this facade, and it is precisely her usual 'normality' that renders these cracks all the more comical, as the writers suggest the impossibility of being the perfect donor/helper and domestic goddess that sitcoms ask for (see Haralovich 1988; Mellancamp 2003; Spigel 1992). Marge has experienced several nervous breakdowns, leading her to hair loss, road rage, alcohol, a gambling addiction, steroids, and even an asylum. Marge is, after all, the ideal sitcom mom stranded in a family with genuine problems, and she serves as a powerful indicator of how harrowed a role domesticom motherhood is. Even beyond her breakdowns, Marge is regularly ignored, humiliated, and under-appreciated, particularly by Homer and Bart. If she inhabits her 'function' more or less unproblematically,

The Simpsons shows how much these functions rely on one another to work, and thus the severe unlikelihood of finding the sitcom family ideal proves itself reality.

As mischievous Huck Finn-like character, Bart also seemingly occupies a role present in every American family sitcom and many folk tales (the young Hansel, or Jack the Giant-Killer), and so, at first glance, may appear a Proppian hero. To a certain degree, this is his role, and as with Marge, he fills it reasonably well. However, as became obvious when Bart was made a focus for a moral panic of sorts about youth rebellion for the American far right and grumbling parents alike, Bart's rebellion is several steps worse than the average sitcom mischief master-mind. Importantly, Bart frequently refuses to learn, and while Marge and Lisa as donors/helpers may regularly feed him with advice, he rarely takes it to heart. If a folk tale or sitcom exists in large part to prove the importance and truth of the opening interdiction, Bart subverts the whole point of the exercise by endlessly shrugging off moral platitudes. In many ways, he is a symbol of the degree to which children cannot be programmed as unproblematically as most American family sitcoms suggest. As hero, then, Bart frequently comes close to cohabiting the role of villain, and at other times renders the helper and donor irrelevant, and denies the closure and happy, rounded ending that any self-respecting folk tale or family sitcom should contain.

And yet . . .

However, while *The Simpsons* attacks the domesticom version of the family, the show is by no means 'anti-family,' nor does it radically destabilize the family unit itself. Homer *can* be a good dad, and, whatever else, always cares deeply for his wife and children; Lisa has her 8-year-old girl moments, and loves her Malibu Stacy dolls as much as the next sitcom girl loves her Barbie; Marge may be driven to bouts of temporary insanity, but overall appears happy with her lot; and Bart occasion-ally listens to his parents, and in the end proves a loving child in most instances. Likewise, while family-affirming endings are nearly always undercut, they are not denied altogether. Rather, in offering a sweet ending, then a sarcastic, parodic pull of the rug, as is their common technique, *The Simpsons* still gives us that sweet ending, if in modified form. Rarely if ever has an episode ended with total misery and/or sting. Occasionally, too, an episode will close with a genuinely sweet ending. As such, we may choose to regard its parody as token only, as a strategy of post-modern hip or cynical chic that, upon further study, reveals itself as hollow and meaningless. To do so, however, would be to sorely misunderstand both parody generally, and *The Simpsons'* domesticom parody in particular. To parody a genre, after all, that genre and its grammar must be continuously invoked. By follow-ing sitcom rules of logic and performance at times, *The Simpsons* fulfils these

59

requirements. Meanwhile, though, its treatment of those generic rules is far from reverential. We may get a happy ending, but we may not. It is this very unpredictability that characterizes parody, and that ensures a critical appreciation of the predictability of regular genre. If, instead, every generic rule were continuously flouted, we would be left with a product wholly unlike its parodied genre; this new product might be boldly radical in its own right, but it would be disarmed of its ability to comment on, criticize, and *teach* the domesticom.

To return to the issue of sitcom time and re-setting, while many sitcom critics rightfully look to the existential circle of the sitcom as precluding the possibility of change, Newcomb and Hirsch (1984) counter with the example of *MASH*. Here, they pose, 'we are caught in an antiwar rhetoric that cannot end the war. A truly radical alternative, a desertion or an insurrection, would end the series. But it would also end the "discussion" of this issue' (1984: 65). Re-setting, in other words, can, in some instances, work within a network of televisual phenomenology and discussion to enact more substantive change than briefer programs with more radical endings, simply by keeping doing what is being done. The issue, then, is one of *what* is being re-set, and *how*. The traditional American family sitcom, with little respite, worked to re-set and re-tell the neoconservative myth of the ultra-happy suburban nuclear family life from the 1950s to the early 1990s. Alongside and opposite it since 1990, though, *The Simpsons* has been re-setting its parodic attack on this myth, reloaded with every viewing: a continuous critical intertextuality. It is not unique in this regard, for *Roseanne* acted as a strong, if less overtly 'parodic,' partner in the early 1990s, and numerous programs have followed in *The Simpsons'* tracks, including, most notably, *King of the Hill*, *Malcolm in the Middle*, *South Park*, and *Family Guy*. But it has been by far the most prominent, continuous, and popular.

Radical alternatives can be imagined, but it is not enough to offer alternatives. Admittedly, few new domesticoms have joined the televisual ranks in recent years, as by and large the sitcom has moved from suburb to city, and from family to friends (see *Friends*, *Seinfeld*, *Will and Grace*), or to decisively non-nuclear families (such as the father and two adult sons in *Frasier*). Even the United States' hugely successful family sitcom, *Everybody Loves Raymond*, rarely features the children, and focuses instead on the adult relationships between Ray and his parents, and Ray and his brother. Similarly, the couple on *King of Queens* have no children. Nevertheless, reruns of the old domesticom bloc still loom large, whether in syndication or in the memory. Parody of such shows therefore remains a vital corrective. Moreover, since reruns bolster nostalgic and televisual constructions of time past (Lipsitz 1990; Spigel 1995; Weispfenning 2003), critique of historical genres can lead to new and less mythologized understandings of history itself. When *The Simpsons* started in the United States, it was at a peak in the domesticom's success, and Fox counter-programmed it opposite the reigning sitcom king, *The Cosby Show*. Effectively, then, for its first few years, its critique was directed at its televisual contemporaries.

Where *The Simpsons* began as a comment on television's present, though, its domesticom parody is now largely a comment on its and our televisual past, and on the potential aftershock on our sense of cultural and familial realities.

Ironically, too, with this shift, *The Simpsons'* popular meaning has intertextually augmented from being 'anti-family values' to being a last bastion of the nuclear family on sitcoms. While Bush, Sr hated the show for 'hating' the family, and while it was even kicked off the air in Costa Rica for being 'anti-family values' (*Loaded* 1996), a decade later, both the Archbishop of Canterbury and Prime Minister Tony Blair expressed affection for it largely because it is one of the few 'pro-family' programs on television (see also Cantor 1999). To some, such ringing endorsements from pillars of conservatism might be read as proof positive of either a weakening of the parody, or a parody that has always been weak. Indeed, at one level, these endorsements illustrate how parody's offers of criticism are precisely that: offers that might be denied. However, *The Simpsons* never set out to destroy the family; rather, it sets out on a weekly basis with a goal of destabilizing and ridiculing the traditional American family sitcom's solitary and peculiar *version* of the way a family should look.

The all-consuming family

Part and parcel of this version of family relations, and one that comes under fire by *The Simpsons*, was and is, as Jones notes, the domesticom's insistence on being a 'Miracle Play of consumer society' (Jones 1992: 4). What is remarkable about domesticom families is their utterly comfortable middle-class-ness. Everyone in the idealized sitcom world is either a happy American consumer and one of 'us,' or suspicious but (and because they are) one of 'them.' Once again, some 1970s sitcoms mark a notable exception, as shows such as *All in the Family* pointed toward the seething anger and conflict simmering beneath American society, but otherwise, the pre-1990s domesticom world is a happy land of plenty. As Haralovich (1988: 57) observes, for example, sitcom mothers (before *Roseanne*) never seemed to spend much time doing chores, freed instead by their many appliances – conveniently advertised in and around the show. Home makeover programs aside, it is the sitcom which tells us how we might better design our homes, or, in other words, what we might buy, what 'a normal family' owns. As Mark Crispin Miller (1988) acerbically comments of the family in *The Cosby Show*, there is a sense in which 'Each Huxtable, in fact, is hardly more than a display case for his/her momentary possessions' (1988: 69), a comment that we could apply to many family sitcoms.

Take the perfect, happy suburban nuclear family and endow them with all manner of consumer goods and one gets the American Dream in one's living room nightly at 7.30 p.m. This picture of the American Dream, Jones (1992) and Marc (1989) note, was vitally important to the nation after World War II – a reassuring message that 'everything's all right' and 'the dream is still alive,' especially in a time when cities were filling with successive waves of new immigrants and racial tensions were increasing (see also Lipsitz 1988). As such, Jones remarks, particularly the early sitcoms 'came to crystallize some of the great American self-dillusions of the 1950s' (Jones 1992: 87), 'the products of profound national confusion masquerading as confidence' (1992: 101). 'The domestic sitcom,' adds Marc (1989: 53), 'romanticized the suburb as an idyllic small town that was located not merely miles from the modern city but the better part of a century as well.' Yet, behind this candy-coated nostalgia lay profound acts of exclusion (Grote 1983: 82) and self-deception that kept the American Dream a very white, by-invitation-only 'dream.' Moreover, lest we believe this to be a trait peculiar to the 1950s sitcom, Jhally and Lewis' (1992) study of *The Cosby Show* points to identical problems and a similar whitewashing of the American Dream in the 1980s.

Ultimately, then, the American family sitcom as genre has a notably conservative history, desperately trying to hold onto and present the American Dream of suburban nuclear families living in a predominantly white, middle class consumer world. Admittedly, not all commentators see the American sitcom as totally system-maintaining. Newcomb and Hirsch (1984) observe that sitcom characters' struggles against imposing power systems may be more important than the inevitable failure of those struggles, or as Lipsitz notes:

> narrative closure is not so easy to achieve. It is difficult to soothe anxieties without first aggravating them, and impossible to predict in any given case whether the emotional appeal of closure will silence the questions and criticisms provoked by narrative's evocation of the real hurts of history.
>
> (Lipsitz 1990: 93)

To some readers, then, the genre may be a powerful voice of dissension. Certainly, moreover, this dissension rose to the surface in the early 1990s, not only with *The Simpsons*, but also with *Married . . . with Children* and *Roseanne*.[7] Nevertheless, while the genre may well have *potential*, and may at times use it well, it is still hard to watch family interaction in most sitcoms, particularly older ones, and not be overwhelmed by the 'family values' glow that permeates every scene. Leading on from Winnicott (1974, 1975), Silverstone (1994) talks of television providing ontological security, and standing in for the mother's breast or the child's security-blanket, and in this light, we should recognize the huge role that the family sitcom plays in rocking us to sleep with the soft and soothing affirmations that everything – the family, the home, the suburb – is just fine, and nothing at all is wrong. Such a message might sound welcome . . . until we remember its racial exclusivity and its patriarchal notions of familial and societal power.

To this end, though, *The Simpsons* also plays with the role of the sitcom family vis-à-vis the 'outside' world. 'Home' can act as a powerful exclusionary concept (Morley 2000), and the family sitcom in particular sets up boundaries of inside versus outside, familiar and safe versus foreign and dangerous. Propp's (1990) schema of functions, after all, begins with the hero leaving home – for in one's true home, lies the suggestion, what could ever go wrong? – and as Grote (1983: 82) remarks, 'One of the most striking, and disturbing, aspects of the family's role in the sit-com is its intense exclusivity,' whereby 'the people from the outside who cause problems are overcome and excluded at the end of every episode.' However, in *The Simpsons*, as we have seen, Homer and Bart are just as likely to play the role of villain and act as genesis of problems, as are any external influences. Similarly, home offers no necessary promise of assistance, much less resolution. As the following exchange from 'The Great Money Caper' shows, Simpsons' family dynamics parodically seethe with discontent:

Homer: A good son would come through for his dad.
Bart: And a good dad wouldn't miss his son's little league games.
Homer: I already told you: I find them boring!
Bart: Well, I showed up for all your stupid interventions!

Home and family, in short, are not quite the warm, enveloping womb-like retreats that they are in *Leave it to Beaver*, *Growing Pains*, *Full House*, or so forth. Numerous feminist critics have pointed out the degrees to which home and family can be the sources of much conflict, coercion, violence, and risk (see Fog-Olwig 1998; Goldsack 1999; Oakley 1976; Segal 1983), and, while significantly more light-heartedly so, *The Simpsons* echoes this disillusionment with the wonders of home and family. As Lisa suggests in 'Like Father, Like Clown,' 'a man who envies our family is a man who needs help,' for in *The Simpsons*, home can cause as many problems as it solves, and the family exacerbate as many dilemmas as they dispel.

Moreover, this reshifting of boundaries of trust and safety extends beyond the family house as home, to the town and suburb as home. Springfield is hardly the ideal family sitcom neighborhood: its populace are prone to mob rule; its leaders are corrupt, inept, and/or evil; it claims the lowest voter turnout ('Two Bad Neighbors') and highest average weight ('Sweets and Sour Marge') in the United States, and its citizens include such dark figures as Mr Burns, the sadistic Mo the bartender, and consummate criminals Sideshow Bob and Snake. Meanwhile, interactions with or comments on the outside world and its people nearly always fall into one of two categories. In the first instance, they reflect more negatively upon Springfield and/or its individuals than on the outside world. Take, for example, Bart's response to Lisa lecturing Homer on not judging a place he has never been to: 'Yeah, that's what people do in Russia' ('The City of New York vs. Homer

Simpson'). Similarly, when in 'Missionary Impossible,' Homer goes as a missionary to a South Pacific Island, the sanctimonious colonialist attitude of missionaries is continually lampooned, such as when the outgoing missionaries proudly report to Homer that they have 'ridiculed away *most* of [the islanders'] beliefs,' and when a small child explains that they wear clothes because the missionaries 'gave us the gift of shame.' The episode ends with Homer introducing the locals to 'his way' of life, making them all violent and alcoholic gambling addicts. Elsewhere, *The Simpsons* have even mounted an episode-long blistering critique on xenophobia, 'Much Apu About Nothing,' in which the town is trying to have all illegal immigrants deported. In a particularly pointed instance of satire directed at the gatekeeper mentality behind white suburbia or 'White Flight,' one scene sees Police Chief Wiggum rounding up deportees with this inversion of the Statue of Liberty's promise: 'First, we'll be rounding up your tired, then your poor, then your huddled masses yearning to breathe free.' In general, the show wastes few chances to point toward the dark provincialism and fortress mentality of suburbia, suggesting that something is wrong with American suburbia, both on screen and off.

In the second instance, in a rather high risk strategy, *The Simpsons* employs what we could call *hyper*-stereotypes. From Scottish Groundskeeper Willie and Quik E Mart owner Apu, to the show's depictions of Japan, Australia, East Africa, Canada, and Brazil in family trip episodes, the show rounds up multiple stereotypes and jams them into one character or episode. The result, although admittedly this is a strategy that passes many by,[8] and hence risks backfiring on itself, is to make the *process* of stereotyping the target, rather than the people themselves. Certainly, while many Australians were offended by a *Simpsons* episode set in Australia, for instance (see Beard 2004), the episode's key targets were American behavior overseas and smalltown American mindsets that view other countries in one-dimensional ways. Beard is right to criticize the show for using other countries and people as mere props to examine America and Americans, so we should be wary of celebrating its difference from wholly insular sitcoms. At the same time, though, by including countless references to the outside world, to a community beyond the family, and to political and cultural events, *The Simpsons* refuses to place Springfield into the nostalgic space-time warp and void that most family sitcoms so keenly set up shop and home in. Ultimately, rather than serve as retreat, Springfield is under the microscope, inviting us as viewers to laugh at it and at the myth of the perfect suburban middle-class America that gave birth to its non-parodic counterparts.

As Spigel (1995) argues, when we consider that 1950s and 1960s sitcoms are some of the most readily accessible 'artifacts' from those decades, their reruns 'haunting' contemporary television and society (see Nelson 1990: 90), we see how sitcoms can not only render the present in conservatively nostalgic terms, but also render the past to us in such terms. Spigel recounts how many of her students 'know' the 1950s, and the role of women at the time, only through such sitcoms, and thus asks to what degree these sitcoms are *making* American history or 'memory' (Lipsitz 1990) more conservative, patriarchal, and sexist (and, we might add, racist). Thus, by combating the domesticom's depictions of family, home, women, and suburb, *The Simpsons*' parody can work toward destabilizing the *de facto* history that domesticoms have told. By showing traditional family sitcoms to be presenting a convenient yet unrealistic, unlikely fairytale, *The Simpsons* could play a small role in provoking a critical reevaluation of that myth, not only as it has appeared on the 21-inch screen, but also as we may have imagined it to have 'actually happened.' Although highly critical of sitcom politics, Jones ends his history of the genre with a note of optimism inspired by the advent of *The Simpsons*, which he sees as 'about the sitcom form itself as much as about life' (1992: 268). 'The mask of illusion,' he argues, 'has been stripped away by creator and audience alike,' robbing the sitcom of its 'alchemical powers' to create reality (1992: 269). While I hesitate to regard parody as turning lead into gold, certainly *The Simpsons* holds great potential not only to criticize genre, but also, given that the media are increasingly our culture's most listened-to historians, to rewrite our conception of history.

Animating parody

Many of the examples and quotations of *Simpsons* parody that I use in this book consist largely of verbal humor. After all, verbal humor is already in words, and thus does not require the same bending of translation that music or images do. E. B. White observed that 'Humor can be dissected, as a frog can, but the thing dies in the process and the innards are discouraging to any but the pure scientific mind' (cited in Wallace 2001: 235), and so, I already risk killing a few frogs. However, if analyzing humor can kill it, trying to explain a joke can often constitute an altogether more inhumane act of torture, and so I have deliberately avoided dealing with too much visual or musical parody. This has the great pity of missing out on some of *The Simpsons*' finest parodic moments. Nevertheless, if we are to do the study of *Simpsons* parody any justice, we must at least mention its visuals, its 'look,' and its power as *animated* parody.

In writing on techniques used by parody, Harries notes the prevalence of transposition, whereby:

> the lexicon, syntax and style of a parodic text operate by way of a complex pattern of shifting in which one or two of the planes work to anchor the parody to its prototext while the other functions to create ironic difference from the targeted text.
>
> (Harries 2000: 99–100)

An animated world is one of perpetual transposition, for anything it depicts is something that we are more used to seeing in live action (except, of course, when it turns its parodic eye to other cartoons). When *The Simpsons* takes *any* visual trope from live action and turns it into a cartoon, it therefore removes that trope a few steps from us, potentially allowing us to see the trope with fresh eyes, defamiliarized. Bizarre camera angles; traditional ways of shooting a given scene or genre; devices such as fast editing, panning, close-ups, and montage; and even how people move or make facial expressions all become defamiliarized in cartoon form. This is part of the magic and wonder of animation, but also part of what allows animated parodies particular powers to comment on and render obvious general strategies of filmic and televisual storytelling. *The Simpsons*, by and large, is 'filmed' like whatever genre it happens to be mocking, with 'shots' put together under the appropriate genre rules, and so *visually* almost everything that occurs in *The Simpsons* is potentially parodic, from the crane-cam shots of the opening sequence to a graduated close-up on a character's eyes for emotional effect.

This defamiliarization extends, too, to the use of pathos, and hence to much of the show's use of music in kick-starting such pathos. When, for instance, we see a character deeply upset, we are faced not with a real person (acting) in despair, just a rather crudely drawn cartoon image. This distance can therefore turn what might otherwise be a touching or sad moment into a humorous one. To say animation *restricts* identification with characters would be inaccurate; however, it certainly *constricts* identification: Homer can cry and bemoan his life, the 'camera' can begin a slow close-up, and sad music can accompany, yet often this only looks funny, and turns our attention to the mechanisms by which live action shows call for our sympathy. To some degree, then, as Wallace (2001: 240) writes, 'It may not be too great a stretch to suggest [. . .] that *The Simpsons* is a sort of Brechtian television show,' for it is a show that *as animation* is always one step back from reality. *The Simpsons* makes use of its abilities not only, as Wells (1998: 6) claims animation can, to 'absolutely resist notions of the real world,' but also to turn around and mock that 'reality,' and, by distancing us and our identification from it, reveal the role that we usually play in allowing such constructions of reality to be set up. Moreover, as Mittell (2004) argues, genre mixing collides two sets of generic expectations, and thus by offering two or more ways of interpreting a given scene, character, or instance, genre mixes tend to draw the viewers' attention to the processes of generic grammar and construction. Consequently, as cartoon genre expectations clash with those of the sitcom, *The Simpsons* stands to provoke closer, detailed attention to the logic and rules of the sitcom.

The Simpsons' existence as an animated show also allows its writers and artists seemingly infinite scope for characters, settings, or effects. *The Simpsons* can go anywhere, add any number of characters,[9] or create any effect without the hassle of building sets, hiring new actors, or contracting a CGI (computer-generated imagery) studio. This gives the writers considerable freedom to set up shop on any generic site with great ease and no economic burden. Furthermore, as Wells (1998: 122) states of animation, 'Abstract concepts and previously unimaginable states can be visualised' and be 'used to reveal conditions or principles which are hidden or beyond the comprehension of the viewer' (1998: 122). We can go inside Homer's reveries of 'The Land of Chocolate' ('Burns Verkaufen der Kraftwerk'), witness Bart's immune system voluntarily give in to the Osaka flu virus ('Marge in Chains'), or go to all manner of other sites that are largely out-of-bounds to live action television. As renowned Czech surrealist animator Jan Svankmajer notes:

> Animation enables me to give magical powers to things. In my films, I move many objects, real objects. Suddenly, everyday contact with things which people are used to acquires a new dimension and in this way casts a doubt over reality. In other words, I use animation as a means of subversion.
>
> (quoted in Wells 1998: 11)

As a tool of parody, then, animation greatly increases scope for exaggeration and literalization, two of the six key strategies Harries (2000) notes that parodies make use of. For instance, Mr Burns, Homer's decrepit and evil boss, can be depicted as a tiny, wiry old man with a long, hooked nose, whose bones are constantly breaking, and whose touch kills plants. Meanwhile, when he and the Springfield Republican Party meet in 'Brawl in the Family,' they can be shown to congregate in a Transylvanian castle (with Dracula in attendance) surrounded by lightning and rain. Not only, though, does animation allow for greater use of exaggeration or literalization, but also its distancing ensures that the show can get away with it. Surely, for example, if we were faced with a live action overweight and drunk Homer meeting his alcoholic friend Barney in the local rat-ridden bar, or if we saw a real person throttling his child in anger throughout the show, the program would lose both viewers and advertisers. When, in a satiric take on family counseling, the Simpsons are offered nerf sticks to hit each other with when one feels emotionally hurt, and Bart removes the nerf in order to beat his family members with hard plastic ('There's No Disgrace Like Home'), animation softens the blows on the viewer's moral sense, highlighting that 'it's only a cartoon.' Animation's distance from reality allows us a few steps back, and with that, allows the writers a few steps forward, and beyond what their live action counterparts are capable of. Wells (1998: 6) argues that animation 'offers a greater opportunity for film-makers to be more imaginative and less conservative,' and this is an opportunity on which *The Simpsons* capitalizes.

As Wells also notes, though, 'The very language of animation seems to carry with it an inherent innocence which has served to disguise and dilute the potency of some of its more daring imagery' (1998: 19). Here we reach a key dialectic for parody's use of animation, for on one hand, as Wells suggests, animation can 'disguise' parody, hence allowing it past otherwise wary gatekeepers. Fool-like, *The Simpsons* can be seen as harmless, and hence gain access to a wider audience than would more overtly 'threatening' shows. In this way, Rushkoff (2004) suggests, it may act as a 'media virus.' On the other hand, as Wells (1998) also suggests, viewers' preconceptions of animation may 'dilute' the strength of its parody. I will return to this dialectic in Part III, but here it must be flagged that a viewer thinking 'it's only a cartoon' may be inclined to take its commentary less seriously as a result: perhaps even more so than live action parody, animated parody may risk failure by virtue of its methods alone.

Meanwhile, however, yet one more virtue of animation as it pertains to *The Simpsons* exists at the level of what it does *not* do. Animation ensures a regularity of appearance, and consequently allows the eye, imagination, and surrounding talk to focus on other elements. In a world where David Beckham's hair, Carrie's shoes on *Sex and the City*, or the furniture in a sitcom character's apartment can attract all the attention, Marge's blue bouffant hairdo and green dress, and the Simpsons' 1990 house and contents deny the world of style and fashion another program and yet more characters to emulate. Nobody in *The Simpsons* ages, and any change in a character's look will be made solely for the purposes of comedy – as when Maggie is dressed in her star-like Christmas costume. Combined, then, with an animation style that, while humorous and effective, is nonetheless unspectacular, *The Simpsons* must rely on its wit and humor for popularity, not on the good looks, sexy or chic clothing, and designer consumables of its characters. In this regard, it rejects the legacy of its domesticom forerunners, offering little room for product placement or the marketing of style, body image, clothes, or appliances. As will be discussed further in Chapter 3, *The Simpsons* is refreshingly anti-consumerist in this regard. Of course, the show has spawned its own army of merchandise, as will also be discussed in Chapter 3. Whereas sitcoms have often centered entire plots around consumer items, though, when *The Simpsons* does so, the item is mythical, not product placement, and the family member's irrational need for it is soundly mocked: Homer's Canyonero SUV ('The Last Temptation of Krust') or Assassin shoes ('Bart's Dog Gets an "F"'), or Bart's love for the computer game *Bonestorm* ('Marge Be Not Proud'), all give rise to criticism of a consumer society, not valorization. Just as Groening's choice not to follow his sitcom predecessors and use a laugh track refuses to demand our laughter, the show also refuses to demand our consumption. On the contrary, as Chapter 3 will detail, the program directs many of its parodic swipes at ads and at hypercommercialism.

THE LOGIC OF TELEVISION
AND AD PARODY

A s Dallas Smythe (1981) has observed, the world of commercial tele-vision is a giant marketplace for advertisers, one in which the viewers are the commodities, and in which spectacle and hypercommercialism often preside (see McAllister 1996). Even most public service broadcasters must either pander to advertisers, as in the American PBS model; live alongside commercial neighbors, and thus all-too-readily adopt the commercial mindset of ratings and shares (see Ang 1991); and/or broadcast multiple programs designed for commercial television systems. The logic of most global television, then, is a commercial logic, one of ad breaks, and of the constant fear of bored viewers reaching for the remote control. Meanwhile, viewer-centered technology such as the remote control, VCRs, TiVO, and DVD players constantly threatens this logic and the marketplace it seeks to serve and protect. Amidst this skirmish, though, television as system leaves itself open to intertextual invasion. Inaugurating intertextual theory, Bakhtin (1981: 39) wrote glowingly of the novel as the prime voice of dialogism, 'made of different clay than the other already completed genres,' but television and the television series have surpassed the novel as hyper-dialogic modes of communication. Textuality is always intertextuality, and the text is always an interactive, intersective phenomenon, but certain media and genres particularly encourage intertextuality and an intertextual reading strategy. Television and the television series are the current crown domains of intertextuality. To even think of a television series, let alone to watch it, demands a complex and involved, inescapable intertextuality. Moreover, within this televisual domain of intertextuality lies fertile soil for critical intertextuality, and for parodic raids, which this chapter will examine.

The fact that television is driven by hypercommercialism should, by this point in television studies' history, be a commonplace observation. But this chapter will examine *The Simpsons'* attacks not only on the ad as genre, but also on the ad and promotional culture as a governing ideology of television. Mapping the program's parody, though, will also involve studying how television as an operating system allows all manner of fissures and fault lines to appear, ones that can be exploited by savvy parodists such as *The Simpsons*. Thus, while arguing that television is a hyper-intertextual environment characterized by its porosity, I will illustrate how *The Simpsons* capitalizes on this environment.

In writing of television, I write solely of television as it has come to be used, not of some form of inherent televisual essence. Technologically determinist models of television are in no short supply (see Baudrillard 1983a, 1983b; McLuhan 1995, 1997; Meyrowitz 1985; Postman 1986), and while these often offer valuable insights into understanding television, they suffer from assuming that television is one thing. All media, Levinson (1997) has argued, have a 'natural history,' and, like all living beings, 'evolve' over time, used in different ways in different times and spaces. Ultimately, Hartley (1987: 122) tells us, 'there is no such thing as "television" – an abstract, general form with invariable features' (see also T. Miller 1997: 1–5), and so my interests are restricted to how television and the television series currently work, how they are consumed, and how they appear to be developing in most Western (and many Eastern) countries. As such, this will also involve updating television scholarship, for many of television studies' landmark texts were written in a different televisual age, in what Ellis (2000) calls the 'era of scarcity,' with few channels on offer. How viewers use television and the televisual text has changed remarkably even since the mid-1990s, and with each passing year, intertextuality seeps even more thoroughly into televisuality, infusing itself as a primary governing principle of television.

In the BBC's early radio days, Lord Reith called for silence or dead-time between programs, so as to discourage idle, leisurely listening; and in television's era of scarcity, the televisual text was presented as an isolated unit, with a more literary-cinematic level of involvement assumed. However, such assumptions are now long gone, as are Reithian levels of control over modes of viewing. As we have moved comfortably into the era of 'availability' and are heading rapidly into a third era of 'plenty' (Ellis 2000), the televisual text and our involvement with it has changed. Today's televisual text is frequently watched in a distracted mode, it is interruptible, and its borders are constantly collapsing around it; even within itself, the text is crumbling. Deep involvement may well occur, but it is no longer the norm, nor even an expectation. All texts are becoming more intertextually vulnerable, and so too, then, is the hypercommercialized logic of television, and its minions of ads, product placement, and promotional culture.

Ads are frequently figured as the missionaries of global capitalism, spreading the gospels of Want and Want More, and, as such, have attracted a long history of criticism within media and cultural studies. A mere survey of such material and theory could take up many a book,[1] but in this chapter, I will look to *The Simpsons* to see how it parodically criticizes the advertisement and the whole culture of consumerism that advertising begets. If our world is a world of ads, so too is *The Simpsons'* Springfield, and yet in its parodically exaggerated presentation, Springfield's advertising culture is rendered even more ludicrous than our own world's, and *The Simpsons* develops its own popular parodic critique of commercial culture that on many points echoes and illustrates several of the more academic-theoretical critiques. In the process, it offers a counter to television's commercialized rhetoric, carving out space within an ad-polluted realm for discourses of consumption critique. Mark Crispin Miller has argued that 'What advertising needs is precisely what TV provides: a site secured against all threatening juxtaposition' (1988: 13). Later in this chapter, I will argue that *The Simpsons* actively works against this security, intertextually threatening advertising; first, though, I will argue that television as a whole is perpetually vulnerable to juxtaposition.

Distracted viewers and the vulnerable medium

As hyper-intertextual medium, television's defenses are always down to a certain degree. A first observation to make of television is that it is frequently watched in a distracted mode, and as Ang (1996: 67) notes, '[i]f anything, viewing today is often more like browsing than reading a book.' Several empirical studies (Collet and Lamb 1986; Gauntlett and Hill 1999; Lembo 2000; Lull 1990) confirm that people regularly do all manner of other things while watching the television: talking, ironing, cleaning the goldfish tank, and so on. We may well, then, not be watching when we are watching, so to speak, and in spite of the constant barrage of statistical reports suggesting that we all spend substantial portions of our lives in front of a switched-on television, qualitative work has underlined the important qualifier that, for much of that time, we may not be paying much attention. Indeed, as Lull (1990: 164) suggests, those who spend the most time in front of a television might also be actively watching it the least. Lull (1990), Medrich (1979), and Altman (1986) all document the degree to which television has become an 'environmental resource' (Lull 1990: 35) to many, serving largely as background noise that only moves to the foreground occasionally. Thus, as Ellis (1993) posits, where a film may ask for the full attention of the 'gaze' (see Mulvey 1975), much television invites the 'glance' (Ellis 1993: 128).

We should not overplay the incidence of distracted viewing to suggest – incorrectly – that *all* television is watched this way, for as Caldwell observes:

> even if viewers are inattentive, television works hard visually, not just through aural appeals, to attract the attention of the audience; after all, it is still very much in television's best narrative and economic interests to engage the viewer. Theorists should not jump to theoretical conclusions just because there is an ironing board in the room.
>
> (Caldwell 1995: 27)

Producers still long to find and capitalize upon 'appointment television,' that Golden Fleece of scheduling. Hence, while television may serve, as Morse (1990) believes, as a nexus of everyday distraction, this is not always the case, and producers work hard to avoid it being the case. Rather, television is watched with varying levels of involvement, a fact that has been obscured by much research. Distracted viewing and its ramifications for the text, in particular, have been downplayed by much audience research in media studies (see J. Gray 2003b). Television audiences, Ang (1991) observes, do not so much exist as they are discursively constructed, and for the purposes of academic study, these audiences are frequently constructed as fans or engaged viewers (see Buckingham 1987; Jenkins 1992; L. A. Lewis 1992), or have been ushered into a room by the researcher and required to watch attentively (see Jhally and Lewis 1992; Morley 1980; Schlesinger et al. 1992). For ease of research, this mode of audience research is to be understood, and such work has greatly illuminated academic understanding of high involvement and of close viewing. For an overall picture of the varying levels of involvement with television, though, audience research's close reader inflection has painted for us a deceptively stable picture of television viewing. Close viewers, after all, can be expected to watch a whole television program, free from distractions and paying close attention to detail. Fans, meanwhile, can be counted on to watch regularly, recording what they miss and reliving the text through discussion.[2] But, of course, many (most?) viewers are not fans or close viewers, will be distracted, and will miss bits.

Not only will these non-fans' level of involvement differ markedly from fans or close viewers, but also, importantly, so will their understanding of the text (see J. Gray 2003b). Distracted viewing, and its correlate of remote control zapping and muting, and general disregard for the sanctity of the produced text's wholeness, riddles the text with gaps, holes, and half-understandings, leaving questions of precisely what form the experience of the text takes for such viewers. As is, television's texts often move too fast for some, causing viewers to miss sections even when paying attention (see J. Lewis 1986), and, due to the nature of the moving image, there will nearly always be more on the screen than the eye can pick up in one viewing. Add a distracted viewer and the remote control, and the televisual text becomes an even more choppy and pieced-together entity. Many of us miss or choose to avoid large portions of televisual texts, so that every time a friend calls and interrupts a program, every time we avert our eyes and mind from the screen to read a magazine, and every time we 'zap' mid-program, the text that we experience has been transformed. TiVO and other video-delay systems may eventually change this, but with subscription rates still small (*The Economist* 2002: 7), no future sea change is as yet in sight. The televisual text, in short, enjoys no firmness of borders or composition, and relies desperately on its viewers to put it together, to *make* it a text.

Following on from an evening of television viewing in Miami, Williams (1974) noted that, as one text flowed into another, what he was watching amounted more to a televisual *flow* than to texts *per se*. 'This phenomenon of planned flow,' he wrote, 'is then perhaps the defining characteristic of broadcasting, simultaneously as a technology and as a cultural form' (1974: 86). After all, television texts are book-ended, to a degree, by opening and closing credits, but they are also interrupted by ads and continuity sequences (such as station identification). American 'half-hour' shows, for instance, are only 22 minutes long, so as to leave room for 8 minutes (or 27 per cent of the time slot) of commercials, station identification, previews, and so on. Indeed, Morey's (1981: 2) statistics suggest that continuity alone occupies as much time on most channels as do dramas, and more time than the news. These sequences do not only occupy time and space in the middle of programs: they are also, and perhaps most importantly, there at a program's end to entice us to keep watching. Program flows into ad, flows into program, flows into station identification, flows into next text all so seamlessly. As with distracted viewing, we should avoid seeing this as always the case, and should avoid totally submerging the text in flow (see White 2003), but as Williams (1974) nevertheless suggests, with television exhibiting such fluidity, we should study flow, not just texts. Williams focused predominantly on planned flow within a given channel, but given the prevalence of distracted viewing today, the flow from one word and image to the next may not be the producer's flow, but instead may be modified by our attention and involvement levels, and by the remote control. A producer may wish scene B to follow scene A, but we may miss B, and hence go directly from A to C, or F, or we may zap from C on one channel to Q on another.

To understand an important controlling principle of televisuality, we must understand the effect(s) of the often under-appreciated technique of juxtaposition. Eisenstein (1998) noted that, when faced with a string of images, the human brain is remarkably adept at piecing them together. Perhaps the most famous example here is that of an experiment carried out by fellow Russian montage theorist Lev Kuleshov. Kuleshov took the same frame of actor Ivan Mozhukhin's face, and then preceded it with frames of, respectively, a bowl of soup, a woman in a coffin, and a girl playing with a teddy bear. When showing these sequences to an audience, they all remarked on the great nuances of the actor's performance, which, they felt, expressed perfect hunger, sadness, and joy respectively (cited in Stephens 1998: 102). What Kuleshov proved with this simple experiment, then, as did Eisenstein in his films, was that objects placed aside or after one another on screen can positively inflect the audience's understanding of each other. The art of montage, of juxtaposition, Eisenstein argued, lay in realizing that 'each sequential element is arrayed, not *next* to the one it follows, but on *top* of it' (1998: 96, original emphasis), '[a]s in Japanese hieroglyphics in which two independent ideographic characters ("shots") are juxtaposed and *explode* into one concept' (1998: 95, original emphasis). One concept or image, in other words, does not merely affect a second: it transforms it and becomes a part of it.

Applying this to television, we can hypothesize that each image or set of images from one textual component has the ability to inflect a reading of that which precedes or follows it. Definitely, then, the art of juxtaposition is one in which all schedulers in particular must be well versed (Paterson 1980), and it is simultaneously a power that they wield. However, the scheduler is not alone in practicing this art, nor can the scheduler completely control its power. Curious juxtaposing incidents happen all the time. For instance, a BBC Two channel identification sequence involving an exploding number 2 upset many viewers in 2000 when played directly before a program on the Challenger disaster. Moreover, distracted viewing introduces a chaotic element into scheduling, as images that were not intentionally constructed to sit alongside one another nevertheless end up together, as the viewer watches distractedly. Cable and satellite television subscription is only increasing (Balnaves et al. 2001; *The Economist* 2002), and as it does, the number of channels available to most households proliferates, inspiring ever more zapping. Where an evening's viewing used to require either channel loyalty or thoughtful perusal of the television listings, it is now just as possible (and, given the sheer size of television listings, probably more *likely*) to rely on the remote's channel up and down arrows as guides.[3]

The chaos and order of juxtaposition

When we examine modern televisual flow, we can easily be led to a picture of chaos. Altman (1986) writes of how the interplay between flow and distraction (or 'household flow,' as he calls it) demands that, to a certain degree, we should talk not of television's form, but rather of its 'for-me-ness' (1986: 51), and although writing of cinema, Staiger (1992: 30) provides the sobering reminder that 'a reader may wish to construct him or herself, not the text, as coherent.' The presentation of television allows, even at times encourages, this disjuncture and, as such, creates the conditions whereby any given text will *physically*, let alone cognitively, be received by different viewers in vastly different ways. As Sloterdijk (1987: 312) suggests, television is a zone in which 'all things can be turned into neighbors,' with any textual shard placed next to another. Therefore, while we may prefer to work with tidy, closed-circuit communications models, as Ang (1994: 203) suggests, we must at least entertain the idea that 'Not order, but chaos is the starting point,' and that consequently, 'not success, but failure to communicate should be considered "normal" in a cultural universe where commonality of meaning cannot be taken for granted' (1994: 198; see also Hall 1980). Here, Ang's (1994) 'cultural universe' is that of communications in general, but given the ways in which many of us view and consume televisuality today, it would not be out of place to regard the televisual as an even more perplexing, complexifying black hole within this universe.

Nevertheless, we can still find ways through this black hole and through the chaos. Ang (1994) is keen to embrace chaos theory, but as she accepts, within every system of chaos are systems of order. Parody capitalizes on this system of semiotic intertextual chaos, but in doing so offers ordered paths through the chaos. It does this at the level of the 'lexia' – the end product of a system of distracted, cross-text, cross-channel flow. Within film studies, numerous scholars have recently expressed dissatisfaction with what they see as the discipline's obsession with narrative (see Barker and Brooks 1998; Barker et al. 2001; Neale 1980), and with the subsequent devaluing of other ordering principles. Television studies have at times suffered from a similar affliction, though, with considerable interest placed, for instance, in how shows end and in what final morals they offer, as if most viewers watched the text closely from start to finish. Televisual flow and distracted viewing fracture the text, though, oftentimes rupturing narrative and displacing the rounded-off story as central pillar of the text. Television is always being broken up, and it therefore may be helpful for us to narrow our focus at times from narrative to image-sound sequence, to what Ellis (1993: 116) calls the 'segment,' 'a coherent group of sounds and images, of relatively short duration,' and what Barthes (1990: 13) dubs 'lexias,' 'brief, contiguous fragments,' that serve as 'the best possible space in which we can observe meanings.'

Television's increasing segmentation and supposed abandonment of, or at least move away from, narrative is easily visible. Turn on MTV or watch the news or ads in particular, and one will be greeted by a fast-paced panoply of images and sounds that work in bursts rather than via slow, careful exposition. As Stephens (1998: 91) explains, much of this 'new video' works on the idea that it is the viewer who should move, not necessarily the photographed objects. In such programs, segments and scenes become the prime units both of subdivision and for analysis. If, as Ellis (2000) poses, television works under the assumption that viewers will watch with a glance-like mode of attention, this is because that is 'all that television can assume of its audiences' (2000: 10, emphasis added). Many programs are already divided into bite-size portions, and information is often densely packed into such lexias, or else the viewing behavior of distracted, zapping viewers itself divides programs into lexias. Many of the lexias encountered as we surf from channel to channel, and phase in and out of attention, will remain disjointed, incomplete and isolated chunks of non-meaning, failing to land on what Grossberg (1992) calls our 'mattering maps.' Nevertheless, those texts and lexias that we do care about are anything but disconnected. Intertextuality – which extends to an 'interlexiality' (as intertextuality of the segment) – ensures that texts and lexias are always connecting, and in the process combining to create meaning.

The television series, as far as any of us know it or can talk about it, is, after all, an intertextual bricolage of lexias. None of us has seen every second of every episode of every show, and yet we still experience little difficulty in creating composites that we can call, say, *The Simpsons*, *The Sopranos*, or *The West Wing*. We actively and continually piece texts together to construct a notion, a gestalt, of the televisual text. One-off programs can exist in a relatively more complete, located, and coherent form, but most television shows demand more of us. They demand a heightened intertextuality which uses not only texts, but also lexias, as its tools and resources, as I will shortly examine. In its flowing, yet lexial and fragmented state, televisual (inter)textuality bears a close resemblance to Deleuze and Guattari's (1988) notion of the 'rhizome.' Deleuze and Guattari argue powerfully and poetically against simplistic notions of purely hierarchical, linear and tree-like connections between and within items and texts. 'All of arborescent culture,' they argue, 'is founded on them, from biology to linguistics. Nothing is beautiful or loving or political [,though,] aside from underground stems and aerial roots, adventitious growths and rhizomes' (1988: 15). Key with rhizomes is that they grow in all directions, frequently in unexpected ways, and continuously so. 'A rhizome,' they state,

> has no beginning or end; it is always in the middle, between things, interbeing, *intermezzo*. The tree is filiation, but the rhizome is alliance. The tree imposes the verb 'to be,' but the fabric of the rhizome is the conjunction 'and . . . and . . . and . . .'
>
> (Deleuze and Guattari 1988: 25)

Rhizomes are active and vibrant entities, rendering it impossible to study them in entirety since such entirety never yet exists: they are only ever in their middles and always in the continuous process of formation. As such, the rhizome serves as a powerful metaphor for the televisual text.

When we talk of books or films, terms such as 'beginning' and 'ending,' 'inside' and 'outside,' 'completely-read' and 'incompletely-read' are easier to assign, for, at least in some way, the text is 'there' for us to work with. The television series, by contrast, exists rhizomatically across time and space, a text and gestalt constantly under construction. Each and every viewer must literally put the text together out of the lexias encountered, in a process that carries juxtaposition over time. No longer is the text made solely of lexia next to lexia, but also of *lexia-remembered* next to lexia. As Fiske notes, the

> segmentation of television allows for connections between its segments to be made according to the laws of association rather than of consequence, logic, or cause and effect. They are, therefore, much looser, much less textually determined, and so offer the viewer more scope to make his or her own connections.
>
> (Fiske 1989a: 63)

Fiske opens the door to semiotic freedom too widely without noticing there is a screen door in the form of *limits* on this freedom, and so I dispute how 'loose' the majority of connections are, and am more interested in the 'laws of association.' Nevertheless, he is right to point out that the televisual text's ontology is produced by the association of segments over time and across space. Juxtaposition combines with memory, as interlexiality and intertextuality constitute the television series and produce what we call the text.

Much of this association occurs at a broadly obvious level, as titles, characters, sets, and styles frequently act as immediate associative linking mechanisms. Thus, for instance, we know if we are watching *The Simpsons* or an ad, *The Simpsons* or station identification, *The Simpsons* or another show: any of the show's lexias' general *Simpsons* 'look' and sound announce themselves as *The Simpsons* and call for associative amalgamation with other obviously *Simpsons* lexias. Here, though, we return to my 'reading through' model of textual phenomenology, for these lexias are not all strung together in time or space; instead, they come to us in snippets over time. As long as a show is still running, in syndication, and/or available on video tape or DVD, its lexias continue to unite in a continuous process of textual (re)construction, with the text always open to potential change. After having read a book or film, one can review it *spatially* as a whole utterance, but unless one has seen every episode of a now-finished series, one never achieves 'mastery' over the text. Rather, its process of textual becoming continues, as does our process of reading through. To rephrase, then, while all texts are intertextual, the longer a text takes to deliver itself and to be consumed, the more vital and determining intertextual and interlexial bricolage becomes, and the more we come to accept and expect that the text will change over time and require subsequent redecoding. Thus, with television series and genres – texts that often stretch over years and years (and remain longer still with syndication) – we witness the ongoing birth of the ultimate intertextual beings.

Space invaders and the laws of association

As part of this prolonged birth, though, other associations may also work themselves into the textual bricolage. Television represents 'interrupted and interruptible space' (Caughie 1990: 50) – 'interrupted' since it is drawn out over time and prone to a distracted, zapping viewership, but also 'interruptible' since its space may be invaded. Therefore, televisual lexiality is intricately engaged in the process of textual becoming. For example, if one has seen two episodes of a television show, and then reads a magazine article about this show, the article will, in all likelihood, inflect how one then makes sense of any third episode. Implicitly updating Williams (1974), Brooker (2001) writes of the pervasiveness of 'television overflow,' as both the production and consumption of the text continue in ads, previews, reviews, interviews, merchandise, spinoffs, fan magazines, websites, talk, media conversions such as books or films, and so forth. Buckingham (1987) provides the example of how newspaper and magazine articles on soap stars frequently feed into the reception of the stars' performances. *EastEnders*, he recounts, at one time had a villain, Den, who was rechristened 'Dirty Den' by the many tabloid press articles extolling the sins of this character. Furthermore, the tabloid press leapt on the fact that the actor had himself served time in prison and the 'resulting composite of [Den and actor became] a contemporary "folk devil" who embodie[d] everything that "we" are not, and whose continued presence in our homes [was] an affront to the decent people whose values the newspapers claim to represent' (Buckingham 1987: 144). These tabloid paratexts interrupted and inserted themselves into the text, so that future readings of *EastEnders* and of Den specifically would be refracted. As this example illustrates, all manner of texts can take advantage of gaps in televisual linearity to inflect the reading process of other texts.

Television is thus the ideal delivery and circulation system for intertextuality proper, and the televisual text is particularly prone to intertextual inflection. Between distracted viewing, zapping, and the large amount of television that many people watch, television presents us with texts and textual lexias at a remarkable rate. Each of us will probably watch thousands or millions of texts or textual lexias over the courses of our lives, and even in one sitting will often expose ourselves to the flow of a great deal of textuality. Television brings intertextuality to us. We do not need to set foot in a library, bookstore, theater, or video store: we only need lay back in our chairs and press some buttons. Televisual flow makes televisual intertextuality *easy*, as it brings together all manner of texts in several thousand pixels. As Newcomb and Hirsch (1984) have characterized it, television is a 'cultural forum,' a site where texts are brought together, and will converse, agree, disagree, and work with or against each other. Importantly, though, this process of textual jostling occurs while many texts are still in the advent of becoming, while their textual boundaries and their interpretations are, by their nature, still open, incomplete and therefore vulnerable. Granted, many texts are uninterested in exploiting others' vulnerabilities. Nevertheless, the medium still creates these cracks and fissures whereby vulnerabilities *could* be exploited, and parody sets to work by doing precisely that. Television, then, is open to parodic reinflection, and open to parodic subversion. As Naficy (1989) explains, a central paradox of television is that, on one hand, producers

> seek constantly to create syntagmatically a seamless televisual flow in order to secure and maintain audiences. On the other hand, their own practice of segmentation and self-reflexivity promotes syntagmatic resonances among the texts themselves as well as paradigmatic resonances with their contexts – both of which tend to undermine the first practice by enhancing potentially subversive readings. In addition, the conditions of viewing, and the technological apparatuses available to viewers, can turn that subversive potential into reality by increasing intertextuality and by weakening the hold of the supposedly hermetic and seamless televisual flow.
>
> (Nacify 1989: 45–6)

Television is a realm of hyper-intertextuality, and, pieced together with associatively linked lexias, paratexts, intertexts, and talk, the structural and ideological integrity of the televisual text is deeply reliant on which associations 'win out' and become dominant, on which interpretive communities form around them, and on how they mediate the text's becoming. So, while critical intertextuality's growth never promises to be easy, if it is likely to thrive anywhere, it is over and through the waves, flow, and talk that constitute television. Parody's powers may seem small and minute if one looks at its presence on television relative to other genres. Undoubtedly, too, many parodies in many instances will speak into a chaotic void with no response. As for more successful parody, though, earlier I quoted Ang's belief that television may work through a fair deal of chaos, but as she states, and as chaos theorists tell us, there is both an order and a tremendous power to chaos (see Kellert 1993). If parody taps into the order and power of the chaos that is intertextuality, borrowing from early chaos theorist Edward Lorenz, we can therefore ask, 'if a butterfly on television flaps its wings, might it set off a tornado in a Texan living room?'

Ad parody in *The Simpsons*

The scheduler-programmed ordered flow of television may well follow and dictate a commercial logic, but as savvy parody, *The Simpsons* is able to work with the chaotic phenomenology of the televisual text so as to swim against the current, offering as it does a counter-logic that is deeply suspicious toward and critical of commercialism. While many of the show's contemporaries write weekly valentines to commercialism, *The Simpsons* revels in ad parody and mockery. In particular, *The Simpsons* often shows us ads on Springfield television, and always so as to deride them. Thus, for instance, as Marge and Lisa watch the Super Bowl on television in 'Sunday, Cruddy Sunday,' we cut to an ad set in the American South-West. Tumbleweed rolls by an isolated gas station, as a nerdy-looking man stops his car, and honks his horn for service. Rock music starts playing, and three scantily clad, curvaceous women saunter out. As they proceed to check the oil, wipe his windows, and fill his car up with gas, all the while performing for him and for the viewer, the ad hits us with innuendo after innuendo. The 'camera' then focuses in on one of the women leaning forward, and we see, glittering between her cleavage, a cross on a necklace. At this, a voiceover announces, 'The Catholic Church: we've made some changes!' Brilliantly, then, the prevalence with which sex is used to sell anything in the advertising world is made fun of, as is a tired advertising sub-genre of sexy women appearing from nowhere as if summoned by the product or service for sale, and, with this, the advertising industry's objectification of women. Reading further, we might note the parodic commentary, through radically rebranding something (making the Church sexy), of how rarely most 'rebranding' amounts to any substantive change.

Cheap sell techniques and over-the-top pizzazz abound in Springfield. Another such moment comes in 'Lisa the Skeptic,' when Lisa discovers what appears to be the fossilized remains of an angel. The townspeople all believe it to be forewarning the impending end of the world, and they gather around it on a hillside expecting Armageddon to follow. With this, they hear a booming voice telling them to 'Prepare for the End.' An awed hush falls upon them, only for the voice to continue: 'The end of high prices . . . at the new Heavenly Hills Mall!' Following this, the mall at the foot of the hill is flooded with light – its grand opening. Lisa complains to the owner/manager, 'You exploited people's beliefs just to hawk your cheesy wares!' and this rebuke could be addressed to many of the town's advertisers, for the constant message in *The Simpsons*' ad parodies is that advertisers will go to and surpass any limits to sell something (see Preston 1994).

Ads are shown to be inescapable in Springfield. Buzz Cola, Lard Lad Donuts, Laramie Cigarettes, and Duff Beer ads can be found everywhere. Yet, far from slipping by as naturalized background, the inappropriate and invasive placement of these and other ads is often lampooned. Thus, for instance, in 'Krusty Gets Busted,' Bart's talking Krusty doll implores, 'Buy My Cereal!' when its string is pulled; and when in 'She of Little Faith,' Mr Burns 'remodels' the church, posters cover its walls, a flashing Vegas-style huge and automated Jesus figure advertises black-jack outside, Reverend Lovejoy is given a Fatso's Hash House robe, his podium has a rotating ad-board installed in it (with such messages as 'Watch *Ally McBeal*. It's Great'), and a corporate mascot delivers a 'special sermon' on 'the sanctity of deliciousness.' Of these many changes to the church, an advertising executive explains to Bart and Lisa, 'We're rebranding it. The old church was skewing pious. We prefer a faith-based emporium, teaming with impulse-buy items.' As if ads in children's toys or in churches are not enough, in 'Bart to the Future,' an episode in which an Indian shaman at a casino treats Bart to a vision of his future, even his vision is interrupted when future-Bart says, 'I guess I am an embarrassment,' and a ghost responds, 'You sure are. But, hey, there's an embarrassment *of riches* at the Caesar's Pow-Wow Indian Casino. You can bet on it!' Here, as with the church ads, *The Simpsons* uses parody with great effect, not only to illustrate how annoyingly and disrespectfully ads infringe on any territory, but also to mock their logic and rhetoric.

Naomi Klein (2002) has written of contemporary corporate society as offering no choice to avoid ads, and no space in which we can escape them. A key concern she identifies, and a continuing dilemma for contemporary society, is how to construct public spaces in which people can just be citizens, not consumers. As malls, 'guerrilla advertising' techniques, endless billboards, product placement, and the attempted takeover of the news by corporate concerns and advertising reaches a fever pitch, Klein notes that we sacrifice any sense of a 'commons' or of unbranded, public, citizens' space. *The Simpsons* illustrates some of Klein's concerns neatly in a Halloween special called 'The Attack of the 50 Ft Eyesores.' The episode begins with Homer driving through Springfield's 'Neon Mile,' marveling at all the ads and giant corporate mascots, and at how not a library or church is anywhere in sight. But an electromagnetic disturbance soon brings the '50 Ft Eyesores' to life and they proceed to ransack the town. Here, then, the episode literalizes the 'destruction' of America by ads. Moreover, Lisa discovers that the ads will only live as long as they are paid attention to, and so their wanton destruction of the town's school, buildings, media, and public places is rendered as a desperate plea for attention. The town defeats the giants through ignoring them, but Springfield's concerned news anchorman, Kent Brockman, closes the episode by addressing his camera, and, implicitly, us as viewers. He warns, 'Even as I speak, this scourge of advertising could be heading towards your town. Lock your doors. Bar your windows. Because the next advertisement you see could destroy your house and eat your family.' At this, Homer pops into frame, adding, 'We'll be right back,' and *The Simpsons* cuts to commercial, leaving the lead-in ad in a precarious position to say the least.

Ad parody often risks drawing yet further attention to its specific targets, as in a famous scene from the film *Wayne's World*, in which the lead characters verbally mock and deride product placement, while displaying numerous brand products. To this end, though, it is noteworthy that *The Simpsons* offers a town largely free from real-life logos. 'The Attack of the 50 Ft Eyesores' involves one sight-gag with a Planters Peanuts type figure, but otherwise none of its logos serve to advertise real-life products. This adherence to a 'No Logo' (Klein 2002) critique on contemporary advertising even extends, amusingly, to one of *The Simpsons'* hit computer games, *Hit and Run*. Obstensively a drive-and-destroy game in the vein of *Grand Theft Auto*, not only does *Hit and Run* include numerous ad parodies – beginning with the game's opening sequence, no less – but also players are required to seek out shortcuts around town, most of which are found by driving through and hence obliterating Buzz Cola billboards. Quite literally, therefore, the ads become targets.

The Simpsons also targets advertisers by frequently showing how immoral they can be in targeting particularly vulnerable groups, such as the out-of-work or children. In 'Homer's Odyssey,' for example, Loaftime, 'the cable network for the unemployed,' runs an ad with a lush jungle scene as backdrop, that beckons, 'Unemployed? Out of work? *Sober?* You sat around the house all day, but now it's Duff time. Duff – the beer that makes the days fly by.' Similarly, this time concentrating on the ethics of advertising to children, in 'Lisa the Beauty Queen,' Laramie Cigarettes sponsor a pageant for kids, and their advertisement shows a young girl who has just been crowned Little Miss Springfield and enthusiastically pipes up, 'What a feeling! I'm as happy as a smoker taking that first puff in the morning!' These examples depict a world with even less (or no) advertising ethics than our own, but it is clearly a world born of our own, and the critique is directed toward a genre that shows little sign of moral sense, instead looking at everywhere as a potential site for advertising, and everyone as a potential buyer.

Ads have become masters of semiotics (Barthes 1973; G. Dyer 1982; Williamson 1978), engaging in careful and ingenious encoding at the level of connotation and mythology. When a given brand of fish sticks can signify being a better mother and wife, clearly the ad industry's prowess in semiotic manipulation proves itself. However, as David Arnold (2001: 253) suggests, *The Simpsons* aims to 'disrupt the stable, easily-interpretable diet of images and ideas that television viewers generally expect, and that the medium tends to encourage.' Connotation and mythology work at full capacity only if they are internalized, naturalized, and can hide their tracks, and so *The Simpsons* attempts to *ex*ternalize, *de*naturalize, and reveal tracks. 'Ads may look "real" and "natural,"' notes Dyer, 'and the connections they make between dissimilar things may have the appearance of a system that is "logical," and belongs to a "real" or "natural" order, but such connections are not inevitable' (1982: 125). *The Simpsons* succeeds by constantly making ads appear fundamentally unnatural, foreign, and invasive. To laugh at many of these jokes is to accept and share the criticism of advertising's modes of address, for the jokes are not just on the internal absurdities but also, externally *and intertextually*, at ads that we have all seen before. In short, *The Simpsons* plays an important role in (un)teaching the advertisement. Its parodic ads, afloat in televisuality's chaotic flow, call for and offer a redecoding of the general language and look of advertising as a genre, and a more media literate decoding position toward future ads (the next time one hears an ad announce

'We've made some changes,' *The Simpsons*' Catholic Church ad may well come to mind and place itself alongside it).

'The media's stupid and manipulative'

While parodying the form, address and (im)morality of ads, though, *The Simpsons* also levels particular comic scorn on stars who 'sell out' to advertisers, using their names and images to make a few more dollars. Krusty the Clown's inclusion as a semi-regular character on the show serves as semi-constant comment on stars who sell out. Krusty will endorse any product. Thus, on the shelves and streets of Springfield, in addition to Krusty slippers, pajamas, cereal, a KrustyBurger Store, and a Kamp Krusty, one can find Krusty Non-Narkotik Cough Syrup, Krusty Sulfuric Acid, the Lady Krusty Moustache Removal Kit, and Krusty Low Income Housing. When, in 'The Last Temptation of Krust,' Krusty changes his act to ranting against capitalism, he is soon wooed back to his old ways by sponsorship offers, and is forced to admit, 'It ain't comedy that's in my blood – it's selling out.'

Krusty's key sin is not selling out, though: it is his continued indifference to the quality of products or services bearing his name, and the means by which they are marketed, particularly when they are aimed at children. Advertisers, of course, use stars' names to cash in on the trust, respect, affect, and/or adulation that people have for them, but none of this means anything to Krusty. In 'Kamp Krusty,' for instance, we learn that the 'Krusty Brand Seal of Approval' goes on short-circuiting electric toothbrushes and clocks that overheat if plugged in, and Bart reveals that his Krusty vitamins gave him a rapid heartbeat. Meanwhile, Krusty Non-Toxic Kologne warns to 'Use in a well-ventilated area. May stain furniture. Prolonged use can cause chemical burns' ('Like Father Like Clown'), and in 'Hello Gutter, Hello Fadder,' Krusty takes time aside on his program to talk about Krusty Brand Chew Goo Gum-Like Substance: 'We knew it contained spiders' eggs, but the *Hanta virus*? Wahew! That really came out of left field. So, if any of you have experienced numbness or comas, send proof of purchase and $5 to Antidote, P.O. Box 14 . . .' In instances such as this, Krusty's complete disregard for both his dignity and his fans' welfare, and the advertisers' complete disregard (or, as in the box-front warnings, parodic over-regard) for honesty in advertising, are exacerbated by Krusty being a trusted and respected children's performer.

Throughout *The Simpsons*, Krusty is depicted as if he was a cult leader, and his hard sell tactics are garish and shocking. At the beginning of his television show, for instance, the children are prompted to pledge undying love for him, chanting on cue that they would kill themselves if he went off the air. Krusty is a master of manipulating peer pressure for the purpose of furthering his own fame and fortune, and of offering himself as caring friend to ensure the same ends, as is particularly evident in the recorded message Bart receives when calling the Krusty Hotline in 'Stark Raving Dad': 'Hi Kids! You've reached the Krusty hotline. If you haven't asked your parent for permission, naughty naughty . . . but Krusty forgives you. $2 for the first minute, 50¢ for each additional minute. Waheheheheh!' *The Simpsons* is by no means hostile to celebrity; on the contrary, its revolving door of guest stars contributes to the deification of celebrities in society. But it is especially critical of those who abuse their celebrity.

The parody involving Krusty also points to another level of selling out that *The Simpsons* is quick to parody: the invasion of seemingly all media by ads. While, as instance of critical intertextuality, *The Simpsons* attempts to invade other genres and inflect their decoding, the program aptly illustrates how the ad as genre has itself already invaded many, if not all, genres. Ads and marketing do not limit themselves to the space between programs; rather, they are themselves textual invaders, and part of *The Simpsons'* parodic attack on ads involves revealing their hiding places in other texts. Therefore, when Bart and Lisa's kids' news show proves unprofitable in 'Girly Edition,' it is replaced with *The Mattel and Mars Bar Quick Energy Chocobot Hour*, mocking how many children's programs have become little more than the ad to the merchandise (see Englehardt 1986; Fleming 1996; Kline 1993). Similarly, in 'Brush with Greatness,' Krusty's show is filmed at Mt Splashmore water park, and begins with a conspicuously flattering monologue and sing-a-long on how great the park is; an Emmy-nominated cartoon in 'The Front' is called *How to Buy Action Figure Man*; and, during Super Bowl coverage in 'Lisa the Greek,' the announcers welcome a special guest, 'whose new sitcom is premiering tonight, coincidentally enough right after the game.'

Even the very form of television as being structured around ads and advertiser demands receives occasional parody in *The Simpsons*, as in 'And Maggie Makes Three.' The episode sees Homer and Marge tell the story of Maggie's birth. When we return from one flashback, though, Bart and Lisa are leaving the room. Homer asks where they are going and Bart explains, 'Dad, you can't expect a person to sit for thirty minutes straight,' to which Lisa adds, 'I'm gonna get a snack and maybe go to the bathroom.' Marge, meanwhile declares that she will 'stay here, but I'm going to think about products I might like to purchase.' Thus, the segment mocks commercial television's incessant pausing for ads, as well as the 'logic' that consideration of product purchase should in any way flow naturally from watching a narrative of some form. Indeed, this joke plays better in a commercial television system, where the show cuts for commercials right after Marge's comment: an immediate and almost-assured instance of critical intertextuality, and indicative of a common strategy behind *Simpsons* ad parody placement that takes advantage of televisual flow to attack actual ads, not just ads as a system. Ads, *The Simpsons* shows time and time again, plague television from commercial breaks, to sports coverage, to children's shows, to the very structure of televisual flow, and *The Simpsons* attempts to undercut these ads by denaturalizing their presence, mode of address, trust-construction mechanisms (such as star use), and their intentions.

If the ad and promotional culture are such frequent recipients of parodic scorn and derision on *The Simpsons*, this is in part due to the show's creators' cynical take on ads and television culture. In interviews, most of the key production staff voice considerable dislike of ads, with writer Mike Reiss, for instance, stating that the show's 'overarching point is that the media's stupid and manipulative' (Rushkoff 2004: 299). Meanwhile, head writer George Meyer repeatedly reveals his hatred of advertising and marketing (see Owen 2000). However, the writers also talk of their prime goal being to entertain, and so we might observe that the ad as form/genre positively cries out to be parodied, effectively wearing an easily sighted bull's-eye on its chest, and hence making ad parody easy.

As has been stated, parody is fool-like in its proclivity to render monologic discourses as dialogic. Consequently, it works best against those genres and discourses that purport to dictate, and that have obvious and explicit pretensions to monologic power. Jenny poses that:

> [I]t is possible to ask whether it is not a given type of form which provokes intertextuality [and o]ne might, for example, propose the hypothesis that it is the most strictly or exaggeratedly encoded texts which provide matter for such [intertextual] 'repetition.'
>
> (Jenny 1982: 37)

By 'exaggeratedly encoded texts,' Jenny means those of Truth, Law, and Definition, those that work the hardest to encode a precise meaning. In this category, we may place history, journalism, science, and any other discourse of truth or persuasion, such as the ad or sales pitch. However, because such texts attempt to nail down meaning, and due to their established and entrenched power, as Jenny points out, they are 'impossible to forget or neutralise' (1982: 59). Texts such as ads are so pervasive and invasive that they saturate television, and public space more generally, constantly calling to us and demanding to be heard. Indeed, although critics of *The Simpsons* often state that its humor requires a high degree of cultural capital, in truth it is mostly its pastiche that requires cultural capital. When Homer or Lisa quote philosophers, a certain education level is required to follow the joke, but everyone is familiar with ad style, rhetoric, and modality. Consequently, intertextuality flourishes around such 'strong' texts, and these texts become the easy and preferred targets for intertextual 'perturbation' (Jenny 1982: 59). Intertextuality 'forces them to finance their own subversion' (Jenny 1982: 59), since they are so universally well-known, and the most reliable of intertexts in the sense that parodists can comfortably rely on their audience's intimate awareness of them and of the ways in which they speak. Effectively, then, as Bakhtin (1981) and Volosinov (1973) argued, the monologic word or text calls out for dialogism. Moreover, there is a sense of joy or pleasure in re-interpreting a text (see Barthes 1995; Fiske 1989c; Jenkins 1992), and in attaching additional and/or illegitimate readings to those whose meanings are supposedly clear. This is the basis of the audience's enjoyment of the fool, and it is what marks discourses such as ads and the news as parodic targets.

Television comedy

Parody's other key move in using commercial television against itself is that it taps into the powers of comedy. Many attempts to take parody seriously forget or overlook that it is *comedy*, that it is something we *laugh* at, so that while Hutcheon (1985, 1988) and Rose (1993) remain two of the most cited authors on the subject of parody, strangely neither discusses the role or effect of laughter in furthering parody's aims. These powers, though, are central to its mechanics. Ultimately, comedy works remarkably well in lexial, segmented units, and can stand alone from whatever narrative these units might be a part of. The spirit of comedy often involves moving from joke to joke in quick succession, and frequently the role of such narrative devices as characters, settings, themes, and plot serve mostly as material out of which the next joke can be fashioned, not as co-developing complexities. Admittedly, great humor has the ability to build upon itself, but comedy as a whole is not as dependent upon narrative, and upon narrative development as are other genres. It builds with largely self-contained blocks, and is inherently and unproblematically lexial and segmented. Therefore, as the remote control hatchets up full programs, comedy is particularly well-built to survive, even thrive, in such an environment. Comedy as a genre can work *with* multiple channels and a quick-firing remote control, and is not as threatened by household commotion and conversation as are many other genres.

Meanwhile, when it works, to state the obvious, comedy makes us laugh. And laughter warms us to comedy, allowing it easy entrance onto our 'mattering maps' (Grossberg 1992). As a genre, it is almost universally liked, for while some hate romances, sci-fi, soaps or reality television, it is rare to find someone who does not enjoy laughing. A strong link between laughter and affect exists, evidenced perhaps most acutely in the prevalence of calls for, or promises of, 'a good sense of humor' in personal ads in newspapers. Laughter, quite simply, makes us feel good, and as Silverstone (1999: 55) writes of our media consumption, not only are we 'drawn to [such] otherwise mundane and trivial texts and performances by a transcendent hope, a hope and a desire that something will touch us,' but similarly, once satisfied, we return to such sites of 'transcendence' again and again. It is no surprise, then, that comedy frequently reigns supreme over Nielsen and BARB ratings (see Staiger 2000). This positive relation between laughter, affect, and popularity can lead to us placing comedy not only on our 'mattering maps,' but also on our textual travel maps, ensuring that amidst all of television's flow, zapping, and surfing, many of us find our ways 'back.'

A large part of comedy's appeal, after all, is its lightness. So many people, places, genres, and situations ask for us to be serious. Similarly, so much *requires* that we be serious: the world can be a dark and ugly place that often gives us little reason for cheer. Thus, it is only natural that we will seek out refuge, and laughter is precisely a zone of refuge. Psychologically, as Freud (1960) observed, laughter allows a release of anxiety. Key to its strengths, too, though, is that it sends a message that 'this is play' and works to exclude the fearful. Serious and/or worried-over issues are by no means excluded too, but comedy is a relatively safe zone in which they can be addressed. As Bakhtin argues:

> Laughter is a vital factor for laying down that prerequisite for fearlessness without which it would be impossible to approach the world realistically. As it draws an object to itself and makes it familiar, laughter delivers the object into the fearless hands of investigative experiment – both scientific and artistic – and into the hands of free experimental fantasy.
>
> (Bakhtin 1981: 23)

We would be wrong to think of comedy as harmless – indeed, much humor *aims* to harm – but the comic zone is a relatively safe one, in which joker and audience can feel somewhat free to play with issues or topics that would otherwise disturb or tax too heavily.

Moreover, comedy lends itself to being remembered well. Perhaps precisely because comedy frequently exists in small, 'lexial' units, comedy stores well. Mixed with its capacity to warm or lighten us, it also gives us a *reason* to store it. In this sense, since, as Silverstone notes, we return again and again to sites of affect and joy, the 'site' to which we return may well be our own memories. Furthermore, comedy plays a large role in everyday talk, and hence provides us with reasons to store it. Sharing jokes is a popular component of friendly talk, and of creating a common ground between oneself and others. Freud noted that 'a new joke acts almost like an event of universal interest; it is passed from one person to another like the news of the latest victory' (1960: 15), and as Bergson observes, there is 'a kind of freemasonry, or even complicity, with other laughers' (1935: 6). The sharing of jokes is in one way or another frequently at the center of many social relationships and networks.

In this regard, 'stored' comedy, and particularly comedy stored from popular and well-loved television programs, becomes a sort of comic capital. In the media's 'affective economy' of which Grossberg (1992) writes, remembered jokes and comedy are blue-chip stock in which many of us hold sizeable shares. Furthermore, due to the sharing of comedy through talk, comedy can spread exponentially, traveling from one person who actually witnesses the comic element to numerous people with whom this person might share the joke. Within a group with similar cultural codes, travel is something that comedy does extremely well. In its frequently small and easily memorable form, it becomes remarkably portable. Moreover, because it is often reasonably self-contained, it can easily be activated wherever it is taken, as my own quoting from *The Simpsons* has shown: in order to recount one of its jokes, it is rarely necessary to provide much 'setup.' Rather, like blue-chip stock, comedy moves well. Of course, the medium through which it moves is the audience and interpretive communities, and thus I will detail this movement further in Part III.

Returning to *The Simpsons'* ad parody, in particular, if the program offers a picture of a television system controlled by ads, and if it attacks ads and promotional culture on a regular basis, never tiring of its favorite target over more than 350 episodes, its critique is relatively empowered by comedy, intertextuality, and televisual flow to become more than just a single dissatisfied voice in a crowd of eager commercial television supporters. Parody enables *The Simpsons'* critique to travel to other texts, to exist in everyday talk, to work through and in the cracks and fissures of televisual form, and, hence, to deliver its criticism with considerable potential power.

The face behind the ad

Meanwhile, its sophistication of critique extends to an interest not only in advertising as products or texts, but also to the forces of production and reception that contextualize and situate ad power. Its parody of advertising, for instance, works hand in hand with its broader satire of consumerism and capitalist culture in general, particularly evident in its attack on the big businesses behind advertising. By way of explaining and extending Marx, Jhally (1987: 50) writes that if advertisers have proven so adept at mythologizing their products, at filling them with meaning, this is because, alongside capitalism more generally, they have already systematically emptied commodities of any other meanings. Ads rarely if ever tell us about the process of production, for instance, or of how the product came to be, instead obscuring details of wages, factory conditions, environmental fallout, the design process, and so on. Thus, as Jhally argues, advertising 'does not give a false meaning *per se* to commodities, but provides meaning to a domain which has been emptied of meaning' (1987: 51). This is part of the genre's ideology. And yet, as part of its parody/satire of advertising, in Brechtian fashion, *The Simpsons* often reveals aspects of production, not only denying advertising its new meanings, but also working toward refilling products and services with their fuller meanings. It works as an anti-advertisement.

The Simpsons frequently shows product designers and advertisers at work, for instance, and rarely if ever depicts them in a favorable light. In 'Trash of the Titans,' the board of Costington's Department Store look for a way to increase purchasing, and one member suggests inventing a holiday with religious connotations, arguing, 'We had great penetration last year with Christmas 2,' to which another member adds, 'Ooh, I know: Spendover. Like Passover, but less talk, more presents.' Meanwhile, 'Grift of the Magi' sees Kids First Industries take over the elementary school, using it as a means to get marketing information from the children, complete with new homework assignments such as 'Design your perfect toy' and classes in which children pick favorite fabric swatches. The company's stunt later results in a television ad that announces 'If you don't have Funzo, you're *nothing*,' and when an incensed Lisa confronts one of the company's managers, the latter can only manage the defense that, 'I know you're mad, but just for a damn minute try to see this from a product-positioning standpoint!' Combining these instances with what we constantly learn of the poor quality and design of Krusty brand products, and with the general ludicrous semiotics of Springfield's advertising (such as the Barnacle Bill Home Pregnancy Test, with free corn-cob pipe), we have a picture of product designers, researchers, and executives who are far from ethical or analytically sound in their work and judgment. Gitlin (1994: 269) has remarked that 'if television is unkind to businessmen, it is scarcely unkind to the values of a business civilization. Capitalism and the consumer society come out largely uncontested,' yet in instances such as these, it is the logic under which such individuals operate that is ridiculed, and the target is clearly business more than it is business people.

At the level of capital's treatment of workers, Homer and the rest of Springfield are continually shown to be meaningless pawns in nuclear power plant owner Mr Burns' game of accumulating ever more wealth. The plant is central to the town and its welfare, and appears to be one of the only places to get a real job, so that when Homer is fired in 'Homer's Odyssey,' or laid off in 'Burns Verkaufen der Kraftwerk,' he struggles to find anything else. At the plant, though, luminous (radioactive) green drops fall from pipes in the ceiling, the plant has made Homer sterile, we are repeatedly informed of how low its safety standards are, and yet the corporate toilet is (literally) palatial, and Mr Burns' home exhibits signs of endless wealth. Mr Burns is the complete caricature of a cold, uncaring, and heartless owner and manager. At one point, he asks his assistant, 'What good is money if you can't inspire terror in your fellow man?' ('Burns Verkaufen der Kraftwerk'); he has an alert light installed in his desk to warn him if employees are ordering room service on the company tab, and a button that opens a trap door in front of his desk; his parents, we learn, died because they 'Got in my way' ('The Mansion Family'); his assistant raises his spirits with thoughts of endangered condors flying into power lines; and after hitting Bart with his car, he instructs his lawyer to remind the court how rich and important he is, defiantly adding, 'I should be able to run over as many kids as I want' ('Bart Gets Hit By a Car'). On top of this, due to creative use of tax loopholes, he pays only $3 in yearly income tax. Thus, while much of this criticism is excessive by nature, as stand-in for corporate ownership, Mr Burns presents a thoroughly avaricious, environmentally and socially indifferent, and exploitative image to the viewer.

I do not wish to overstate here, for *The Simpsons* does not perpetually adopt a *Socialist Worker*-style voice, but in its portrayal of Mr Burns and other managers, it does refuse to leave such figures rose-colored, or, perhaps worse yet, wholly absent from the picture, as does advertising. As Jhally (1987) observes, advertising is a genre that works by refusing to talk of production, counting on it remaining a blank and void, and yet *The Simpsons* surrounds its own parodic treatment of ads with a satiric-parodic reflection upon production, and in doing so, adds this reflection to the televisual flow.

The pleasures of consumption

If a genre's ideological position is important, though, so too is its audience, for this is the ultimate site of any construction of meaning, and of any success or failure of any genre's power or effects. *The Simpsons*, however, rarely lets the audience go free from its parodic attack on advertising. Rather, the show implicates the audience as allowing advertising to work, and as often getting too caught up in advertising's spectacle and rhetoric to ground themselves and realize what is going on. 'Ads do not simply manipulate us, inoculate us, or reduce us to the status of objects,' notes Dyer (1982: 116); rather, 'they create structures of meaning which sell commodities not for themselves as useful objects but in terms of ourselves as social beings in our different social relationships.' Ads, in short, are not (just) about the products – they are about us, but as Weinstein (1998: 62) notes, 'Not only does *The Simpsons* dismantle and examine realistic television form and content, but it also probes the effects of television on viewers' psychic realities: their thoughts, fantasies, dreams, desires.'

Thus, for instance, in the aforementioned angel hoax used to advertise the new mall, after Lisa expresses her outrage at the owner's exploitative advertising tricks, she tries to turn the townspeople against the owner, but instead the unphased crowd charge to the mall, hoax forgotten. Similarly, when Krusty opens his show at Mt Splashmore water park clearly as a promotional tool, Lisa notes, 'This is a rather shameless promotion,' to which Bart replies, 'Hey, it worked on me.' Lisa adds, 'Me too,' and the kids are soon asking their parents to take them. Here, the show honestly reflects upon the pleasures of consumption in a way that is lacking from many early, heavily Marxist-inflected scholarly critiques of advertising (see

Williamson 1978, for example). However, *The Simpsons* also jibes at how we as audiences can allow this pleasure in the advertised object to blind us to the methods employed to sell it. It mocks and highlights how we not only put up with, but hence validate and ensure the continued life of, invasive and hard-sell advertising tactics.

Ultimately, much of *The Simpsons'* parody of the role audiences play in advertising centers around Homer, as über-consumer. Homer must and will buy almost anything an advertiser recommends. In 'Homie the Clown,' for instance, Homer gets excited that all the new billboard ads are out, and proceeds to drive around town seeing what they say, so that he can follow them to the letter. 'This year,' one reads, 'give her English Muffins,' to which Homer replies, 'Whatever you say,' and a few scenes later he is seen with English Muffins. Similarly, in 'Realty Bites,' upon seeing a billboard ad for Lumber King, he intones, zombie-like, 'Lumber . . . we need lumber.' Meanwhile, after seeing the *Saving Private Ryan*-style Buzz Cola ad described in the Introduction, and as Lisa ponders aloud if such a silly ad could actually work, Homer dashes to the lobby to buy some Buzz.

Homer represents every advertiser's and CEO's dream consumer – the ultimate feeble-minded purchaser, Adorno's perfect hypodermic audience specimen who has endowed the advertising media with talismanic powers to tell him what to buy and what he needs to improve his life. To a certain point, then, we are encouraged to laugh *at* Homer, or treat him as stand-in for others we may believe are like him. However, as Barthes argues of Charlie Chaplin, 'To see someone who does not see is the best way to be intensely aware of *what* he does not see' (Barthes 1973: 40, original emphasis), and so, too, with Homer. Homer is incapable of separating rhetoric from reality, product plug from personal need, and so the jokes on him are often also on us, or at least directed our way, and on the degree to which all of us are, at times, guilty of Homer's crime, both as individuals and, importantly, as an entire, rampantly consumerist society. As my audience research subjects were often quick to point out, there is a little Homer in all of us, allowing the shiny veneer of ads to get the better of us. Cantor notes that '*The Simpsons* is based on distrust of power and especially of power remote from ordinary people' (1999: 745), and while the advertiser's power is arguably *The Simpsons'* favorite – and most successful – target, the program also shows how ordinary people create that power on the advertiser's behalf.

Nevertheless, *The Simpsons* avoids adopting an overly crude model of ad power. While the show pokes fun at particularly Homer's devotion to the gospels of advertising, precisely because Homer is so mindless a drone, the show also mocks notions of ads as being all-powerful. If we turn to Williamson (1978), for instance, in her study of *Decoding Advertisements*, she employs Althusserian conceptions of ideology, interpellation, and appellation (Althusser 1971) to argue that 'Appellation [. . .] gives us imaginary blinkers in preventing us from looking sideways and recognizing other people, contiguous to us; it only allows us to see forwards, into the ad' (Williamson 1978: 54). Ideology and its minions of advertising are pictured as a huge *Star Wars*-like traction beam, 'hailing' and luring us unknowingly into the Death Star that is capitalist ideology. Let us compare this, though, to Homer's desire to be a clown. In 'Homie the Clown,' Homer sees a billboard advertising clown college, and while at first he discredits and discards the idea, he soon becomes plagued with visions of clowns. Everywhere he looks, he sees clowns, with his new-found ad-programmed obsession boiling over until finally he announces that he will train as a clown. This is Althusser in action: monkey see, monkey do. While, as I have said, part of the humor in such situations lies in recognizing a degree to which we *can* or *might* allow ads to influence us so directly, moments and episodes like this clearly also mock conceptions of consumers as wholly passive and unthinking. Surely, such humor suggests, *nobody* is quite as absurdly weak-minded as is Homer (see Nava and Nava 1992; Schrøder 1997), and thus at the same time as *The Simpsons* parodies the strength of ads, it wisely avoids falling back on an oversimplified and largely unhelpful notion of brain-dead audience reception.

The Simpsons as advertiser

To posit the ad industry as the unmitigated bad guy, and consumers as the poor, afflicted victims is too simplistic. Likewise, to posit *The Simpsons* as waging a tooth-and-nail battle against advertising would be similarly incorrect. The show deftly exploits televisual form so as to mock, ridicule, and take parodic swipes at advertising, but in doing so, it is aware of the complexity of advertising's infusion into contemporary culture, and calls on audiences to acknowledge their own complicity. Of course, though, the show is also, in no small way, complicit itself with advertising. Few television texts in history have spawned as much merchandise as has *The Simpsons*, nor have many other texts been able to capitalize on their success so lucratively by offering their 'stars' for ads. *Simpsons* characters can be found in Master Card, Kentucky Fried Chicken, 1–800–COLLECT, Doritos, Intel, Ritz Bits, and Butterfinger ads, and so while they might mock advertising in the world of Springfield, in the world of the ad break, they often hawk products themselves. Groening has even said that the program's mere existence and Fox's final decision to sign them on relied upon a pre-arranged deal to have Bart serve as Butterfinger's spokesperson (Turner 2004: 19). One could worry, then, that its message of ad and consumption parody is diluted or wholly erased by its ad and merchandise progeny. Groening claims to favor product licenses and advertising that is itself somewhat self-parodic and distant (McAllister 2004), but the show's merchandise and involvement in ads still greatly mitigates any excited proclamations of its anti-consumerism that one might wish to make.

Nevertheless, as I have suggested in this chapter, individual viewers and inter-pretive communities must piece together their own gestalt/metatext of what *The Simpsons* or any other text or genre means, and, hence, of what it is saying. As Jenkins (1992) illustrates with the case of fan productivity, audiences are not always locked into the entirety of a text as put forward by the producer, and in constructing their personal or communal metatexts, they can ignore or downplay certain episodes, segments, or paratexts which they do not see as fitting their desired (meta)text. With *The Simpsons*, then, while it is evident how the program's complicity with advertising may be seen by some audience members as a complete Faustian bargain, nullifying an anti-consumerism message elsewhere in the text, for other audiences, its messages from within the show may be of prime importance. Meanwhile, we must avoid the trap of assuming audiences of its parodic lexias will necessarily *try* to form a metatext: rather than always being an audience of *The Simpsons*, any given viewer may instead be an audience of its individual jokes and lexias, responding to them as they come, unconcerned with creating in their mind some perfectly coherent notion of what the show is and what it is saying. To such a viewer, the show's involvement in ads and merchandising may be television business-as-usual, whereas its lexias of parody and critique could stand out and beg attention.

We could also respond to the dilution of its consumption critique with a strain of sober realism, as does McAllister (2004), noting that, as far as consumption critique on commercial television goes, in many ways, *The Simpsons* 'is still the best we have.' I will return later, in Chapter 6, to an examination of the show's commen-tary on its commercial complicity. For the time being, however, *The Simpsons'* multiple and varied salvos fired at advertising from its weekly new episodes and daily reruns show us how parody can use television against itself, or at least against its sponsors. Television, as Caughie (1990: 50) notes, is 'interrupted and interruptible space,' a space of continual intertextual collisions, and of lexial fragmentation and juxtaposition. Parody, though, uses this system to its advantage. Thus, if a predomi-nant and overarching logic of television is that of commerce and of the perpetual marketplace, good parody such as *The Simpsons* can work with this logic so as to render it illogical.

Chapter 4

NEWS PARODY AND
THE PUBLIC SPHERE

I F ADVERTISING HAS FORMED A PREDOMINANT LOGIC OF commercial television, a rival logic, much-lauded by many media scholars, and followed in theory by public broadcasting systems, is that of the creation and maintenance of an active public sphere. Jürgen Habermas' ideal of the media serving as a space where 'private people come together as a public' (1989: 27), is well known, and despite the many criticisms of Habermas' thesis,[1] the notion that the media should serve the public interest is an enduring and noble ideal, at least in theory built into many countries regulatory policies. In recent years, though, the USA's Federal Communications Commission and other international (de)regulatory bodies have instituted policies that often weaken the media's ability and producers' commitment to serve citizens as citizens, not merely as consumers (Bagdikian 2004; Hesmondhalgh 2002; McChesney 2004). As Dahlgren neatly describes it, the public sphere is

> a space – a discursive, institutional, topographical space – where people in their roles as citizens have access to what can be metaphorically called societal dialogues, which deal with questions of common concern: in other words, with politics in the broadest sense.
>
> (Dahlgren 1995: 9)

However, many critics follow Habermas in believing that today, 'the public sphere has to be "made": it is not "there" anymore' (1989: 201). The public sphere is widely believed to be ailing, if existent at all. In this chapter, though, I will examine the role that parody can play in helping to foster 'societal dialogues' and to nurture a public sphere. I will focus on *The Simpsons*' news parody, and on its critical evaluation of what has long been seen as this most important of televisual genres.

Entertainment and the public sphere

As a character in Don DeLillo's novel *White Noise* notes, there is a degree to which, 'For most people there are only two places in the world. Where they live and their TV set' (DeLillo 1999: 66). The news plays a key role in bringing the rest of the world and information on the state of it to our TV sets, so that we might know of the world, and thus its importance cannot be understated. The news is seen as where we learn what is going on around us, what political, economic, and/or social forces are shaping our lives, and is (thus) a crucial component to the construction of ourselves as active citizens. It comes as no surprise, then, that, when writing on the public sphere and on television's 'public knowledge project,' as Corner (1996: 283) calls it, many media studies scholars focus on the news. Echoing Habermas (1989), many critics look to the news as the all and end-all of a public sphere (albeit a damaged one, in many versions of the tale), so that to many, 'the media' becomes wholly synonymous with the news media. For instance, for all the bold promise of its subtitle, Herman and Chomsky's *Manufacturing Consent: The Political Economy of the Mass Media* (1988) looks solely at the news.

Following Habermas' insistence that the public sphere be 'rational,' much radical political economy in particular has looked fetishistically to factual broadcasting, information, and the news as bastions of the promised land, and to entertainment as variously the distraction, the 'sugar on the pill,' or the 'circus tent' that not only lets down the side, but also frequently contaminates information, making it nothing but dreaded 'infotainment.' This would seemingly allow little if any room for an animated and often silly comedy such as *The Simpsons* to contribute anything substantive to a public sphere. But, as Dahlgren notes, 'any model of communication which tries to eliminate the arational, in the end risks becoming irrational' (1995: 86). Even Dahlgren, though, follows the scores of 'infotainment' detractors by stating that the entertainment – information distinction is breaking down because entertainment is seeping into and 'swamping' information (1995: 38), yet he ignores the fact that information might also have seeped into entertainment. Entertainment is embarrassingly misunderstood and under-valued by too many who write of the public sphere, and it is long overdue that media and cultural studies reappraise the value of entertainment to the average citizen.

Of course, some have already championed this cause in one way or another. Hartley, in particular, writes of the radical nature of much infotainment and of the tabloid press (1996), of style magazines (1996), and of television entertainment (1999). He notes that some of the more important issues facing the modern citizen, such as environmentalism, gender relations, and peace-seeking politics, receive more attention outside of Habermas' traditional rational public sphere and in the zone proper of entertainment (Hartley 1996: 58, 1999: 180). Gillespie's (1995) work with Southall teens has similarly illustrated how citizenship can be fostered through such programs as soap operas and ads, and through their viewers' talk about such programs. Livingstone and Lunt (1994) offer television talk shows as instances of a televisual public sphere, albeit limited, while Glynn (2000) tracks the resonant meanings and political discussion, or at least expression, in 'trash television' such as *The Jerry Springer Show*, *Cops*, and tabloid news. Bolin (2000), too, has charted the construction of a public sphere among swappers and fans of violent films in Sweden; Meijer (1998) looks to a public sphere surrounding ad discussion and consumption; while Maigret (1999: 6) shows how a public sphere of sorts has formed around comic book readers. These writers' work serves as evidence of how entertainment and the 'irrationalities' of character identification, aesthetic appreciation, style, and narrative can work just as well as documentaries or the news to build and maintain a public sphere. Their work also demands that *cultural* citizenship be taken more seriously, and not solely seen as an also-ran to political citizenship.

Habermas' romanticization of the nobility and purity of rational communication, notes Peters (1993: 565), 'leaves us both with an impoverished account of how communication in fact works and impedes the imagination of alternative forms of participatory media.' Amplifying this latter point, Stallybrass and White (1986: 43) suggest that 'It is indeed one of the most powerful ruses of the dominant to pretend that critique can only exist in the language of "reason," "pure knowledge" and "seriousness".' Rational discourse, they point out, is traditionally the tool of the powerful middle classes, and thus to require that all meaningful discussion take place in this realm is automatically to cut off many others' chances of taking part in this discussion. This, as Peters (1993) comments, is to rule out the very alternatives that *are* open to those groups and individuals. As Foucault would note, this is to play a cruel game of discourse, whereby only a certain group of individuals have access to a speaking platform, while those who lack the cultural and educational capital remain as excluded and irrelevant to the subsequent public sphere as those who, two hundred years ago, never had access to Habermas' beloved coffee houses.

I will not be arguing that *The Simpsons* has *replaced* the Habermasian coffee house, nor will I suggest, ludicrously, that it could or should replace the news. However, as I have already shown in Chapters 2 and 3, parody works by talking of genre, and it can inspire ridicule of a genre through discussing that genre's inner mechanics. Consequently, while *The Simpsons* does not tell us what is happening in Capitol Hill, Westminster, or the Sudan, it calls for a critical appraisal of those televisual voices that do tell us (or at least try to tell us) of world news. *The Simpsons*' news parody, while neither as pervasive nor as sustained as its ad or sitcom parody, can, in its own small way, contribute to a shared teaching and learning of the news, and thus it hails us not solely as news *consumers*, but as *citizens* trying to make sense of the news and of 'what happened.' In this chapter, I will, therefore, first analyze its discussion of the news, and then argue for how this contributes to a public sphere, and, as such, constitutes a mainstream and popular media literacy education of sorts.

Kent Brockman and *The Simpsons* report

While many critics regard the news as of primal importance, few see the genre as functioning in healthy Habermasian fashion. As Langer (1998) notes, there is a general academic 'lament' for news, a lament that spans a great deal of work.[2] In its political economy form, this lament points to countless structural problems, whereas other researchers have added to the list that news programs are constructed poorly (J. Lewis 1986) and thus that they confuse many people and/or are improperly understood by many (Richardson 2000); that the news alienates many, and is often of questionable relevance (Groombridge 1972); and, simply, that people generally do not enjoy watching the news and find it a frustrating duty to perform (Hagen 1994: 203; Perse 1998: 59–60). Many of these and other critics lament different things, but in common is a dissatisfaction with how this supposed bastion of political-discursive dissemination is failing its public. Similarly, though, *The Simpsons* often criticizes the news for its many foibles. In doing so, it follows two key tactics. The first sees it reveal the news' strategies of reembedding trust. Borrowing from my discussion in Chapter 2 of Giddens' theory of trust in contemporary society, we see that the news as genre must continually convince us that it is trustworthy, and *The Simpsons* illustrates several means by which it attempts to do so. Second, it disembeds that trust. By depicting the artificiality of the news' reembedding strategies, and by suggesting alternative explanations of how and why the news works as it does, *The Simpsons* works to engender or further nourish a suspicion and distrust of the news. As critical intertextuality, *The Simpsons* plays fool to the king of the news.

In the world of discourse, the news aims for coronation. The news is fundamentally a discourse of Truth, Fact, and History: if a tree falls in the forest and no reporter is there to see it, the tree makes no noise, as the news has become the *de facto* Office of Public Records . . . or at least aims to be. The news would have us believe that it is neutral, merely passing on objective fact altruistically, and hence serving a laudable role in society. As such, if it succeeds in winning us over completely, and if we believe in its oracular abilities to speak the truth, we grant it, and the individuals and corporations behind its production, immense power over us, and over our perceptions of reality. Once again, this is the reason why the news has attracted so much academic and critical attention. This is also the reason why the genre as king is in dire *need* of fools. As previously noted, Jenny suggests that certain genres 'provoke' (critical) intertextuality and parody, particularly those that are 'exaggeratedly encoded' with firm generic rules, and that claim to speak The Truth (Jenny 1982: 37). Such genres – and advertising and the news are obvious among them – cry out for parody.

Much of *The Simpsons*' news parody centers around the recurring character of KBBO newsman Kent Brockman, and his news programs, *Eye on Springfield* and *Smartline*. First and foremost, *The Simpsons* illustrates that these programs are *shows*, and, as such, operate under the same logic as any other entertainment program: get an audience and keep that audience. The news on *The Simpsons* is anything but an earnest attempt to inform Springfield's citizenry, and Kent Brockman is shown to be an entertainer, not an educator, nor the great midwife of Springfield's own Habermasian public sphere.

Operating under the proper aegis of commercial television, *The Simpsons*' news plays what sells. Thus, the opening sequence of *Eye on Springfield*, as shown in 'Flaming Moe's,' is a high-paced sequence with more cleavage than news, and several shots of Brockman enjoying himself in a hot tub. The sequence firmly posits the program as spectacularized entertainment in which sex and action take precedence over any remnant of news. The sequence then opens up to Brockman promising several interviews, 'But first, Part Seven of our eye-opening look at *the bikini*,' and in this it joins countless other instances of mindless, spectacularized trash making the news in Springfield. In 'Radio Bart,' a reporter leaves the now-old story of Bart stuck down a well in favor of a tip on a squirrel resembling Abraham Lincoln; in 'Grade School Confidential,' Bart promises to get the media's attention (and succeeds) by calling in an escaped octopus on the school roof; and other Brockman stories include reports on a wave of towel-snappings (which, 'experts say, will only get worse before it gets better'), and on a nudist camp for animals. When Kent believes that his show may be ending, in delivering a farewell broadcast, he lists 'a few of the events that brought me closer to you: the collapse of the Soviet Union, premium ice cream wars, dogs that were mistakenly issued major credit cards, and others who weren't so lucky' ('Sideshow Bob's Last Gleaming').

Not only does the news in *The Simpsons* pander to silly, tabloid material, but also it is incapable of drawing a distinction between matters of real importance (the collapse of the Soviet Union) and slightly amusing trivialities (canines with credit cards). Likewise, then, in 'Call of the Simpson,' reversing 'special report' protocol, the news cuts off a presidential address in favor of a report on Bigfoot. In 'The Computer Wore Menace Shoes,' Homer becomes an Internet news reporter, manufacturing all sorts of stories, and when approached with proof that the school's science class is dissecting frozen hobos, he responds, 'Real news is *great*, son, but I'm getting a thousand hits an hour with Grade A bull plop.' However, while this episode takes a swipe at the romanticization of indy media, lest television news appear better by comparison, after Kent defends local TV news as 'the real news [. . .] delivered by real, officially licensed newsmen like me,' Brockman announces, coming up, 'how *do* they get those dogs to talk in beer commercials? Cowboy Steve will tell you.' Springfield's, KBBO's, and Brockman's news priorities are remarkably and exaggeratedly misplaced, with right versus wrong, and important versus trivial, subsumed to interesting versus boring, so that we as viewers can laughingly reflect on our own news channels' failures to provide what is important.

In the episode 'Girly Edition,' Lisa learns first hand what makes particularly local news channels tick, when she and Bart are given the task of producing a children's news show. While Lisa dedicates herself to hard-nosed investigative journalism, Bart quickly becomes more popular with his flashy sports report, replete with props and sound effects. Bart is then promoted to co-anchor with Lisa, and learns a lesson from Kent on how 'human interest' stories win the awards. To teach Bart how to construct such a story, Kent pops in a tape of one of his reports:

> Hear that? It's the sound of children's laughter. Silenced. That's because tomorrow this old carousel, which has delighted young Americans for, lo, these past six years, will be torn down to make way for the future: a store that sells designer mouse pads. Well, I guess there's no room in this modern world for Old Blackie [,pointing to a carousel horse], but if you don't mind, this reporter is going for one last ride.

Sure enough, then, and to Lisa's chagrin, Bart goes on to produce a series of highly successful stories on 'Bart's People,' including a report on a man who feeds ducks that do not exist.

In making fun of the news, *The Simpsons* also attacks the overblown rhetoric and form of news programs. The need for reporters to sell every story, so as to keep viewers watching and the ratings meter ticking, often receives comic treatment. Thus, for instance, the 'bait' technique is aptly mimicked when Brockman announces in 'Bart Gets Famous,' 'tonight, a certain kind of soft drink has been found to be lethal. We won't tell you which one until after sports and the weather with funny Sonny Storm.' Or, in 'She Used To Be My Girl,' he promises car chases every night, and that the weather girl will wear a tube-top, or else 'you get a free pizza!' Likewise, the news' proclivity to market every story as the biggest is wonderfully parodied in 'Kamp Krusty,' when, in reporting on problems at a children's summer camp, Kent declares: 'Ladies and gentlemen, I've been to Vietnam, Afghanistan and Iraq, and I can say without hyperbole that this is a million times worse than all of them put together.' Furthermore, *The Simpsons* exhibits a fundamental problem of the news: that since death and misery sell, and since it will therefore always be in the news' best commercial interests to provide death and misery, this can easily lead to a resounding amorality, even bloodlust, on behalf of reporters. Clearly, when the news is shown to take an excited interest in 'a real life Noah,' accused of *killing* two of every species, as in 'Das Bus,' *The Simpsons* encourages little faith in the moral sense of news programs.

This questioning of journalistic ethics extends to *The Simpsons*' criticism of reporters' frequent abuse of interviewees. When Brockman interviews Marge on her doorstep in 'Miracle on Evergreen Terrace,' he asks if her 'husband or lover' is present, exhibiting a knee-jerk tendency to scrape for muck with the suggestion that she has a lover. In inquiring about the theft of their Christmas presents, he asks, 'So, when you realized Christmas was ruined, how did you feel?', hence displaying the reporter's art of asking hurtful questions with obvious answers, all in the name of the soundbite. Or, in 'Bart vs. Thanksgiving,' Brockman delivers a 'heartfelt' report on the plight of the homeless on Thanksgiving, ending with the guilt-trip that 'every year, on one, lone, conscience-salving day, we toss these people a bone – a turkey bone – and that's supposed to make it all better.' However, when the camera stops rolling, Kent thanks the homeless people for their help, saying 'this reporter smells another Emmy,' and then races off with the news team. His concern is thus revealed as a pose, with selfish motives and a lust for misery behind it, not honest empathy for these people's situation. Interviewees, *The Simpsons* shows, can easily become dehumanized resources to a largely uncaring if spectacularizing news machine.

The newscaster's well-worked image of caring, parent-like, calm, all-knowing, assertive and personable friend is taken to task by *The Simpsons*' use of Kent Brockman, who is depicted as a bad-tempered, spoilt, overweight, and overpaid *prima donna*. He regularly overreacts with outlandish assumptions, such as in 'Deep Space Homer,' when pictures from a space shuttle show escaped ants from the onboard ant farm, and he assumes a race of giant insects has taken over the shuttle and is soon to arrive on Earth to do likewise. Furthermore, he panders to owner- ship. Thus, believing that world domination by giant insects is inevitable, he adds that, 'I, for one, welcome our new insect overlords. I'd like to remind them that as a trusted TV personality, I can be helpful in rounding up others to toil in their underground sugar caves.' In a similar situation, while reporting on the leader of a new cult in 'The Joy of Sect,' when handed a note saying the station is now *owned* by this man, Kent flip-flops from calling the sect 'almost certainly evil' and a 'way out and wrong religion' to welcoming him and imploring him to 'Continue to improve our lives!'

In yet another parody of the content of news being adversely affected by ownership, money, and power, in 'Homer Defined,' when challenged by Mr Burns on reports of a nuclear meltdown at the plant, Brockman apologizes, 'Well, sir, your point about nuclear hysteria is well taken. This reporter promises to be more trusting and less vigilante in the future.' Such instances echo Bourdieu's (1998: 16) acerbic comment that, 'It is important to know that NBC is owned by General Electric (which means that interviews with people who live near a nuclear power plant undoubtedly would be . . . but then again, such a story wouldn't even occur to anyone).' Corner (1995) notes a general slippage in terminology whereby 'the news' comes to mean both the *events* and the *presentation*, and thus the news as latter, 'as the particular set of professional operations [. . .] enjoys a measure of social invisibility, being perceived as so closely related to the events themselves as not to warrant separate identification' (Corner 1995: 54), but *The Simpsons* works against this dangerous elision. *The Simpsons* illustrates that the news is a show, carefully put together for entertainment purposes, dutifully obeying the (sometimes *dis*information) objectives of its owners, and still as much a product as any ad or item of merchandise. When, in 'Homer Defined,' Lisa notices the front page headline of Homer's *USA Today*, 'America's Favorite Pencil: #2 is #1,' she criticizes the paper as a 'flimsy hodge-podge of high-brass factoids and Larry King.' Homer defends the paper by arguing that it is a paper 'not afraid to tell the truth: that everything's *just fine*.' *The Simpsons*, then, shows how often the news is wholly toothless, sacrificing journalism for sales, and leaving us not with important public information, but with America's Favorite Pencil.

With the above example as rare exception, Kent Brockman is the focus of much of *The Simpsons*' criticism of the news. Thus, the program may appear to suffer from focusing too much on the individual, rather than on the system. However, I believe that this would be to misread *The Simpsons*' critique of the news. After all, many viewers trust television newscasters above any other story source (see Gauntlett and Hill 1999: 61). As Hermes (1999: 70) argues, 'the news, like other media genres, functions through its central personalities,' and thus newscasters are rarely true individuals. Rather, they are a matrix of much of the news production team's efforts to reembed our trust in what they are telling us. In Giddens' (1990) terms, the newscaster becomes the 'access point' whereby we see the system – the glittering point of 'facework' designed to win our trust, and the genre's form embodied. Consequently, any attack on the newscaster is by nature an attack on the system. In choosing Brockman as the focus of its news parody, *The Simpsons* undercuts this mythification of the newscaster. In this regard, arguably some of its best 'news parody' comes at those moments when Brockman is shown *not* at work, but as just another person in a crowd, for at these moments, he is denied his symbolic power as ethereal, remarkable figure. He, and the news by extension, is shown to be (un)remarkably human, and as no great King of Truth. Admittedly, Brockman could be seen as the anomaly to the rule, and he could be seen as funny precisely because he fails to live up to the austere norms and integrity of newscasters; however, if Brockman is a poor newsman, *The Simpsons* never shows us what a good one might look like, as instead it regularly lampoons the news and its shoddy delivery.

Public theory

While *The Simpsons* has less overall news parody than ad or sitcom parody, the show has produced several episode-long critiques of the news. One of these, 'Homer Badman,' begins with the Simpsons' baby-sitter publicly accusing Homer of sexual harassment. As soon as the news breaks, Homer is set upon by a story-hungry media. First, Godfrey Jones of a show called *Rock Bottom* offers to help him tell 'his side' of the story. In broadcast, though, Jones puts together a highly edited and incriminating, cut-and-paste version of his interview. For maximum effect, too, the interview is introduced as such:

> Tonight, on *Rock Bottom*, we go undercover at a sex farm with sex hookers [. . .] But first, she was a university honors student who devoted her life to kids, until the night a grossly overweight *pervert* named Homer Simpson gave her a crash-course in depravity: 'Baby-sitter and the Beast.'

When Jones asks if Homer has anything to say to defend himself, *Rock Bottom* cuts to a paused hideous picture of Homer (complete with pause-line across the screen) and over the picture we hear Jones cry, 'No, Mr Simpson, don't take your anger out on me! Get back, get back! No!!' At high speed, another voice intones, 'Dramatization – may not have happened,' and thus ends Homer's interview. This part of the episode alone stacks the news critique high, as it mocks the 'dramatization,' the abuse of interviewees and treatment of them as mere resources, the spectacularizing impulses of some news programs, and the news' general love for polarizing any story to make it more appealing to the public.

Outside of *Rock Bottom*, Homer is no more safe from the news. A news helicopter captures a picture of Homer wrapped naked in a shower curtain, and the next 'Simpson scandal update' displays the picture, with the script that Homer 'sleeps in an oxygen tent which he believes gives him sexual powers.' Later, too, Brockman reports on 'hour 27 of our live, round-the-clock coverage outside the Simpson estate.' As we are given an aerial view of the Simpsons' house, Kent reminds viewers to tune in later, 'for highlights of today's vigil, including when the garbage man came, and when Marge Simpson put the cat out, possibly because it was harassed – we don't know,' and we then see heat vision footage of the house. At the episode's original airing date of 1994, and for a considerable while after, such pictures, phrasing ('the Simpson estate'), and general hoopla offered obvious commentary on the media circus surrounding the OJ Simpson trial. Even for those viewers not picking up on this commentary, though, the generic criticism is still clear, as *The Simpsons* parodies the level to which the news media make big stories out of small ones, and will engage in all manner of trivial practices (endless aerial shots of an inanimate house, heat vision cameras, tracking the cat's movements), and all manner of outlandish speculation just to keep the story big, alive, and to keep viewers.

Ultimately, as Lisa explains to Homer, 'The media's making a monster out of you because they don't care about the truth. All they care about is entertainment.' While we must be wary of adopting a crude view of truth and entertainment as mutually exclusive concepts, *The Simpsons* levels serious criticism at the news for constantly placing the latter above the former in importance. This episode, among others, lampoons how the news tries to convict regardless of evidence. In an instance of particularly pointed criticism, Brockman announces 'some results from our phone-in poll: 95 per cent of the people believe Homer Simpson is guilty. Of course, this is just a television poll, which is not legally binding . . . unless Proposition 304 passes, and we all pray it will.' However, lest *The Simpsons* leave all of the blame with the media, here it also implicates the audience (those who phoned in). Then, at the episode's end, once Homer is cleared, *Rock Bottom* announces next week's show, an exposé on the man who cleared Homer, and Homer remarks, 'That man is sick,' reasoning, 'listen to the music: he's *evil.*' If the news places polarization, spectacularization, and simplification over reality or any attempt to investigate the truth, *The Simpsons* argues that the audience must take some of the responsibility for allowing this to happen. The episode's closing 'moral,' then, is that, as audience members, we should heed its criticism of the news and remember it as a critical intertextuality as we watch the news.

One of *The Simpsons'* more recent episodes, 'Fraudcast News,' focused on media conglomeration. Mr Burns decides to buy all of Springfield's media outlets in order to control their output, and thus news stories quickly lose any critical edge, and become littered with glowing references to Burns. The episode unambiguously criticizes the FCC's torrent of deregulation, and slyly mocks *Simpsons'* parent company News Corporation's own Fox News. The implied parallel between Burns and Springfield's media, and Rupert Murdoch and his own news empire, is rendered explicit when, in one scene, Burns and Smithers trade Murdoch compliments, while looking fawningly at the camera. This direct attack on Fox News also extends to a brief sequence in 2004's post-election, 'She Used To Be My Girl,' when a cavalcade of news trailers is followed by a huge Fox News trailer, sporting a massive 'Bush-Cheney 04' decal on the side and victoriously playing 'We Are the Champions.' Or, in another sequence from 'Mr Spritz Goes to Washington,' a Fox News ticker runs across the bottom of the screen, full of pro-Republican and pro-establishment 'news,' such as, 'Do Democrats Cause Cancer?', 'JFK Posthumously Joins Republican Party,' 'Oil Slicks Found to Keep Seals Young, Supple,' and 'Study: 92% of Democrats are Gay.'

Ultimately, *The Simpsons* serves as a mouthpiece of what we could call 'public theory.' Granted, the show hardly develops or substantiates its critique of news form to the degree that academic theory requires, but embedded in *The Simpsons*, and as

103

seeds of its humor, are statements on, for example: the excess speed and ensuing incomprehensibility of news that we find in Justin Lewis (1986, 1991); the role of news graphics in truncating complex issues found in Ellis (2000: 97); the questioning of journalistic ethics that we find in Dahlgren (1981), Moeller (1999), or Seib (2002); the news' often inherent conservatism found in Bagdikian (2004), Hallin (1994), and Herman and Chomsky (1988); news hype, ahistoricity, and the primacy of entertainment found in Postman and Powers (1992); the power of the market in deciding what is news, detailed by McManus (1994); the news' essentializing treatment of its subjects documented in Brunsdon and Morley (1978) and Couldry (2000); and how the news appeals for our trust that we see in Hartley (1982). Moreover, these lessons, as visual parody, are illustrative and are theory applied – theory *prêt-a-porter* – rather than declarative theory in the abstract. Buckingham (2000: 18) suggests that 'Rather than attempting to measure the effectiveness of the news in communicating political information, we should be asking how it enables viewers to construct and define their relationship with the public sphere.' In *The Simpsons*, we have a program enabling viewers to construct and define their relationship *with the news itself*, not only so that we can forge a relationship with the public sphere through this, but also so that we can be better equipped to read through and *filter* through, political information as it is presented to us.

The rational carnival?

In doing so, parody defies Habermas' stipulation that the public sphere must be rational. As comic, and at-times ludicrous, silly, and irreverent, parody speaks in an 'irrational' language and tone. However, we must question how clear the division between rational and irrational discourse indeed is, for with *The Simpsons*, we have a case in which 'irrational' language is used both to lodge rational complaints, and to inspire rational thought and commentary about the news (and ads and the sitcom). Examination of *The Simpsons*' news parody therefore points to the inadequacy of theories of the public sphere that look only to the news and to wholly 'rational' discourses to foster societal dialogue and critical thought. It also points to a deficit in media studies in understanding how comedy works. To move discussion of the public sphere forward, we must grapple more convincingly with comedy and its prospects for critique.

In the previous chapter, I wrote of comedy's 'lexial' quality, and, hence, of the ease with which it 'moves' intertextually. Yet, comedy always has particularly appropriate sites of (re)activation. Comedy sees us laugh *at* something or someone, and thus it is fundamentally transitive, aiming itself at some other site. Comedy is often explained psychologically as a *defense* against anxiety (Freud 1960), but it also goes on the offensive, poking fun at other discourses. Comedy relies on certain levels of competence with these 'target' discourses, precisely because at activation or – through memory – reactivation, it works by attaching itself to these discourses and toying with them. Comedy works most often by wedding sense and the expected to the unexpected, by colliding discourses and moving one into the realm of the other. This is, as Jerry Palmer (1987) calls it, the 'logic of the absurd.' Palmer provides the example of a gag from Laurel and Hardy's *Liberty*, in which an elevator lands on a policeman, and rises again to reveal a midget in full uniform. Here, Palmer (1987: 39) says, one strain of logic (immense pressure compresses an object) collides with another (an elevator landing on a man would kill him) and produces a hybrid logic, the logic of the absurd. In other words, comedy subjects something that seems natural to an external logic. In doing so, it carries with it at least the potential to reevaluate the seemingly flawless logic of many instances of hegemonic 'common sense' (see Stewart 1979).

As an intricately intertextual, transitive genre, comedy works on the ground of other genres, discourses, and/or individual texts, as is best evidenced by the fact that we must know of these sites in order to understand what the joke *is*. Thus, while I write of comedy moving well, the main obstacle to its motion would be lack of understanding of its target's 'logic' or cultural coding, since this logic is the ground upon which it works. One is only likely to laugh at a joke about lawyers if one knows what lawyers are – what they do, how they work, how they are perceived. Without such knowledge, the joke would fail, because it would be 'groundless.' Ultimately, then, although comedy is self-contained, it must take us somewhere, and parasitically it relies on other grounds. All comedy works through provoking us to laugh at something, and the 'at' in this process serves as propulsion, moving the comic lexia into other territory. Frequently, this other territory is within the comic text more broadly (a joke at a character's expense, for example), but just as often it takes us out of the text, and toward other knowledges and other texts. Comedy is inherently intertextual, and by colliding disparate discourses, always invites at least some degree of critical intertextuality, for when we laugh, we acknowledge having moved with the joke to other territory, and having been treated to an alternative view of that territory. While comedy works on other genres', other texts', other logics' grounds, then, it also brings them back forcibly into its zone of play for potential study. As Bakhtin writes:

> Laughter has the remarkable power of making an object come up close, of drawing it into a zone of crude contact where one can finger it familiarly on all sides, turn it upside down, inside out, peer at it from above and below, break open its external shell, look into its center, doubt it, take it apart, dismember it, lay it bare and expose it, examine it freely and experiment with it.
>
> (Bakhtin 1981: 23)

105

The level, type and degree of 'experimentation' will vary from joke to joke, but comedy's logic demands at least some.

Comedy is perhaps best understood as setting up inside and outside positions. The inside position – that of being 'in' on the joke – is one of comfort, and of a certain degree of personal empowerment. To understand the joke situates us on the knowing inside of comic space, looking and laughing out. As such, comedy flatters us, our competence with the world and our critical understanding of it. The inside position is at base a critical (even if playful) one, of the outside, for while situated in this inside space, we look out at the butt of the joke with critical 'understanding.' My scare quotes here, though, point to an important proviso: comedy may lead only to *perceived* understanding. By no means is all comedy ideologically pleasant, and by stating it is personally empowering, I attach no necessary positive value to this, for the basis of the inside-outside might be racist, sexist, homophobic, or otherwise regressive critical commentary and *mis*understanding.

As the case of bigoted humor reveals, though, while comic space's inside is a position of empowerment, its outside is one of disempowerment. As Bergson (1935) writes, laughter creates a form of freemasonry, and Freud (1960: 108) adds that, whereas jokes frequently reveal a certain amount of 'disguised aggressiveness,' 'every joke calls for a public of its own and laughing at the same jokes is evidence of far-reaching psychical conformity' (Freud 1960: 151). Thus, any disguised aggressiveness is shared and communal among the inside laughers, and is directed outwards at the object(s) of mirth or derision. We may note how hard it is to respond to being the object of a joke: because comic space is one of play and the absurd, rational criticism is often ineffectual (witness any wooden politician attempt to respond to comic critique). All that is left open to those inhabiting the outside space is either to shut down and silence the inside through censorship (should they have the means to do so), or to create their own comic space, and 'return' the joke with one of their own (see J. Palmer 1987: 199).

However, comedy's ability to create insides and outsides is precisely one of the qualities that renders it politically potent. Consequently, although this potency may lead to exclusion and bigotry, it also has great positive potential. After all, one of comedy's most frequent targets is the taken-for-granted, the 'common sense' of everyday life. As Ellis notes of television comedy, comedy in general 'thrives upon recognition, which is often slightly uncomfortable, of orders of discourse presented in disorder' (Ellis 2000: 118). Comedy works through a form of defamiliariza-tion, whereby that which regularly goes unnoticed, because assumed 'natural,' is re-presented as irrational. Comedy can take that which in everyday life is on the safe inside, and put it on the outside of comic space. The object of this reversal of fortunes, or *perepeteia* (see J. Palmer 1987), and turning inside-out may range from the deeply political to the banal, but common among all instances is a critique of 'normality,' for as Bergson notes, comedy 'expresses an individual or collective imperfection which calls for an immediate corrective. This corrective is laughter, a social gesture that singles out and represses a special kind of absentmindedness in men [sic] and events' (Bergson 1935: 87–8). Comic space is one in which the world can be turned inside-out.

In this regard, it is helpful to see comedy as a form of what Bakhtin (1984) calls Rabelaisian 'carnival.' Rabelais situates his fictional world within the carnivalesque, a marketplace world of bawdy humor, profanities, fooling around, excessive bodies, licentious behavior, comic reversals, the grotesque, and an overall absence of regulation from above. As Stam quaintly summarizes, the world of carnival is one of 'orgiastic egalitarianism' (1989: 90). This world, as such, becomes 'a second world and a second life outside of officialdom' (Bakhtin 1984: 6), in which all manner of societal rules are struck down, allowing an experimental space for transgression, criticism, and liberation. Carnival is licensed, but is controlled by the people, by its participants. According to Bakhtin:

> Carnival is not a spectacle seen by the people; they live in it, and everyone participates because its very idea embraces all the people [. . .] It has a universal spirit; it is a special condition of the entire world, of the world's revival and renewal, in which all take part.
>
> (Bakhtin 1984: 7)

Moreover, amidst the transgression of everyday rules for reality and communication, 'This temporary suspension, both ideal and real, of hierarchical rank created during carnival time a special type of communication impossible in everyday life' (Bakhtin 1984: 10).

Humor and comedy act on a similar level to carnival. Comedy on television is definitely more of a spectacle, and less participatory than Rabelaisian carnival; moreover, as spectacle, any individual will have the choice of whether to participate, and hence many will not. Rabelaisian carnival, if it ever had a real-life referent, no longer exists in pure form. Nevertheless, televisual carnival can require considerably more participation and activity on behalf of the 'spectators' than one might first believe. Comedy provides a space outside of ordered reality, and becomes that 'special type of communication' of which Bakhtin writes, a communication that involves viewers and 'belongs' to them, not only to the comic 'producer.' Furthermore, as Neale and Krutnik observe, comedy's generic conventions '*demand* both social and aesthetic indecorum' (1990: 3, emphasis added), so that indecorum becomes an expected part of comedy. Space is of vital importance to transgression, and thus is of vital importance to an understanding of what comedy provides. Following Foucault's (1977: 141) observation that 'discipline proceeds from the distribution of individuals in space,' Stallybrass and White note that:

Each 'site of assembly' constitutes a nucleus of material and cultural conditions which regulate what may or may not be said, who may speak, how people may communicate and what importance must be given to what is said. An utterance is legitimated or disregarded according to its place of production and so, in large part, the history of political struggle has been the history of the attempts made to control significant sites of assembly and spaces of discourse.

(Stallybrass and White 1986: 80)

Outside of comedy, indecorum is not given much space, or time, and is strictly hemmed in. By contrast, though, carnival-like, comedy offers a relatively open and inviting space in which indecorum and difference are not just tolerated, but actively sought after. The transgression of everyday boundaries is the comic agenda, and as such, comedy provides fertile ground for criticism of any kind, whether playful or with bite.

To invoke carnival theory, though, we must address its most common criticisms. A key rebuke is with regards its potency, asking to what degree we actually transport what we learn in comic space *outside* of that zone and back into everyday life. Bakhtin (1984) quotes a circular letter to the Paris School of Theology from 1444 about carnivals, which argues that they are harmless, for

wine barrels burst if from time to time we do not open them and let in some air. All of us men are barrels poorly put together, which would burst from the wine of wisdom, if this wine remains in a state of constant fermentation of piousness and fear of God. We must give it air in order not to let it spoil. This is why we permit folly on certain days so that we may later return with greater zeal to the service of God.

(Bakhtin 1984: 75)

As space for indecorum, carnival is criticized as a strategy of the powerful designed to maintain power, for the very reason that this letter-writer approves of it: the idea being that comic space is walled in, with transgression and indecorum restricted from exiting with comic space's visitors.[3] Worse still, the argument goes, carnivals may prove 'functional for their respective "establishments" in that their very continued existence proclaims the openness and liberality of those establishments' (Powell 1988: 101). The zone of play, in other words, may work too well, prohibiting lessons learnt from crossing over into 'reality,' and becoming 'the only terrain in everyday life on which [people] can compete with or resist social controls of the powerful' (Powell 1988: 103), yet ensuring its participants walk away happy. Carnivals end, comedy shows end, and, according to comedy's critics, so does the potential for transgression.

A second criticism sees comedy as holding potential for transgression, yet rarely realizing it. If, by transgression, we mean political resistance, this criticism is entirely valid: people slipping on bananas hardly threatens to change the world order. Thus, when I write of transgression, I do not necessarily mean political resistance; rather, just the violation of, and working against, an established rule or norm. After all, banana peel gags transgress rules of bodily sanctity and dignity (especially if our victim is of high rank in society). The question, though, becomes when and in what instances is comedy harnessed to do more than just play with bananas?

Parody provides significant opportunities for more meaningful transgression, and whether it is of sitcoms, ads, or the news, *The Simpsons* in particular presents countless instances of comic criticism and of a fundamentally *rational* criticism worded 'irrationally' as comedy and play. Precisely because this parody is playful, is a form of spectacle, and is measured critique, it rarely amounts to a blistering attack: *The Simpsons* is by no means leading a vanguard of news criticism as we know it. Nevertheless, as will be explored further in Part III, we would be wise never to underestimate the powers of comedy and parody to nudge a viewer toward greater understanding of and even involvement with an issue. As Jerry Palmer (1987) notes:

> political opposition does not consist essentially in the rational criticism of one's opponents – central though this may be to political success – it consists essentially in the will to oppose, the will to say 'No.' Thereafter it may well be necessary to define the grounds of such opposition, but the essential moment is the simple recognition that one does not want *that*, that what one wants is something different: the essential moment is no more than the will to opposition. To mark something with the indelible seal of ridicule is intrinsically to indicate the will to oppose it.
>
> (J. Palmer 1987: 199, original emphasis)

Parody can offer such moments of recognition, and in doing so, contributes to the public sphere as a popular media literacy educator. Jameson (1984) has infamously pronounced the death of parody in a postmodern era, arguing that it has now dissolved into pastiche, and 'a neutral practice of such mimicry, without any of parody's ulterior motives, amputated of the satiric impulse, devoid of laughter' (Jameson 1984: 116). This is powerful writing, but as I have shown, *The Simpsons* exhibits multiple moments of ulterior motives, satiric impulse, and laughter. Parody faces several obstacles that will be discussed further in Chapter 6, but *The Simpsons'* news parody is a clear example of at least an attempt to speak to a public sphere.

Public pedagogy

Parody is a fool of sorts, but it is also a teacher (if indeed the two can be separated!), and its joking lessons and reminders amount to a public pedagogy, acting as a powerful theorist and illustrator of media studies. While some commentators see television's educative capacities as largely nefarious in practice, or even see television and education as incompatible, with television as a threat to education (Postman 1986), parody suggests that television is remarkably capable of offering positive and empowering lessons. With media saturation a basic fact, and thus media literacy of vital importance to meaningful participation in contemporary society, parody, as a form of critical intertextuality and as a teacher of media literacy, is a sterling example of what Hartley (1999) calls 'democratainment,' or entertainment with a democratizing, public sphere component.

Far from being a mere supplement to more institutionalized media literacy lessons, or a vaguely amusing illustration, parody is capable of teaching media literacy in ways that elude more traditional methods. Schools and universities only prove so effective in teaching the news, for instance. First, learning happens in all sorts of locations and via all sorts of means, and as Illich (1971) points out in his radical thesis on *Deschooling Society*, it is one of the more damaging notions of contemporary society that true learning only happens in an institutional setting. Illich's belief in the consequent need for the closure of public schools is an oddly extreme position which I do not share; nevertheless, he is astute to observe that serious learning happens outside school walls. And since we must go to school, whereas the media comes to us, the media often proves a key – and more continuous – site of pedagogy. Thus, while the fact may be humbling to those of us teaching in schools and dedicated to our own educative missions, as Eco (1979: 24) states, 'A critically oriented education has to recognize the fact that television exists and is the principle source of education for adults and young people.'

'Theory,' writes Henry Giroux, 'has to be *done*, it has to become a form of cultural production and not merely a storehouse of insights drawn from the books of the "great theorists"' (1997: 240, original emphasis). This is one of parody's greatest skills – that it can *do* theory. As any teacher who has used video clips or magazine clippings in their classes could attest to, the ability to show the media in action while theorizing it is frequently important in effective teaching. Parody is continuous illustration, for it talks through the body of that which it mocks and aims to teach. Therefore, when the effectiveness of much education relies upon showing relevance, so that 'the importance of relating classroom knowledge to the everyday lives of students cannot be overemphasized' (Giroux 1994: 121), parody is always-already applied and relevant. Furthermore, its lessons are taught from within the media flow that it wishes to tell us of, rather than from the often media-sterile and altogether distant environment of the classroom. Parody's presence in the television alongside its targeted discourses may prove a literally timely reminder. In challenging our trust in the news as discourse of truth, *The Simpsons* helps us not only to understand the news better, but also to understand what we are committing ourselves to as consumers of the news.

Institutionalized media literacy classes, when they are well taught, undoubtedly hold far greater potential to educate students than do any episodes of *The Simpsons*, but they are hardly perfect, and are fraught with their own problems. In particular, such classes can suffer from alienating their students. On one hand, as Giroux (1994) notes in an autobiographical preface to *Disturbing Pleasures*, school itself can be a foreign setting that lacks connection to lived realities. Of his childhood, he describes:

> My friends and I collected and traded comic books, learned about our desire through the rock and roll of Little Richard and Bill Haley and the Comets, and drank to the blues of Fats Domino [. . .] We felt rather than knew what was really useful knowledge. And we talked, danced, and lost ourselves in a street culture that never stopped moving. Then we went to school. Something stopped us in school. For me, it was like being sent to a strange planet [. . .] The language we learned and had to speak was different, strange, and unusually verbose. Bodily and intellectual memories disappeared for working-class kids in this school [. . .] This is not to suggest that we didn't learn anything, but what we learned had little to do with where we came from, who we were, or where we thought, at least, we were going.
>
> (Giroux 1994: ix–x)

As talk by some critics of 'the ivory tower' or 'academia' as if they were foreign planets suggests, schools and universities can indeed be a different world. While the distinct advantage of this different world is that it provides a space for critical distance and reflection, its distance may also at times prove alienating. Where schools may alienate, therefore, television and parody might welcome. Of course, parody and television will themselves exclude as well, but they provide other options.

Moreover, where, as Foucault notes, 'Any system of education is a political way of maintaining or modifying the appropriation of discourses, along with the knowledge and powers which they carry' (1981: 64), we as academics are both naive and arrogant if we believe our universities and schools only ever 'modify' discourses. It is no accident that one of *The Simpsons'* other key targets is the education system itself, for it is in schools and universities that trust in all manner of other discourses is frequently taught. If, therefore, *The Simpsons'* prime 'message' is, as Groening says, 'That your moral authorities don't always have your best interests in mind' (quoted in Chocano 2001), it is only proper that schools and the family, as the authorities

111

that often teach us of all other authorities, figure so heavily as the targets of its humor. Television might be 'tainted' by its political economy, but we should never assume academia itself is untainted and therefore a 'pure' zone from which to teach. The point here is not to devalue traditional institutional education, but rather to accept that just as schools and universities can teach in spite of their flaws, so too can television.

Meanwhile, media literacy classes in particular suffer their own problems, and can also be profoundly alienating. Too often, notes Morgan (1998), such classes begin with assumptions of weak and vulnerable students, clever and protective teachers, and a 'bad' media. 'Media,' he notes, 'are the active force in the relationship,' whereas, 'students, on the other hand, are *done to* – acted upon, manipulated by, exposed or vulnerable to – are victims in essence' (Morgan 1998: 118, original emphasis). The teacher, of course, though, remains magically immune. Theorists of media literacy education are increasingly arriving at the consensus that an 'inoculatory' or 'demystification' approach to media literacy not only perceives the media in crudely simplistic terms as a force of darkness, but also risks insulting students with its patronizing belief in the superhuman media defenses of the instructor and the weakness of individual audience members. Furthermore, as is suggested by Giroux's (1994) comments on his childhood, the media can be dear to many of us. Thus, inoculatory media literacy classes walk the thinnest of high wires, risking putting students immediately on the defensive by alienating (and angering) them through adopting a too overtly anti-media stance. By contrast, a cultural studies approach to media literacy (see Bazalgette 1997; Buckingham 1998a; Giroux 1994; Kubey 1998; Masterman 1997) realizes that audiences' relationships with the media are complex, and sees media literacy education as a means of helping audience members interrogate and analyze their experiences with the media themselves, not solely subordinate them 'to the teacher's tastes, the text's immanent meanings, or the dominant views of the majority' (Masterman 1997: 26).

Ultimately, Morgan (1998: 128) suggests, we need to stop seeing 'media literacy' strictly as an awareness and protection project, and start seeing it as a continuance of and an involvement with meaning. He thus suggests that what is needed is not Media Education but a 'media education in small letters' (Morgan 1998: 128). Again, parody proves useful here, for its lightness of tone and its aversion to sanctimonious preaching may allow it to occupy the middle ground between teaching and not patronizing. Inevitably, this 'media education in small letters' involves compromises, as well as a need for brevity that often entails simplification. But with public pedagogy, we can never just ask which teaching method says more and uses more detail: we must also ask who is listening and who has been alienated. Meanwhile, to talk of who is listening raises another issue regarding media literacy education, and that is one of the prestige, or lack thereof, of media studies classes. Media studies ranks low on the distinction scale of courses, and with this, then, particularly at the elementary and secondary levels, media studies is undertaught and in need of assistance. Media literacy courses may well be important, but with many teachers, politicians, parents, students, and curricula refusing to accept this, a public pedagogy such as that offered by parody is all the more necessary.

'Consciousness is power,' notes Fetterley (1978), continuing that:

> To create a new understanding of our literature is to make possible a new effect of that literature on us. And to make possible a new effect is in turn to provide the conditions for changing the culture that the literature reflects.
>
> (Fetterley 1978: xix–xx).

Thus, we should not undervalue any form of public pedagogy that aims to increase consciousness, and to model new effects, nor should we underestimate any form's powers. As Giroux surmises, 'The struggle over meaning is no longer one that can be confined to programs in educational institutions and their curricula' (1994: 22). Rather, he argues, we must make 'the pedagogical more political by reconstructing the very concept of pedagogy as a social practice' (Giroux 1994: 64), and we could look to parodies such as *The Simpsons* as complementary tools in the media literacy project. Parody and critical intertextuality work alongside our own efforts to teach the media, and we would be wise to acknowledge and respect these efforts. Eco states that 'if you want to use television for teaching somebody something, you have first to teach somebody how to use television' (Eco 1979: 15), but parody finds a way to teach viewers to use television *on television*.

The Simpsons and/as 'quality television'

Of course, as a form of 'public theory,' *The Simpsons*' comic statements are as prone to shortcomings as is any other theory. To point one out, *The Simpsons* is too keen to write off tabloid-style journalism as inherently laughable and a waste of televisual time and space. Glynn (2000), Hartley (1996), and Langer (1998) have all written powerfully of the important narrative, cultural, and political roles that tabloid or 'trash' journalism serve. Hartley (1996) in particular points out that the division between 'real' journalism dealing with 'hard' issues such as money and politics, and other forms of news dealing with more 'lightweight' material is a perilous one to make, for, *'events are semiotic,* as well as being public and political, and equally, *semiotic developments are political'* (Hartley 1996: 83–4, original emphases). *The Simpsons'* relentless parodic criticism of tabloid news replicates this error of assuming that what Langer (1998) calls 'the other news' is worthless drivel cluttering the way of 'real' news. Glynn (2000) shows that much of television's 'low' forms give voice to many working class and otherwise marginalized discourses in a way that few other genres even consider. Tabloidism, he argues, 'creates media space for the circulation of alternative knowledges as it caters to the disreputable tastes of alienated and relatively disempowered social formations' (Glynn 2000: 227), and he characterizes the elitist mockery and 'Call for the eradication of media "junk food" such as "trash TV" [as] a kind of cultural liposuction that would like to eliminate unsightly social differences' (2000: 104).

In the face of this defense of tabloidism, *The Simpsons* can indeed be too quick to disregard this type of programming and its possible meanings. While the show slightly tempers its attacks on both the sitcom and ads, no qualifications are attached to its news parody. Consequently, *The Simpsons* could be seen as adopting a wholly ambiguous relationship to the issue of 'quality' on television. On one hand, the show revels in high culture, awash with high art references, and implicitly inviting the censure of low brow taste, as it attacks infotainment. On the other hand, this is a show that uses belching and mooning for steady laughs, and that, as both Skoble (2001) and Arnold (2004) suggest, is quite anti-high brow at times, celebrating the common person. Furthermore, through its casual referencing of popular and mainstream media texts that is rivaled in density and frequency by few other texts in history, the show builds something of a temple to low brow American media at the same time as it waxes high brow with Norman Rockwell, Jasper Johns, or Stanley Kubrick references. Thus, although the show's parody denigrates 'trash television' without analyzing it further, and at times plays too easily into established taste hierarchies, it is also a powerful deconstructor and an occasional champion of these same low brow taste hierarchies.

A risk that all defenses of culturally disrespected genres run, as is evidenced in particularly Glynn (2000) and Hartley (1996), is that we make it impossible to talk of quality – or to discuss how we would like to see media content reform – without labeling ourselves elitists. Parody, such as *The Simpsons'* news parody, will therefore *appear* elitist at times, and actually *is* elitist at other times, but if this is the price it must pay to discuss quality, and to call for a better public sphere that offers its citizens – whether high, low, or middle brow – more than it does at present, this price is perhaps a necessary cost of existence, even if regrettable.

However, even while it denigrates tabloid and 'trash' television, *The Simpsons* is attacking an elitist discourse of quality that often pervades media studies scholarship. After all, to see parody such as *The Simpsons* as teaching media literacy and as actively contributing to the public sphere is to recognize that mainstream popular entertainment can form an important part of a healthy media diet, and hence can be 'quality television,' even as, elsewhere in the same program, toilet humor is prevalent. This view is at odds with many scholars within media studies who have posited the mainstream, commercial media as a force to be worked against, never with, especially in the incarnation of entertainment and fun. Here, I include not only those theorists who Hartley (1999: 133) has characterized as 'Camp Fear,' theorists such as Gerbner et al. (1994), Herman and Chomsky (1988), Mander (1977), Philo and Miller (1998), and Postman (1986), who see the mass media as a dark and sinister force. I also include Camp Fear's supposed counterfoil of active audience theorists. While this latter group of theorists have, I believe, successfully challenged the text- or technological-determinism of their opposites by charting activity on the media *consumer*'s side, their base assumption is still often one of the media *text*'s ultimate political conservatism. If, as Morley (1992) suggests, active audience theory involves a 'curiously Christian' assumption that 'the sins of the industry (or the message) are somehow seen to be redeemed in the "after-life" of reception' (Morley 1992: 30), it is a radically Calvinist Christianity, assuming outright that all texts are born sinners in the eyes of God. Popular culture, Fiske is clear in explaining, is 'formed always in reaction to, and never as part of, the forces of domination' (1989c: 43), and thus readers and texts are posited as opposing forces: the goodies and the baddies. Jenkins (1988: 87) concurs when he writes of fandom as 'a vehicle for marginalized subgroups [. . .] to pry open space for their cultural concerns within dominant representations [. . .], a way of transforming mass [read "bad"] culture into a popular [read "good"] culture.' Active audiences, Fiske, Jenkins, and de Certeau tell us, are 'guerrillas' (Fiske 1989c), 'rebellious children' (Jenkins 1988: 86), and 'poachers' (de Certeau 1984), making authors the strategic dominant forces, authoritarian parents, and evil landowners. Thus, mass media texts are still seen as things to be resisted, and definitely not trusted, or listened to too carefully.

This characterization suffers from assuming that all texts fall headlong into the hegemonic, dominant fold, and it produces a polarized picture of power and ideol- ogy that gives too much credit to network ownership as being omniscient and omnipotent. But it also forgets about art and artists. While one might personally dislike much of their output, many of the people involved in creating media texts consider themselves artists. And many artists have a vision, have ideas that they wish to share. In other words, 'production' is not all about corporate messages: it is also about artistic ones (see Hesmondhalgh 2002). Granted, these artists work in a system, with both direct and institutional pressure from above to create a certain product. But some of our world's greatest art has been produced in equally hostile environments. Numerous novelists and poets worldwide, for instance, must write from jail and/or in countries with heavily repressive censorship. Yet, many still find ways to get their messages across; indeed, it is often observed in literary studies – a discipline more sympathetic to allowing for the existence of art – that greater restriction often produces greater creativity in finding ways to circumvent such restriction. Certainly, a lot of media texts are fairly mindless, but so too are many pieces of music, poetry, and sculpture. Perhaps one of our discipline's problems is one highlighted by Charlotte Brunsdon: that we do not like to talk about quality. Brunsdon's (1997: 124) own fear is that this failure yields the floor to the most conservative ideas of quality, but to this I would add that we paint all media texts with the same lackluster brush. Thus, as Caughie suggests, it is perhaps no surprise that media and cultural studies has grown increasingly interested in readers, 'our fascination with the audience [. . .] due, at least in part, to a lack of fascination with the texts' (Caughie 1990: 54).

The point is not at all that there is nothing to be concerned about, nor that hegemony is just a bad Gramscian fairytale. As *The Simpsons* itself points out, television and its genres often drown in conservative values, hypercommercialism, and messages aimed solely at consumers not citizens. Thus, corporate power and dominant ideology are real, active, and often successful in exerting their will over their products, and it therefore follows that careful and insightful criticism of this process is absolutely necessary, and that a large serving of pessimism is required. However, the media also teach and have a benevolent, resistant side. At first sight, to agree with Hartley's (1999: 32) seemingly heretical statement that decent teaching might be conducted as much by the likes of Rupert Murdoch as by Richard Hoggart or any other academic would appear to be the ultimate proof of member-ship in what Morley (1992: 11) calls cultural studies' 'don't worry, be happy' school of cultural optimism. But the point, as Hartley says, is not to make us as critics 'love Rupert as [we] might an honoured teacher, but simply [to] ask that the dismissive default setting be toggled off for a while' (1999: 32). Hartley correctly observes that 'there's now a rather too militantly drawn line between education and media with KEEP OUT! signs all round formal schooling' (1999: 43). However, if we turn the default setting off and move beyond the Keep Out signs, one of the texts we find is *The Simpsons*, parodying and satirizing its televisual colleagues, such as sitcoms, ads, and the news, often with considerable sophistication.

Part III

TALKING WITH
THE SIMPSONS

Chapter 5

PARODY AND/AS INTERPRETIVE COMMUNITY

To some degree or other, all texts transcend their textual homes, also becoming part of common culture and of everyday life. Thus, television texts do not exist solely in their moments of transmission. Ang (1985: 83) noted of *Dallas* in the 1980s that it 'became as much if not more so a practice as a text,' and *The Simpsons* finds itself in a similar situation today. Consequently, it is not enough for us to study parody as a wholly textual being, for it is equally sociological. While in previous chapters, I have looked at how *The Simpsons* moves through other texts and genres, intertextuality and critical intertextuality work not only through texts but also through memory, interpretive communities, and talk, and so to track this intertextuality, we must also move into the realm of audiences. Thus, in this chapter and the next, I will examine how a group of 35 *Simpsons* viewers talked of their interaction with the show and with its parody, and I will study how *Simpsons* viewers make sense of and activate the program both individually and as groups. The 35 viewers I interviewed by no means represent the entire *Simpsons* audience, and therefore this chapter makes no claim to representativeness, but it provides a window into how *some* audience members deal with the program's parody and humor, and with some of its contradictions brought on by its status as popular, mainstream parody.

First, I will examine how most of these viewers belonged to an interpretive community of sorts – a 'parodized' group of young people eager to analyze, criticize, and ridicule. I will next elaborate upon this community and discuss what 'membership' entailed, regarding interpretation. Ultimately, I will then use the interview data to study nagging allegations against parody that see it as mere bread and circuses to placate the crows, as preaching solely to the converted, and/or as being complicit with the powers it would seem to be ridiculing. I consult 35 audience members, in other words, to make sense of parody's life and obstacles beyond the text, in the chaotic realm of the audience.

The interviews: methodological issues

The interview data come from a series of approximately 45 minute interviews about *The Simpsons* conducted in 2001 and 2002. During this time, I put up posters asking for willing interviewees in Goodenough College in central London, a residence with approximately 500 residents that caters to postgraduates from overseas. Concurrently, I employed a 'snowball' technique (see Hermes 1995), which yielded several other interviewees outside of the college. I gave the interviewees the choice to be interviewed individually or with a partner or friend. All interviewees were between 22 and 38, with most younger than 33, and the mean age being 27. There were 15 men and 20 women. It was a predominantly white group, but the mix of nationalities was more varied: Canadians, Australians, and Americans were the three largest groups, but there were also interviewees from South Africa, Britain, and Greece, and others who were part or full Singaporean, Danish, Chinese, Indian, Indonesian, and Japanese. All were middle class. As for education, this was a well-degreed group, with 12 with or working toward a PhD, 18 with or working toward a Masters degree, and 5 with a Bachelors degree; 12 were working, with the rest in full-time education. Finally, I interviewed 8 people in pairs, but the rest individually.[1] For reasons of privacy, all names have been changed.[2]

My interview schedule was loose, adaptive, and open to accommodate other interests or radically different progression. As a result, some interviews involved a great deal of play with *Simpsons* quotes, references, and voices, and others reached topics of *The Simpsons'* importance and politics in just a minute or two. All interviews, though, began with simple contextualizing questions, regarding how closely they followed the show, how they tend to watch it, whether they talk about it, and how they use television in general. I then asked if they had favorite or least favorite characters, lines, and episodes, and why. After a few 'warm-up' questions like this, in varying order, all interviewees were asked the following set of questions:

- Why do you watch? What do you like about it? (or, why don't you like it?)
- Has your viewing relationship changed to it over time? If so, how? Do you find the same things funny?
- Some say the show is getting worse: do you agree? Why or why not?

- What is wrong with the program? What would 'ruin' the show? At what point would you stop watching?
- Does it have politics at all? If so, what are they?
- Do you think the show's humor has any particular 'targets'? If so, what are they?
- Does its humor stick with you, or is it fleeting?
- Do you like the animation? What effects does it have on the program?
- Why do you think the show is so popular?
- What, if any, other shows are like it? How?
- How would you compare it to other shows?
- Rupert Murdoch has said it is the most important show on television. How would you respond?
- Has this interview asked you to talk about *The Simpsons* in a way you wouldn't normally?

As for my own presence and role in each interview, on one level, I too am a *Simpsons* viewer who enjoys the show, and on another level I was a PhD student writing (as most of my interviewees paraphrased) 'a thesis on *The Simpsons*,' and I cannot pretend my fandom and the academic pretext of the interview did nothing to shape discussion. However, and in spite of the countless work on the 'ecological invalidity' brought on by the researcher's presence (see Bell 1983; Clifford and Marcus 1986; Hammersley and Atkinson 1983), I believe my dual role (fan and academic) helped me in the interview process. Many of the interviewees came into the interview room rather tentatively, and most of my transcripts record quick (tense?) answers in the early going. However, I had set up the interview schedule accordingly, starting with purely informational questions, and questions regarding favorite episodes, characters, and lines. Here, not only could the interviewees relax by describing or mimicking humorous lines, but also in joining in to complete a forgotten line, add a reply, or so on, I could shift my role somewhat from student-with-recorder-and-questions to fellow-*Simpsons*-watcher. Thus, I found my interviewees were sitting and talking in a considerably more relaxed manner by the time we got to some of the more thought-provoking questions. Particularly since I was interested in *Simpsons* talk, I was keen to set the tone for talk-and-conversation rather than question-and-answer, and so this move proved successful. As Lull (1990: 179) notes, it is important that research subjects 'be confident that they are not being judged or evaluated by comparison to an external behavioural norm,' and my involvement also promised more of such confidence.

Ultimately, I was trying to access how *The Simpsons* is *talked about* in these interviews. To regard audience research as being able to provide access to 'actual' meaning would be rather foolishly optimistic, for as Sperber notes of any ethnographer's account, 'The resulting description is actually what the ethnographer selected from what he [sic] understood of what his informants told him of what they understood' (Sperber 1991: 15; see also Bloch 1998; Geertz 1993: 9). Just as Part II represents a reading of *The Simpsons*, Part III represents a reading of *Simpsons* talk.

I focused on this group largely due to previous personal exposure to the degree of popularity *The Simpsons* has with the 20- to 30-something university and college community, both as watched text, and as subject of considerable conversation. The show's characters and situations are easy shorthand among most students – references one can *expect* others to pick up on. Moreover, my initial act of choosing *The Simpsons* as case study for parody and critical intertextuality in general was motivated in large part by the many conversations I have had with or overheard between my peers about how smart it is. Thus, it seemed appropriate to return to this group to ask about *The Simpsons*, and the uses of parody. Of course, *The Simpsons'* audience goes well beyond just this age group, but for sheer breadth of *Simpsons* awareness, and frequency of *Simpsons* references, I knew I could rely on this age and education group. Studying this group, though, raises numerous contentious issues, for they are not the usual cultural studies subjects, and I will address these issues later.

For now, though, let me be clear that, despite this group's mostly shared affection for *The Simpsons*, this is not a study of a fan community. As I have argued elsewhere (Gray 2003b), there is much to be learnt of texts and of how their meanings are determined outside the realm of the text by studying viewers of various engagement levels. Consequently, this project was set up to encourage a spectrum, and my poster advertising for interviewees explained, 'ANY level of involvement with the show welcome, whether ultra-fan, casual viewer, or whatever (*even those who hate the show*).' Admittedly, Vivi proved to be the only staunch anti-fan, but the rest fit into a broad range from viewers who had watched closely since *The Tracey Ullman Show*, to recent arrivals and those who watched only occasionally. A large number, too, had gone through various phases of viewership, sometimes devoted, sometimes casual, and several interviewees stated clear preferences for other shows. While a small number preferred to watch without interruptions from start to finish, the majority found watching only small segments or with interruptions perfectly acceptable.

I did not ask the interviewees to 'rate' themselves on some form of 'fanometer,' but many were quite clearly casual viewers rather than fans. Indeed, many of the fan practices of much fan studies work were largely missing from this group, and their interpretations of the text and acts of consumption faced little of the social censure and concurrent subcultural existence of traditional 'fandom.' I therefore encourage my readers not to see in this group a collective of 'textual poachers' (Jenkins 1988, 1992), but rather to see a group of dispersed individuals who enjoy *The Simpsons* and talk of it, and find it significant and/or important for many of the same reasons. I will later detail some of these reasons, but first I will argue that the individuals I talked to exhibited clear signs of belonging not to a fan community but to an interpretive community nonetheless. And interpretive communities, I will further argue, can form important lynchpins in critical intertextuality's success or failure.

Interpretive communities

Much has been written of how individuals construct personal identities, 'lifestyles' (Chaney 2001), or 'supercultures' (Lull 2001), in part by bringing together various media texts and meanings from the global flow of mediascapes (Appadurai 1995), a process Hartley calls 'DIY cultural citizenship' (1999: 178–9). If such work is open to criticism, though, it is because culture cannot be created by the individual – a group must be involved. When it comes to television, while we all have our personal meanings, and our private guilty pleasures, the vast majority of textual meanings must to some degree face others and their interpretations. Thus, while I have written of the dialogue between texts, equally fascinating is the dialogue between viewers. Sperber points out that:

> Every day each individual builds thousands of mental representations; most of these are almost immediately forgotten, and are never transmitted. Very few mental representations are expressed, that is, transformed into public representations and thus transmitted to others.
>
> (Sperber 1991: 30)

Thus, a key question is, 'through which process of selection, as a function of what factors, does a tiny fraction of all the mental representations that humans build become shared cultural representations, and invade, either temporarily (rumors, fashions), or lastingly (traditions), the networks of social communication?' (Sperber 1991: 30), and it is not enough to study personal constructions of meaning. This leads us to the interpretive community.

First proposed by Stanley Fish (1980a), interpretive community theory explains how, given textuality's inherent polysemic qualities, people can still agree on textual meanings. Fish's reader response theory radically poses that texts and authors exist only as reader constructs, that 'the reader's response is not *to* the meaning; it *is* the meaning' (Fish 1980a: 3, original emphasis) and that interpretation is not something that occurs after reading, but is something that *shapes* reading and that *makes* the text (1980a: 13). Such a proclamation seemingly betrays a bizarre intrepretive relativism, whereby nothing exists to stop either *The Simpsons* or *King Lear* from being about elementary bricklaying and/or the Chinese Opium Wars. However, relativism relies on any reading being possible, *and* on the reader being free to

123

choose among readings, but although Fish refuses to allow either text or author a limiting function, he still maintains that neither situation exists. Far from arguing against 'ordinary' or 'literal' readings, Fish argues *for* 'the normal, the ordinary, the literal, the straightforward, and so on, but [. . .] as products of contextual or interpretive circumstances and not as the property of an acontextual language or an independent world' (1980a: 268). If there is always a literal meaning, this is 'because in any situation there is always a meaning that seems obvious in the sense that it is there independently of anything we might do. *But that only means that we have already done it*' (1980a: 276, original emphasis).

Reading and interpretation are thus constrained by situation and by what Fish calls 'interpretive communities.' The interpretive community is

> made up of those who share interpretive strategies not for reading (in the conventional sense) but for writing texts, for constituting their properties and assigning their intentions. In other words, these strategies exist prior to the act of reading and therefore determine the shape of what is read rather than, as is usually assumed, the other way around.
>
> (Fish 1980a: 171)

Here, we may think of Thomas Kuhn's (1970) theory of scientific paradigms – as long as we are in them, their reasoning seems normal and factual, but should we experience a paradigm shift, then the old interpretation is revealed as just an interpretation, whereas our new one now appears factual 'reality.' Thus, apparently nonsensical readings do not point to the borders of justifiable meaning; they only suggest that 'there is as yet no elaborated interpretive procedure for producing that text' (Fish 1980a: 345). Meanwhile, to Fish, consensus or majority opinion is not proof of an undeniable presence in the text: it is solely evidence that the interpretive community behind that reading enjoys a large membership.

Fish (1980a) sees interpretive communities as wholly too essentialist and essentializing, and thus his own theory insufficiently explains how interpretive communities are formed and how one can move in or out of them; moreover, his act of totally vacating the text of inherent meaning is insupportable, and has thus justifiably brought him under attack from many angles (see Pratt 1986; Ray 1984; Scholes 1985). Nevertheless, the basic idea behind Fish's (1980a) notion of interpretive communities retains significant theoretical purchase, particularly if we merge this theory with that of intertextuality and parody. When we arrive at a text, it is with the knowledge and patterns gained from other texts that we can make sense of it. The spirit of the interpretive community as concept dictates that, regardless of what is *in* a text, we will arrive at it with certain reading strategies ready to be deployed, while the spirit of intertextuality as concept allows that other texts may construct those interpretive communities or strategies, and in doing so, positively inflect us toward reading a text in a determinate way, and with other determinate texts in mind. Effectively, then, while Fish saw interpretive communities as always preceding and circumventing the text, they can in fact be powerfully directed by the text, and by intertextuality. The interpretive community, in other words, can become just as effective a motor of critical intertextuality as can parodic texts themselves, and when interpretive communities and parodic texts work *together*, the parody's interpretive work and games can continue after (and before) direct textual experiences. In doing so, the interpretive community can bring together interpreting individuals to propose general, shared, and socially activated meanings.

Particularly when the arena in question is discussions of the media, media talk is rampant. Celebrity gossip, and what wisdom, stupidity, or hilarity was offered by this or that program forms the backbone of many conversations. Media talk today plays a huge role in social situations, strengthening links and bonds between people who already know each other, and providing common ground for strangers to share. Such talk allows the sharing of interpretations and of interpretive strategies. Patricia Palmer (1988: 149) has written of children's play and talk about television 'as a way of deciding with friends what to learn from TV and how to regard it,' and interpretive communities work in a similar manner, determining, redetermining, and predetermining what, in this case, *The Simpsons* has to offer and what it has to say. As opposed to Fish (1980a), I do not see this process as occurring independently of the text, but it is nevertheless a process that must work *with* any critical inter-textuality for the latter to work. Later in the chapter, I will examine this success, but for now, let us examine the group and the existence of the interpretive community itself.

Simpsons-speak

To begin with, many of the interviewees talked about *The Simpsons*' ability to bring people together and to form a community of sorts. Several interviewees' first real contact with *The Simpsons* came through an encounter with a quite literal *Simpsons* community. For instance, Cleo explained that she was dating a man who

> watched it every week, religiously [with friends] in the TV room, and there was a pilgrimage [. . .] It was kind of a cliquey viewing thing and I was told that, you know, if I wanted to spend half an hour with [him] on Sunday nights, I had to come watch *The Simpsons* [. . . But] by the third episode, I was pretty much into the group.

Similarly, Jesse would watch *The Simpsons* with his college-mates weekly, and joked that his partner Susan had joined the group only to 'pull' him. Meanwhile, viewing groups were quite common with other interviewees: Joanne's office ground to a halt whenever *The Simpsons* was on; several interviewees were at one point part of a university viewing group; and Janet was referred to me by someone who explained that she must know all about *The Simpsons*, since her house had been *the* place to watch *The Simpsons* in Sydney throughout university. Moreover, and equally telling, at the end of the interview, many interviewees recommended (quite hopefully) that I should set up some group screenings, saying this would be a great way for them to meet other people.

Beyond the actual communities in a room, many interviewees operated with clear assumptions of an imagined community of *Simpsons* viewers, where *The Simpsons* served as a helpful litmus test for someone's personality. Alyson, for example, explained that:

> For me personally, so many friendships I have started because, 'Oh, you like *The Simpsons*? I like *The Simpsons*,' and so we're off and running. It really has become one of those acid tests for me. Someone who doesn't like them, it's like shorthand for me [. . .] Maybe we won't *hate* each other, but this is not someone who I'm really going to be in simpatico with.

Not only is *The Simpsons* a personality litmus test for her, but she values it greatly for playing this role. Or, more bluntly, Carrie asked, 'how could somebody not like it? If they don't like it, then they're obviously screwed up [*laughs*].' Here, although Carrie did not consider herself a diehard fan, liking or disliking *The Simpsons* and being part of its audience or not could clearly decide, if not one's 'normality,' as she joked, at least how close she would choose to get to one.

While Alyson and Carrie represented the more stark expressions of a *Simpsons* litmus test, they were not alone. Charlie felt that watching the show and *how* one watched the show said a lot about a person, and would clue him in to whether they shared 'a common sense of nuttiness.' Or, perhaps most amusingly, the fact that Janet brought Ryan to a *Simpsons* interview as part of an early date is a telling indicator of *The Simpsons* litmus test's utility. Throughout the interview, the young couple appeared to be using their answers to present certain sides of themselves to the other: Ryan, in particular, was obviously trying to play up his affection for *The Simpsons*, sensing, perhaps, that the future of his and Janet's relationship might rely upon it! Clearly, to many viewers, *The Simpsons* has served as, in Alyson's words, 'shorthand' for a type of person(ality), playing a key role in community-forming. As Tina half-joked, 'it's kind of a chicken-and-the-egg thing: I don't know if I like my friends because they like *The Simpsons*, or if we all come together 'cause we know a lot about it [*laughs*].'

Beyond bringing people together, to many of the interviewees, *The Simpsons* is a common conversation topic. Reid explained, 'I talk about it with most of my friends,' examining together 'how it relates to something that happened that day, or at that moment – it'll be, like, "Oh, that's like the *Simpsons* moment when X or Y happened."' Or, as Ling stated, 'it comes up in conversations a lot. It's always, like, "Oh!" and something reminds you of *The Simpsons*: "remember when they did that, that, that?"' As both Reid and Ling suggested, it is not (only) as if *The Simpsons* is set as the topic of conversation; rather, it just sprouts up. It is not, explained Sonia, 'that we just sat down and said "let's talk about *The Simpsons*," but [more that] something about *The Simpsons* comes up.' Anything, seemingly, can invoke *The Simpsons*, so that, as Angie glossed, 'we don't specifically say "Okay, topic of conversation: *Simpsons*," but it does kind of seep through.'

Certainly, *The Simpsons* has worked itself into the 20- and 30-something lexicon, so that it can at times seem, as Charlie noted, that 'there are certain moments where everybody knows.' Precisely because of this, Joanne observed, *The Simpsons* is 'something you can *easily* discuss and use catch-phrases from with your friends' (emphasis added). In *Using the Force*, Will Brooker (2002) explains how the language of *Star Wars* facilitates discussion between *Star Wars* viewers, even when complete strangers, and *The Simpsons* works in a similar way. Just as there are segments of Brooker's transcripts, then, that would mystify readers unfamiliar with *Star Wars*, whole sections of my transcripts would likewise read as some alien tongue to non-*Simpsons* viewers. As Jesse noted, 'it's got that whole cult following thing, so you're always talking to your friends in *Simpsons*-speak.'

The discussion of cults and the language of religiosity abounded in *Simpsons* watcher self-descriptions. Whitney, Todd, Ling, Al, Carrie, and Cleo all spoke of watching it 'religiously' for a while, Angie talked of becoming 'a convert' to the show, and words such as 'cult,' 'devotion,' and 'follower' popped up in many interviews. Hills (2002) notes the contradictory use of a vocabulary of religiosity within fan cultures, as on one hand, fans use the words themselves to distinguish their activities and communities as beyond regular, yet on the other hand, they do so ironically aware of how they are not a cult. Ultimately, Hills observes the construction of a form of 'neoreligiosity,' whereby

> religious discourses and experiences are re-articulated and reconstructed within the discursive work of fan cultures, meaning that cult fans cannot ever 'cleanse' cult discourses of religious connotations, but neither can fans' use of religious terminology be read simply as an indication that fan cultures *are* fan 'cults' or 'religions.'
>
> (Hills 2002: 129)

Several interviewees carefully distinguished between themselves and fans who they felt were more devout members of this pseudo-cult, often through referencing superfan friends who could quote *The Simpsons*, as Cleo noted of a friend, 'line and verse.' Yet, in discussing these acolytes and apostles, and by the mere use of a vocabulary of religiosity and cult followings, particularly by many viewers who were *not* fans, the interviewees reflected upon their own membership in a *Simpsons* community, albeit of a lesser intensity of involvement than the superfans.

When asked if she would prefer to watch *The Simpsons* with anyone in particular, Katy said rather plaintively that there were people 'I would *love* to watch it with, but I don't necessarily live with them,' adding sadly, 'they're not even in the same country as me,' hence suggesting the degree to which *The Simpsons* and watching *The Simpsons* serves as a friendship glue of sorts. Many went so far as to talk of the program as a generational touchstone, so that Jesse, for instance, in answering if *The Simpsons* was important, noted that 'our generation's gone through with it,' and he spoke at length of how not only the text, but also its language and community – 'a common lens for looking at the world,' as he noted – have been with his generation for a good ten years or more.

If *Simpsons* watchers feel part of a community, though, this was particularly evident to those who did not watch. As a 'latecomer' to *The Simpsons*, Rhys explained that, before he started watching, 'I felt kind of left out. You know, everyone was talking about it, and it got kind of annoying. I wanted to see it.' Later in the interview, upon being asked whether he felt *The Simpsons* was in any way 'important,' he noted that 'everyone else watches, and so it's important to watch yourself.' Here, he spoke as one who was now on the inside, but his comments were echoed more resentfully by Vivi. Vivi's husband Thanos was a *Simpsons* watcher, and although she herself disliked the show, it was her who wanted the two of them to be interviewed, because, she told me, 'I really wanted an opportunity to express my opinion about this problem [*laughs*].' The 'problem' was the show's ever-presence in the language of her peers. As she told it:

> To be honest, I wanted to watch *The Simpsons* for many years now, since I was in Leicester doing my Masters, because *everyone* was talking about *The Simpsons* [. . .] and I didn't know about them, and I felt as though I was excluded [. . .] This is unacceptable [*laughs*]: 'How can you be unaware of *The Simpsons*?' So, for me, it was an obligation to watch *The Simpsons*.

Interestingly, though, despite disliking it, she did indeed learn about it, and could even comment on and analyze aspects of it with great detail. Answering my question regarding the show's 'importance,' then, she replied:

> The characters exist not only in the TV, but they are now in jokes, and how people speak [. . .] because everyone knows this. It's here in our lives, apart from TV. You see, even though I don't watch this show, I don't *like* this show,

uh, I have to know about it to a certain degree . . . otherwise I will be excluded from the conversation of my friends.

Vivi's analysis, then, suggests that, at least among a certain age and education group, in addition to the inclusive sphere of being a *Simpsons* watcher, there is a second, larger sphere, into which some such as herself fall, of being conversant and literate in *The Simpsons* as a cultural artifact and language. Rhys, too, noted that even before watching it, he 'had a whole set of expectations, and knew a lot about it and what it was all about,' since some of his peers talked of the show with great regularity.

Ultimately, then, while the viewers were not united by fandom and intensity of viewing, the text had clearly taken on a dense set of meanings for almost all of them (meanings which we will examine shortly), and had imbricated itself into their everyday lives and conversations. Moreover, it had done so as – and the community was regarded as being about – more than just some shared opinions, and in this respect was fan-like, for as Hills (2002: 129) notes, 'fandom is about more than just "interpretive community" or a rational(ised) system of meaning; it is also about the dialectic of value – the interplay between intensely subjective, personalised value and objective/communal accounts.' Thus, while I believe we should continue to regard the *Simpsons*' university-educated, 20- or 30-something group as a form of interpretive community, complete with its own logics of what *The Simpsons* means and does, there was also an emotional, attitudinal element to this interpretive community, a notion that Laura most helpfully put her finger on when she talked repeatedly of a shared '*Simpsons* attitude,' and a '*Simpsons* way of looking at things.' It is now, therefore, to this attitude that I turn.

Watching (for) parody

After initial start-up questions, my first substantive, open-ended question to each was why they watched *The Simpsons*, and what they liked about it. Time and time again, I heard variations on the same answer: it is 'funny but smart,' or 'smart but funny.' Judy offered that she watches, 'I suppose because it's entertaining. Partly because it's entertaining. *It's clever*. I think it's clever the way they do it: *that's* what I like about it, actually.' Meanwhile, Daphne stated that 'It's a very sophisticated piece of fluff,' and Rhys noted, 'It's funny. It's clever. It's smart. It makes me laugh, but it's also . . . you don't feel dumb watching it.' Beyond these statements, many spoke highly of its smartness, so that, for instance, to Richard, 'it's just so clever. It's incredibly clever. I guess I don't watch it because it's stunning animation or anything like that: it's just – it's more than a sitcom'; Zach offered that 'A lot of people say this and I'm sure you've probably heard this a lot, but it's on two levels: it's on a purely visual level, and there's a deeper level'; Katy echoed that 'I think it's one of the cleverest shows on television. It's, umm, clever *on all kinds* of different levels'; and Thanos said, 'I think I like the kind of humor, umm, in *The Simpsons*. Umm, I find it very clever sometimes and very direct to the point.'

A large part of *The Simpsons*' value, both personally and communally, was therefore that it is smart and not just funny. As Lucia elaborated:

> I'd rather watch programs that completely rot my mind when I'm just in a vegetative mental state, or else it's the complete opposite, where I'll look for something that is stimulating, that will give me something more to think about. And *The Simpsons* fall toward that end.

Later, she glossed that 'it's something that you don't have to be ashamed about talking about around the dinner table,' since 'it's a more sophisticated show than Homer just walking around going "d'Oh!"' Mary, meanwhile, reasoned that the show would not be as popular among academics and students if this were not the case, for 'they wouldn't be addicted to it if it didn't have that [. . .] more intellectual humor to it, I don't think you could get us watching it as much.'

Of course, a substantial danger with interviewing such a well-educated group is the risk that they over-intellectualize every consumption decision. Conversely to Glynn's (1996) experience of interviewing kids about *The Simpsons*, where he found them resisting his attempts to produce knowledge about them, this group could be expected to want to over-contribute to the production of knowledge about them. Much media consumption may be relatively meaningless (see Hermes 1995), yet students and academics may seem a group adverse to the notion of any practice being meaningless, especially when done by themselves. But, as Eliasoph (1998: 20) wisely observes, 'the ways [people] explain [their] opinions, are part of what "holding an opinion" means.' Thus, if some *Simpsons* viewers describe their viewing experiences in a very academicized manner, and offer notably intellectualized explanations of what they feel or believe, this suggests that such vocabulary and theory are part of how they think of, react to, and make meaning out of those viewing experiences. Hills (2002: 67) is right in pointing out that some such scripts become unthinking and deflective 'discursive mantras,' used to respond to any and all inquisitors, and thus may still require suspicion. Overall, though, I was still left sufficiently confident that little of the intellectualization I was hearing was being produced solely for my benefit. If they intellectualized, in most cases I believe this was because they *are* 'intellectualizers,' not because a minidisc recorder was in the room.[3]

Much audience research uncovers the substantial guilt felt by many viewers watching fiction, or simply watching anything except the news, and Geraghty (1998: 150) even poses that the interview process may play a key role in helping 'absolve' viewers of such guilt. However, my own interviews were devoid of expressions of guilt, nor did I feel called upon for absolution. Moreover, these viewers had not wholly rejected high-brow mythology of bad televisual fiction and good non-fiction altogether: rather, *The Simpsons* was seen as smart television, and so exempted from the criticism many of them held for the other 'crap' on television. There is perhaps a touch of narcissism here, whereby an image of the self reflects off the program, so that the act of declaring *The Simpsons* smart and intelligent television implicitly posits the speaker as smart, whereas to declare it banal would suggest a banal speaker. Nevertheless, what is of more importance is *how* (and how *easily*) these interviewees talked of *The Simpsons* as smart. The perception of its smartness came out particularly in the common discussion of the show's various 'levels.' There was consensus that the text has a 'simple,' 'visual,' or 'elementary' level of Homer's stupidity, Bart's wisecracks and slapstick; and a 'deeper' level of smart, parodic-satiric commentary.

To most, what this 'deeper' second level consisted of was relevant and topical parody and political satire. '[T]hey know what's going on in my world,' offered Sujata; Ling echoed that 'it works because it keeps on referring to what's going on'; Cleo characterized *The Simpsons* as conducting 'a weekly political critique of some kind'; and, to Al, 'it's smart because it, it finds ways of using irony to make political statements.' Irony and satire were much-invoked terms, with Janet reflecting what many others told me when she said, 'I think the satire is why I find it so funny. *And*, that's why it keeps being so funny [. . .] If it was just Homer being dumb, it would probably get pretty boring.' Not only, therefore, were irony and satire being invoked, but they were elided with *The Simpsons*. To Al, for instance, 'satire is really their umm, umm . . . I think it's their principal credo,' while to Alyson, 'obviously they didn't create irony. But they kind of honed it.' Moreover, most interviewees felt this irony and play pooled around certain topics or targets. I had intended to ask all of my interviewees whether they felt *The Simpsons* had any favorite targets, or ones that particularly stood out. Interestingly, though, many subjects beat me to the topic, as my question regarding why they watched led quickly and naturally into discussion of who and what was being comically attacked. This discussion of targets led to several usual suspects, as each of the following were offered by at least ten interviewees: consumerism/capitalism, American suburbia, the family, television and the media, Fox and/or Murdoch, politics and politicians, corporations and big business, itself, sitcoms, schools, and religion. With the exception of the latter two, we should note the echo of Part II. I have no wish to repeat my textual analysis here, but will nevertheless recount some discussion of *The Simpsons'* targets for the dual purpose of illustration and elaboration.

'Television and the media' were easily the most mentioned targets. To Rhys, 'It's a comedy show about TV. The way TV frames our lives, and its control and so forth. Yeah. You certainly couldn't do it outside of TV.' Todd offered, with sarcastic understatement, 'there's a fair amount of TV satire, which I like: the kind of sensationalist news, and so many aspects of TV that they've covered.' Al said that the show

> looks to other television shows and to principles of structure, principles of morality, principles of umm, sponsorship, principles of err . . . you know: how it's put together. And it grossly generalizes them sometimes, but as a way of exposing the structure that's underneath that a lot of shows will try and hide. So, you know, certainly – how can we look at *The Waltons* again in the same light after seeing *The Simpsons*? [. . .] They know that they're a creature of television.

Carrie joked about how whenever the Simpsons are watching television,

> it's just absolute crap on, and they're all excited about it. Lisa and Bart are just mesmerized by [*laughs*] the Krusty variety show. The shows are just always God-awful [*laughs*], and then Homer's always just sort of watching whatever kind of crap is on TV and it's always dumb commercials or really bad, but it's like a drug so they have to watch it.

And Harold, too, noted that, 'There are moments when it's definitely about American TV [. . .] Like, commercialism and all that, or children's TV and violence with Itchy and Scratchy – it's TV, but also about American life . . . that we consider that appropriate and allow it.' Proving parody's intertextual nature, in discussing *The Simpsons* and why they liked it, most interviewees ended up engaging in long discussions of other television texts that the program ridicules.

Certainly, my question about *The Simpsons*' targets often opened a can of worms of complaints about television, and yet *The Simpsons* frequently occupied protected ground precisely because it complained alongside them. Here, I quote at length from Niraj's interview, as he described to me how much he hated most television, but exempted *The Simpsons*:

Niraj: [TV is] almost entirely horrendous [. . .] It's really manipulative, and I think it's the arm of larger groups that wanna manipulate, largely advertisers, but advertisers, of course, are working for corporations [. . .] TV's aim is to create a dissatisfaction.

JG: Dissatisfaction with?

Niraj: Inside oneself [. . .] The sense that my life is not quite what it ought to be. Or, it doesn't even have to be an actual physical product. 'If I watch this show . . .'

[. . .]

JG: So where does *The Simpsons* fall in this?

Niraj: Yeah, I think that's very interesting, because I think there are a few shows that are either aware of it, and they don't take that path [. . .] and it's just a little different, in the *intent* it's different, and I find that *The Simpsons*, I just get a feeling that they're aware that this is what TV does. Umm, and they're sort of honest about it, and they *play* with it [. . .] It's *clearly* playing with that issue of 'This is a TV show,' umm, 'and this is TV's place' [. . .] I think there are quite a lot of episodes where they blatantly make fun of television, or of their very network, Fox [. . .] And even, you know, making fun of the Troy McClure guy, or the news guy, or the politicians. I mean, they're making fun of anyone who's got an image, because it's all about image, you know?

Clearly, to Niraj, as to the other interpretive community members quoted above, *The Simpsons* is not just a television program, but a program about television programs, and about their many structural, aesthetic, and/or ideological flaws.

Echoing Part II, three of the areas around which this 'anti-TV-ism' was seen to cluster were sitcoms, ads, and the news. Thus, of the former, many interviewees pointed out that the sitcom's awkward structure was often an object of ridicule. Leo, for instance, noted that 'they have, like, really cheesy endings to episodes where they're all standing around laughing, and it's, like, a piss-take on other comedies like that,' or as Laura observed:

it's a sitcom in terms of its structure, but it makes that obvious and it plays with that. I mean, there are some episodes when they [. . .] had the music and they had the laugh-track, and so on, so they're drawing attention to their own structure as a sitcom, and they, umm, every episode will start with a certain event, and yet after five minutes it'll inevitably shift to something different [. . .] but it's almost one level removed because it makes fun of it as well.

Such comments go hand in hand with critically astute observations of sitcom form and its effects on aesthetics, as what Al calls the 'ludicrous scenario of, after you've taken out commercials, a twenty minute slot' is ridiculed and hence rendered more obvious by *The Simpsons'* sitcom parody. Through talking of *The Simpsons'* parody, these viewers frequently engaged in lengthy scripts on the problems with much commercial television.

From parody to satire

Beyond noting explicit commentary on structure and form, though, the discussion of *The Simpsons* as critical of sitcoms also involved talk of the show's ironic contrast

133

of the family to traditional sitcom families, and hence to traditional domesticom ideology. Mary observed that:

> It can be a funny show, in terms of the slapstick sort of nature of it, but I think it also does have a darker message to it, umm, so yes it is a family sitcom, but it's definitely not as 'everything's all wonderful' as, like, *The Cosby Show*, or, like, *Full House* and those horrible ones that used to be on. It's *much* darker, in that everything doesn't turn out.

Leo echoed that many TV shows argue 'why we should put it on, or that this is virtuous, like *The Waltons*, a striving family working together [. . .] But this is more about the slightly negative sides.' 'Even the way Springfield is drawn in the cartoon,' observed Wei, 'it looks strange, it's not real, and everything is just . . . kind of like that show, *Truman Show*.' Every genre has its own reality separate from lived reality, and many interviewees spoke of *The Simpsons* as highlighting the difference between the two, in particular pointing out the stark mythology and optimistically patriarchal idyll that is the traditional American domesticom. I was often told that *The Simpsons'* depiction of family life was 'more realistic,' but if we take this notion apart, clearly a family whose father, for instance, has been to Space, met several presidents, and can eat a 16 pound steak at one sitting is hardly realistic: rather, the comment is fundamentally intertextual, pointing to the show's illumination of how equally or even more *un*realistic the domesticom view of family life is.

There, too, lay so much of the appeal of *The Simpsons*, particularly when it came to Homer. After all, Homer draws a great deal of his comic appeal from being so unlike his sitcom counterparts. As Cleo explained:

> he's a pretty revolting character, but therein lies his charm. I mean, he is a lot of unchecked appetites, which is Rabelaisian and hilarious of course. Not endearing, and not anything you want to identify with, and not anyone you put at the hero epicenter of your show, which is, of course, hilariously what's done there. I mean, he's the dad, and in *Family Ties*, or *Family Affair*, or – I'm trying to think back – *My Three Sons*, it's the dad who's supposed to be pinning things together.

Many of my interviewees appreciated him as what Whitney called 'the classic anti-hero,' or even a rare 'everyman' in a televisual sea of super-dads. In comments such as these, or Leo's above-quoted criticism of shows that tell us 'why we should put it on,' or in Niraj's attack on the selling of dissatisfaction, we can hear substantial resentment of the traditional domesticom and its ideology, a resentment that *The Simpsons* seems to channel and even to teach, or at least to highlight. In this, then, the show's parody of television easily expanded to comment on issues outside of television, for as Lucia noted, 'it's showing a more subversive side of American. I mean, your main family *isn't* the Flanders: your main family *is* the Simpsons, and so it's very, it's very much anti-traditional.'

Certainly, Lucia's comment is representative of how much the Americanness of the show – or, more properly, of the show's targets – was discussed. Perhaps naively, given that my interviewees were an international group watching an American product, none of my questions were concerned with 'Americanness,' and yet the vast majority of interviewees brought the matter up, making it clear that, to most, *The Simpsons* was a parody of *American* television, sitcom, news, etc. And just as Homer was valued as the antithesis of the sitcom's exported version of American fatherhood, as I have discussed elsewhere (Gray 2003a), many valued how the show provided an inverted and/or, as some suspected, a more brutally honest version of the American family and the American Dream than have the vast panoply of exported domesticoms.

We should also pause here to note a general slippage between parody and satire in the interviews. As detailed in Chapter 2, while parody attacks form, and ideology *through* form, satire attacks ideology directly. However, the word 'parody' is strangely absent from all but a few of my transcripts, which in a project on parody and critical intertextuality may at first seem cause for concern. That said, as the above-quoted comments on the sitcom render obvious, parody was still being discussed, and in considerable and sophisticated detail, even if not named as such. The fact that many interviewees spoke of 'sitcom *satire*' or 'news *satire*' is, I believe, an encouraging sign of its success. After all, if satire is popularly accepted as having sting in its bite, its common replacement of parody indicates the degree to which many interviewees felt *The Simpsons* has bite, and is more than mere pastiche or gentle play with form. Consider, for instance, Laura's discussion of Homer being so popular because of

> the way in which that character pokes fun at American life. He's an alternative, too, cause a lot of other characters on television, they take themselves so seriously, and we're expected to as well, and there's no real satire. I mean, they're funny, and they're comedies, but it's not a satire. So, and I think that's what Homer offers.

This followed a lengthy explanation of Homer as non-traditional sitcom dad, and thus Homer is valued because, through his *parodic* distance from and commentary on traditional domesticom dads, he becomes a powerful *satiric* character. Parody, in other words, begets satire, and the relative absence of talk of 'parody,' in favor of 'satire,' shows how this link had already been made by most interviewees.

Returning to the substance of this parody/satire, several subjects mentioned the news too, and here discussion of *The Simpsons* as parodic teacher was particularly noticeable. Thus, Joanne explained:

It makes you think, is that how I treat television? [. . .] The Kent Brockman and satire of the media . . . like when the ants came, the ants in space, and he was like 'Hail ants!' [*laughs*] and then it's picked up on. He's probably said 'Oh, the humanity!' more than five or six times at different points [. . .] And when Bart had his human interest stories: [. . .] Mike McCartle on BCTV [in Vancouver, Canada] used to do stories just like that. 'People come and feed the ducks,' and he actually did stories about ducks, so when I saw that story, it was like [*laughs*]. You just sort of see . . . it's easy: it's not hidden messages from you. It's very obvious.

Joanne greatly valued *The Simpsons'* ability to parodically comment on the news. Nor was she alone in mentioning the news, as many others made explicit references to it, including, amusingly, journalist Reid, who, in reference to 'Girly Edition,' spoke rather bashfully of how such parody shows

the ludicrous nature of, you know, what we do in a lot of things. The kids news with Bart and Lisa: I mean, you see them do really stupid stories about the news, and 'news you can use,' and 'how to get rid of your sheets when you wet them.' I mean, people really *do* stories like that.

Both Joanne and Reid's comments illustrate another common attribute of these interviews, as *in context* they were able to reel off numerous examples of *Simpsons* parody. I was often met with pained expressions of forgetfulness when, earlier in the interviews, I asked for favorite lines or episodes. Once the context and parodic site of landing were set, though, the lines and episodes rolled off the tongue with great ease. This supports my contention in Chapter 3 that comedy travels well, particularly parody as comedy that always has a precise destination. Asking after the parody at its site of origin (*The Simpsons*) frequently stumped my interviewees' memories, but by shifting to the site of parodic attack, the memory blocks were lifted, suggesting, therefore, the degree to which parody operates as described in Chapter 2, attaching itself to a host text or genre and doggedly refusing to let go. *The Simpsons'* parody, in other words, appeared quite successful in invading contemplation and interpretation of other texts and genres. Alongside the domesticom and news, though, if another genre's ideology was seen as particularly under siege, it was the rampant consumerist capitalism of the advertisement and of promotional culture, but for reasons of space and efficiency, I will refrain from quoting examples of the ensuing scripts.

The 'obviousness' and value of *Simpsons* parody

It should also be highlighted, though, how much of a 'no-brainer' *The Simpsons'*
attack on corporate culture, the sitcom, and television proved to be in discussions.
All but a few participants quickly threw at least one of them forward as a target,
before slowing to think about what else might be targeted, or to list minor targets.
The effect here was akin to what we might expect if we asked somebody to name
the current England football squad, and they unflinchingly offered Beckham,
Scholes, and Owen before slowing to contemplate who else was on the side. *The
Simpsons'* parody / satire of ads and consumerism, television, and the media were
often considered so obvious as to not even be the point of my question. Judy, for
instance, answered, 'I suppose there are things, but to me they're quite *obvious*
things, like television, the policemen and Mr Burns.' Richard, meanwhile, rolled
off in one breath, 'the school system, television, the church, Mayor Quimby, the
police, Burns,' before I had even finished the question, as if to add them to the
question, not to offer them as an answer. Todd replied, almost apologetically, 'I
guess the nuclear family and the TV – there's a fair amount of TV satire, which I
like,' then asked himself, 'What else though?' and Laura also quick-fired, 'American
politics, religion – but I don't think it's a target as much, TV, "family values"
entertainment, consumerism. Umm, let's see. What else?' then slowed to a pause.

Perhaps the best illustration of the taken-for-grantedness of *The Simpsons* as a
parodic voice, though, came from Vivi. As detailed, Vivi did not like the show, and
even resented it, and thus had only watched it a few times, never for more than two
or three minutes. Her husband Thanos even spoke of having to take the television
into another room when *The Simpsons* came on! Yet Vivi had a clear picture of the
text as parodic. Following her husband's comment on *The Simpsons* as parodying the
American family, Vivi herself offered:

> Well . . . from the very few times I've seen it, I think the *media* is one of the
> targets. I got this impression. I don't know if I am right, but in every episode
> there is something or someone from the media, or, the media is always there,
> and [. . .] there's always a hidden comment on them. Even if it is the family in
> front of the TV, or someone with a microphone getting an interview from
> Homer.

Despite being an anti-fan, whether through her limited personal viewing, talk with
her husband, and / or through public discussion of *The Simpsons*, Vivi had a natural
sense of the show as media parody. She may have also had objections to the show,
but Vivi showed the degree to which *The Simpsons* is commonly and widely accepted
as a parody / satire of media corporatism and the televised version of the American
family.

Indeed, although I have already mentioned that the commonly noted guilt of the fiction-watcher was absent from the way these interviewees talked of watching *The Simpsons*, some had taken this guilt to its polar opposite, and I frequently heard comments suggesting a snobbery and elitism of sorts. Of course, fan groups often invert the value system of textual consumption and distinction, creating what Fiske (1992) calls 'popular cultural capital,' whereby knowingness and familiarity with the cult or popular text is highly valued and respected (see Barker and Brooks 1998; Hills 2002). Here, though, I often found the statements of '*Simpsons* snobbery' were quite commensurate with existing value systems and distinction, especially since the show was valued for lashing out at what many saw as the other 'crap' on television. '*Simpsons* snobbery' also frequently took the form of proud declarations of being able to see the show's 'deeper levels' that many others were supposedly unable to see. Whitney, for instance, spoke of 'the secret smugness of getting a joke,' whereby, 'Even though [the show is] amazingly popular, you kind of watch it thinking, "Ah! I bet 99 per cent of the other people watching it won't have got that gag."' Similarly, Angie said that 'the reason why I appreciate it is because [. . .] I don't think most Americans can appreciate that sort of double irony, twistedness. So they see it on one level, but they don't see the other level *behind* it.' Scottish Ryan, meanwhile, was amazed that a Channel 4 poll had seen Homer voted for as top TV character of all time, since he 'didn't think a British audience [. . .] were intelligent enough.' Charlie, too, spoke of being able to watch the show with anyone, 'even people who you don't think [*laughs*], aren't that bright, or something,' because while they could not enjoy the deeper level, 'Homer does all this crazy shit [. . .] and yeah, that's funny too.'

Clearly, then, some viewers adopted a cleverer-than-thou posture to their viewing and enjoyment of *The Simpsons*. At one level, this should serve as a rejoinder that *Simpsons* viewership, and the interpretive community of which I write, is hardly an all-enlightened utopian community. In Chapter 4, I noted that *The Simpsons* as text can too easily replicate established taste hierarchies, at times blind to the political and social meanings within some supposedly 'lower' art forms. However, in interviewing these individuals, all of whom possessed considerable cultural capital, I saw evidence that their consumption of the text frequently perpetuated these taste hierarchies, rather than challenge or deconstruct them. On another level, though, we should not just write this posture off as 'bad' elitism, and we should challenge Caldwell's (1995: 253) acerbic commentary that by perceiving the show as hip, one justifies one's student loans. Their posture not only serves as a powerful indicator of the degree to which *The Simpsons* is appreciated as an intelligent, subversive, and non-traditional television text, but also may have some truth to it. After all, these are well-educated viewers, and to deny that their education has heightened their critical abilities in any way whatsoever would be to engage in a bizarre form of anti-intellectualism (see Gripsrud 1989).

Similarly, lest their consumption appear to be wholly perpetuating taste hierarchies, let us remember that, to some outside this project, watching and enjoying *The Simpsons* would in itself classify as 'barbarous' taste. Alters' (2003) reception study of *The Simpsons*, for instance, found mothers who tried to regulate their children's access to the program precisely because they saw it as lower class. As I will expand upon later, many of my interviewees regarded this half-hour animated comedy as significantly more important, poignant, and intelligent than many genres that in theory should inhabit spots considerably higher up a bourgeois taste hierarchy than does *The Simpsons*. As noted in Chapter 4, then, once again we see how complex, and often contradictory, *The Simpsons*' and its viewers' relationship to cultural capital and taste are.

As might be expected, moreover, not all viewers indulged in the text as a smart, intelligent program, and to some its criticality was clearly irrelevant to their consumption and enjoyment of the text. Lembo (2000) notes in his research into working class television viewers that many liked to use television

> to create a kind of mindful space for themselves, one in which they did not have to think about any one thing or be *held responsible* for their thoughts and actions in the same way they typically had to throughout the day (or night) at work.
>
> (Lembo 2000: 153, original emphasis)

I heard similar sentiments expressed by a few of these middle-class interviewees. Eric, for instance, talked of television as there for 'R and R' for him: 'If I went to bed, or tried to go to sleep when I came home from work, it just, all you think is about one thing reoccurringly [sic]. If I have my half hour of TV or whatever, it just makes my mind relax.' In line with this, he preferred to enjoy *The Simpsons* as a relaxing laugh, and any time I asked him to discuss it on another level, my question was either met with a furrowed brow, or a game but flippant answer. These answers showed that he certainly could talk of *The Simpsons* on multiple levels, and he was by no means surprised by my questions, but he would rather not talk of *The Simpsons* in this way, instead 'protecting' its meanings and associations for him and claiming, with a self-ironic smile, 'I'm a pretty simple guy at the end of the day, I guess.'

All interviewees were aware of the show's criticality, and none objected to an interpretation of the text as parodic satiric. Eric and a very few others, though, did not *care* about this criticality, and preferred the show as light entertainment, or, as he noted, as 'a nice show about stupid people like Homer doing stupid things.' Undoubtedly, in a viewing audience the size of *The Simpsons*', many other Erics exist, so clearly the interpretive community of which I have been writing is by no means all-encompassing, and my interview with Eric showed how easily viewers can belong to other interpretive communities with regards *The Simpsons*. To restate, then, this is likely not a 'representative' study, nor do I claim to have found a universal reading of *The Simpsons*.

Nevertheless, to the overwhelming majority of these viewers, *The Simpsons* was a smart, intelligent program that not only engaged in critique itself, but also fostered critical discussion. Certainly, with great frequency, many interviewees claimed to analyze and share analyses in discussion with each other. When I asked if the interview had required them to talk about the show in a way they would not normally, five claimed to talk only rarely about the show anyway, and a few found my questions regarding whether *The Simpsons* was 'important' as unusual. Otherwise, *Simpsons* analysis was common. Tina, for example, nonchalantly replied that 'I've had these same conversations before,' and Alyson laughingly noted, 'It's kind of ironic, 'cause I've had conversations that were exactly like this, except a tape-recorder wasn't running. I often find myself having these very long, complicated discussions about *The Simpsons* and their importance.' Even for those who were stepping outside of normal conversation, as noted earlier, many claimed to activate the text in context, a practice that in itself points toward a close critical mastery of *The Simpsons* and its parody/comedy. Ultimately, then, as members of an interpretive community of sorts, this community shares in most instances, and albeit to different intensities, common interpretations of what *The Simpsons* is, does, and means. Central to these interpretations is the notion of an intelligent and critically aware text that parodically/satirically and intertextually is targeting other genres and ideologies pervasive on television. Far from just sharing interpretations, though, this interpretive community acts as an amplifier, for through discussion and group analysis, *The Simpsons*' critical intertextuality lives, breathes and grows.

Admittedly, this is a highly educated group, and not only might we hope for them to engage critically with texts, but also some readers might find the choice of subjects peculiar in this sense, preferring a lesser-educated, lower-class sample. My interviewees are, indeed, not cultural studies' usual suspects for audience research. From Hoggart's (1957) milkbar teens, to Morley and Brunsdon's (1999) shop stewards, and Radway (1987), Ann Gray (1987), and Hobson's (1987) housewives; and from Willis' (1977) lads and Hebdige's (1979) punks, to Jenkins (1992) and Penley's (1997) female slash fiction writers, and Buckingham's (1987, 2000) school children, media and cultural studies audiences have traditionally been disaffected, disempowered, or marginalized in some way. By contrast, almost all of my interviewees were financially stabile cosmopolitans well on their ways to powerful jobs, most were white (two were ethnically South Asian, and four East Asian), and all hailed from affluent nations. Thus, it would take a great deal of imagination to consider these interviewees as particularly 'afflicted.' In addition, most were highly media literate – some were even film or media students. However, there are several reasons why such a group requires study.

Arguably, since the beginning of the mass effects models of media audiences, the most frequent subjects of research have been those who are perceived as vulnerable. Thus, whether the individual research project has taken the form of *attributing* vulnerability to certain groups (for an infamous example, see Bandura 1971) or of *defending* such groups' media savvy and use (see Buckingham 1987; Fiske 1989c; Radway 1987), much of this work is about Others (see Blackman and Walkerdine 2001). Effectively, middle-class educated viewers have traditionally been the unseen and unremarked because already assumed. Exceptions exist, and sociological work into youth culture on the dance floor is a notable instance (Thornton 1995). Similarly, as Hills (2002) points out, they have frequently enjoyed a *phantom* and underground existence behind fan studies, as much of this work projects academic concerns and ideals onto fan communities. By and large, though, the well-educated 20- and 30-something crowd have often disappeared off the map in terms of television audience research. This is hardly an insignificant group, though. With the ever-increasing numbers in western universities, this demographic is growing, and with it then, casual supposition of it is also growing. Media studies must examine not only the other and the 'them,' though, but also the (perceived) self and the 'us.' More generally, if university or college is depicted or imagined by so many to be the borderland between being an impressionable youth and a discerning adult, and if education is similarly popularly imagined as a key process by which media and cultural literacies are taught, surely more research is required into those liminal beings on such borders.

Many other groups, and hence other potential interpretive communities, have been overlooked in this study, but perhaps due to their relatively dominant status, university and college students have been able to construct one of *The Simpsons'* most notable interpretive communities, one that sees *The Simpsons* as parodic, and one that enjoys, eagerly anticipates, and discusses its parody, in the process circulating critical messages and evaluations of contemporary televisual genres, form, and address.

Chapter 6

'THE *SIMPSONS* ATTITUDE'

So far, I have shown how my interviewees responded to the show only as smart. Earlier, though, I noted that many of them talked of *The Simpsons* as 'funny but smart' or 'smart but funny,' and so in this chapter, I will turn to its funniness; importantly, to that conjunction 'but;' and to examining how 'funny' and 'smart' were seen to be concepts that must be delicately balanced, rather than simply conjoined in any available quantity. The almost-interchangeability of the explanations that *The Simpsons* is 'funny but smart' or 'smart but funny' suggests that being *either* too smart or too funny could be a liability, but I also heard suggestions that the nature of parody can allow it to rise above these dangers. In short, while I quoted Laura talking of 'a *Simpsons* attitude,' I now wish to study precisely what that attitude entails, and what it might tell us of parody's prospects for success beyond the television screen, in the lived realities of its viewers.

The good, the smart, and the funny

To begin with, in addition to their admiration of its intelligence and media savvy, almost all of my interviewees glowed with approval at its funniness. The show is, after all, billed as a comedy. Thus, before mentioning anything about its cleverness, Reid said he watches it because 'It makes me laugh. I laugh out loud, hysterically at times,' while Tina explained, 'Honestly, the best answer I can give you is just because it's *howlingly* funny.' To say that this laughter surrounded the parodic humor would be only a partial truth; instead, many of the interviewees claimed also to be fond of the show's slapstick and/or silly humor. Al stated, for instance, that, 'On a very, very basic level, it really makes me laugh and it appeals to umm, really vulgar and [*laughs*] profane sort of instincts inside my own humor base.' A deeply cynical reading of such comments could see this as the truth behind the 'narcissism' mentioned in Chapter 5, and claims of the show's intelligence could be seen as the 'front' for the low-base desires. Such a reading, though, could only be sustained by ignoring how matter-of-factly and openly such desires were expressed. Not a single interviewee offered these statements in an apologetic tone: they were simply noted as elements that the show provides, and should continue to provide. Rather, then, these comments illustrate a considerable tension between zany funniness, and intelligence. Hence, as opposed to completely disregarding the cynical reading, I believe there is *some* truth to it, not at the level of using the appeal of the zany to *discount* the appeal of the intelligent, but at the level of seeing one as *allowing* or mitigating the other. Most interviewees discussed *The Simpsons'* zaniness, but were keen to 'defend' the show with reference to its intelligence, as discussed earlier, meaning it is funny, but not just funny – 'funny but smart' – yet most also saw the show as intelligent but also appealing to their senses of humor – 'smart but funny.' Of these two equations – funny but smart, smart but funny – the former is perhaps the easier to grasp, seeing that dominant taste hierarchies habitually rank smart above funny. By contrast, smart should seemingly be enough without needing funny. So how did my interviewees describe *The Simpsons'* smartness and funniness to make sense of the importance of laughter?

The first warning sign that 'smart' is not enough came when I asked why they watched television. Here, I was trying to make sense of what Lembo (2000: 101) calls the moment of 'the turn to television': what hopes and expectations they bring to the set, and what role(s) they are asking it to play (see also Bausinger 1984). Admittedly, all answers were framed by the interviewees' knowledge that this was a *Simpsons* interview, and thus in other contexts, they might answer differently. Nevertheless, all interviewees spoke highly of entertainment and of programs that made them laugh. Even the few media students avoided the 'proper' Habermasian answer that television was primarily there to inform and educate. Joanne, a former communications minor, was even explicit about this avoidance, as she answered in a put-on, nerdy student voice, 'I think it should be entertaining, and educational, and I think it should bring a family together,' before dropping the voice with a laugh to answer, 'I think it should be entertaining.' Joanne's key requirement of entertainment was shared by many, often explained as a desire to relax, and to 'turn your brain off and kill time,' as Rhys put it. To Susan, 'I treat it as a relaxation thing, just to switch off from the world'; to Richard, when 'you come home absolutely knackered at the end of the day, you just wanna veg out: it's great for that'; or to

Daphne, television is simply 'PhD avoidance,' and a chance to move the brain down a few gears. Most interviewees gave some variant or other of this response. And with their brains geared to a slower pace, what many really wanted was entertainment. Thus, as Zach noted, 'with television, you can just relax and let it entertain you. So, I'd say that's what it is,' or as Sonia said, 'Predominantly for me, it's been to entertain. You know, you come home from work and you don't want to think about really complex things. You want to unwind.'

At the same time, these viewers were by no means hostile to information and education on television, often listing this as something television should definitely provide. However, many of them determinedly placed it after entertainment in terms of importance, and several were also guarded about informational programming. Katy, for instance, noted that 'when you have a news program on the television, there's only a certain amount of time, and it's not conducive to any meaningful, in-depth understanding of any particular issue.' Meanwhile, Ling told me that 'Of course there are educational programs, which are interesting and I find those interesting, but sometimes I want to relax, and to laugh, and they're not doing much for me then.' Many interviewees expressed wariness of the news media, whether through distrust of its ulterior motives or through sheer lack of interest, whereas entertainment and humor came through as more likely to reward their attention. Entertainment and humor were seen to have their own problems, as many talked disparagingly of the large amount of 'crap' on television, but such complaints were clearly directed at specific programs, rather than – as with educational programming – at an entire mode of programming (or, simply, at the appropriateness of that mode to a tired student turning on the television at the end of the day).

These general comments on television connected with later comments on *The Simpsons* in particular, as many were reluctant to talk of *The Simpsons* as a *predominantly* serious program. As opposed to Eric, for instance, who talked of the program *only* as light entertainment, most would happily talk of it as a comedy with bite and intelligent commentary, but it was always comedy first. Thus, I heard numerous instances of interviewees recouping the serious into their comfort(able) category of entertainment. Carrie, for instance, noted that 'it is, like, making fun of the whole genre of TV's situation comedy and all that. Umm, but, at the end of the day, it's still entertainment.' Reacting to my question on the show's politics, meanwhile, Charlie said, 'I suppose I hadn't really sat down and thought about *The Simpsons* in a different slant, but that's probably a good thing, right? Cause you still want it to be entertainment at the end of the day.' Joanne, too, insisted, 'when it comes down to it, it's still a cartoon to me. I think there's important things that they say, but . . . [*trails off*],' and Harold told me, 'I don't think it's important at a big, deep, philosophical level. I don't think they're hitting "big" truths. I think it's really hard to do that in a half-hour show, and, hey, it still has to make me laugh, right?'

Comic criticism

This insistence on *The Simpsons* as being entertainment and comedy before politi-cally savvy show also took the form, at times, of pointing out its political and/ or parodic limitations. Some, for example, felt *The Simpsons'* parodic edge was blunted somewhat by being animated. 'When you watch it,' said Wei, 'you do feel like you're in an alternate universe, where the social conventions you're accustomed to don't really migrate into that alternate universe,' or as Ling suggested, while the show has strong commentary, to others, because it is a cartoon, 'you could *take* it as being lighter.' Hence, some felt *The Simpsons'* commentary was in a way contained by its generic boundaries. Eric also noted an ambivalence to some of the show's parody, giving the example that while 'they have a fair go at celebrities,' 'the flip side of that is the people they're having a go at – and they're having a *good* go at them sometimes – are doing the voice, so [. . .] they reap the praise for it.' Or, a different complaint came from Joanne and Mary, who felt the show could verge on overdoing Mr Burns' evil capitalist caricature, and similarly inject too much self-righteous politics into Lisa, in the process trying to be too serious and straying too far from the zone of entertainment.

With such criticism, and with some (albeit rare) expressions of incredulity at the idea that *The Simpsons* might be political in any way, we should observe two things. First, is an honest and straight challenge to *The Simpsons'* critical intertextual-political element, pointing out real limitations, not only to *The Simpsons* in particular, but also to parody in general. Parody can indeed risk becoming contained, fawning, and/or sanctimonious. Second, to some interviewees, the comment that *The Simpsons* is entertainment 'at the end of the day' may have meant less that it is intel-ligent and parodic in a comedic body than that its parody is, in their eyes, a minor part of the program. *The Simpsons* is not just parodic, and in some episodes there is little parody. However, while not wanting to interpret all of my interviewees away from this position, and while marking it as a possible reading of some of their comments, it is contradicted both by other comments and by the tenor of their supposed criticisms. After all, as illustrated in Chapter 5, most of my interviewees talked at great length about, and with great respect and fondness for, *The Simpsons'* parody. This leads us, then, to the tenor of the comments.

Here, an attached CD is almost required, for with every instance of 'it's still entertainment,' the inflection with which the comments were voiced made it clear that *The Simpsons* was being complimented, not criticized. For instance, when Carrie remarked that the show was anti-sitcom but still entertainment, her tone made it clear not that the sitcom critique was a plus and the entertainment was a minus, but rather that the entertainment was a plus *on top of* the anti-sitcom. Similarly, Harold's remark that the show hits no 'big, deep, philosophical truths' intoned these words with such gravity as if to suggest only Stephen Hawking or Plato could achieve such lofty goals, goals moreover that would involve sacrificing the entertainment and humor he clearly valued. Even Ling's statement that *The Simpsons* could be taken as lighter rang with the suggestion that she appreciated this escape hatch from the utterly serious and 'heavy.' This sense of not being too smart or clever was then explicitly stated by Katy and Al. To Katy, 'it's more entertainment. I don't sit down to watch *The Simpsons* to be informed. That's a nice side effect that happens, and it just makes me think about things in a slightly different way, but I watch it to be entertained.' To Al, meanwhile, upon asking him what could make him stop watching, he balanced off, 'if they stopped looking at themselves as being a satirical show' with, 'or, if they tried to, you know, tried to be too clever for their own good, and lose that sense that at the root of all this is a family and a fun show.' Later in the interview, he reiterated that the show is great precisely because 'It doesn't try to be too clever.'

I heard numerous further expressions of this defense of entertainment and weariness of that which tries to be too clever when I asked my interviewees to comment on *The Simpsons'* politics, if they felt it had any. The word 'politics,' of course, has a vague referent, and as both Bhavnani's (1991) and Buckingham's (2000) studies of young people's engagements with 'the political' render clear, the word has different definitions to different people. True to Bhavnani's (1991: 21) findings, for most of my interviewees, 'politics' appeared haunted by notions of parliamentary process and party politics, but as they spoke of these politics, a different politics emerged – one of comic criticism, a politics that many felt *The Simpsons* shared with their own sensibilities.

As far as parliamentary/party politics went, most viewers (correctly, I believe) detected a marked left-of-center thrust to the show. As Whitney dryly pointed out, *The Simpsons* is 'generally less Republican-friendly,' or as Rhys said, 'It's a rather left-wing kind of show, I think, politically.' With many interviewees listing capitalist and consumerist society as one of the show's key targets, its leftist slant appeared obvious to most, even to anti-fan Vivi. Vivi's husband Thanos had just told me the show was leftist when she interrupted, 'Yeah, it's very obvious.' Interestingly, four interviewees professed right-of-center politics, yet none of them felt there was a dominant political slant. Jesse and Susan related more to the show's zany humor than to its parody to begin with, and saw no politics in the program. Richard, meanwhile, tellingly talked himself into a bit of a corner, saying defensively 'it's not left,' and then taking the example (from 'The Old Man and the Lisa') of when Mr Burns goes bankrupt, but regains his millions with entrepreneurial flair, selling sea slurry, turning 'into this environmental monster, with his greed overpowering all . . . but I don't really know if they make a judgment on whether that's a good or bad thing – it's just the way it is.' Richard may not tie the ends himself, but Burns becoming 'an environmental monster,' consumed with greed, indeed sounds like a firm judgment and 'a bad thing,' even in his telling of it.

Aside from a rather willful misreading, though, if a conservative viewer like Richard could still enjoy the show *and* engage with its politics, this would seem to be because of another level of *The Simpsons'* politics on which Richard, Harold (a Republican), and most other viewers agreed: its anti-establishmentism, and its proclivity to mock anything deemed worthy of ridicule. Even those who saw leftist politics in the show noted a broader politics of mischief and deconstruction. Hence, Cleo noted that it has

> a much more left slant than anything else on, but I think that they're very careful not to label themselves as a Democratic mouthpiece, say [. . .] And I think the point of the show is to be able to make fun of *whatever* politics don't make sense in the eyes of the writers. [emphasis added]

Todd similarly offered, 'it strikes me as left-wing, but in a kind of, err, in a kind of restrained way [. . .] It will knock both sides of politics.' Or, as Angie posed, 'I think it's anti-every establishment.' Comments such as these echoed some of the broader answers to my question regarding the show's targets. While many saw television and the media, politics, religion, the news, the family, American life, and schools as particularly in the cross-hairs, Niraj summarized that, at root, 'They're making fun of anyone who's got an image.' Sonia similarly stated that 'they're picking up on, like, culture and social constructions,' making fun 'of things that people are afraid to make fun of, [and] so they make them accessible.' And to Tina, 'I think it goes after falseness a lot: it likes to take the air out of false people.' More than just staking a particular (party) political ground, *The Simpsons* was talked of as going after artifice (which, of course, is parody's modus operandi), embodying Barthes' dictum that 'the best weapon against myth is perhaps to mythify it in its turn' (1973: 135).

There are two elements of this expansive-critical approach that particularly won approval. As Al explained:

> everyone and everything is fair game. Including themselves. Umm, and I, I think that they're very, very clear that they don't want to [. . .] try and get too . . . a political agenda or a political sort of standing block, because it's, ultimately it's futile, because [*laughs*] who are they to say that? It's a bunch of drawn, yellow people who live in a false world, so who on Earth are they to tell us how to live our lives?

The first element here is that of 'everyone and everything' being 'fair game,' and a concurrent cynicism that everyone and everything might be in need of ridicule, while the (related) second element is a bristling desire to avoid hypocrisy and/or being patronized. In what remains of the chapter, I will take each in turn and

147

examine several issues surrounding them that might enlighten how critical intertextuality works and what value it has to its audience.

Everything in need of ridicule

Turning to the first element, Al's comment was repeated by many others. To Leo,
'they take the piss out of everyone, including themselves'; Susan felt, 'It plays
everyone out'; Sujata said, 'I think it's everything goes [. . .] Yeah, cause they make
fun of whoever's in power'; and Ryan noted that 'it seems to attack everyone.' Or,
as Carrie elaborated:

> everything's kind of got an ironic twist on it, it's got a lot of political satire in
> it, and it sort of speaks, I think, to a certain demographic, I feel, or it speaks
> to me. They kind of . . . everything's a joke, and they make fun of everything.

These statements were all offered with considerable approval, as *The Simpsons'* ability
to turn its parodic gaze on seemingly anything was highly valued. Furthermore, as
Carrie suggests, appreciation of this parodic mode was seen as in part constitutive
of group identity for this 'certain demographic' or interpretive community.

Moreover, this satiric-parodic mode was often spoken of as 'important.' On
asking about its importance, I quoted Rupert Murdoch's assertion that *The Simpsons*
is perhaps the most important show on television (see Garrett 2001: 7), and asked
for comment, hence deliberately placing the notion alongside a popularly disliked
figure so that those who wished to discard the notion could feel comfortable in doing
so. Also, as with 'politics,' 'important' is a vague word, and I was keen to see how
viewers might define it differently. Surprisingly, though, only a few interviewees
threw out the idea, and many quickly agreed. After pointing out that the show hits
no 'big, deep philosophical truths,' Harold underlined that *The Simpsons* mocks and
parodies so much of everyday American life and, in that sense, '*is* important, 'cause
we may need a little wake-up call.' Angie, meanwhile, asked, 'Important in getting
people to think about social issues? [. . .] In terms of entertaining in a smart, clever
way? Sure. It's important. I'd say it's good at it,' and Tina offered that:

> I think it is an important show, simply because it offers some sort of filter, and
> offers some sort of organizational tool for, kind of looking back at our culture
> and figuring out what it's all about. So I think in that sense it's important,
> because the things that it chooses to satirize are always current.

'The key thing about *The Simpsons*,' Alyson told me, 'is that you just have to be
observant to what's going on around you,' and others felt that *The Simpsons* takes

'the things that go on around us' and re-contextualizes them, or 'defamiliarizes' them, in Shklovsky's (1965) terms. Hence, Todd talked of its 'capacity to make regular people think about, you know, their lifestyles in a new light, and not take everything for granted.' Mary felt its sitcom and consumer culture parody was particularly important, because 'I think it can burst your bubble of, you know, constant progress and everything's gonna get better, and everyone's moving toward this common American Dream or whatever, and so I think that sits with you.' Sujata, meanwhile, said *The Simpsons* could contextualize what she saw on television. She told me, for instance, of how, when she watched the show more frequently:

> I would turn off, and it would really make me think about things in a way that I had never before [. . .] So, it's not really a thing where I turn off and the show goes away, since those kinds of things, umm, do sit with me for a while. And then I bring them up with other people, and they do mean something for us all, sometimes at least.

Later, when I asked if the show was important, she observed that it is 'probably because I have a sense of it being an important show that I still watch it more than anything else.'

Here, Sujata walked me through the stages of parody and critical intertextuality: she would watch, then carry the text with her to critically operate on other texts and to continue ruminating on it, and, along the way, activated the parody in discussion with others, allowing its power to germinate and grow beyond the screen. Sujata was not alone, however, as others noted similar processes. Charlie, for example, spoke of how, due to *The Simpsons*, 'I *expect* more of other shows.' Tina said, 'It probably sharpens you up.' Carrie joked that she has watched it for so long that she has a *Simpsons* 'voice' in her head as she watches other shows, and Al stated:

> what they've done for me is they've exposed a kind of structure that these kind of shows will often adhere to, a kind of pretension [. . .] and then [they] force *the viewer* to speculate on how generalized or how accurate that generalized notion of that pretension is.

Or, Lucia felt that *The Simpsons* is one of the most important shows on television, and just as important in its own way as the news, because 'it's the flip-side of the news, and it's the commentary.' Thus, to Lucia, *The Simpsons* was almost an organically connected part of the news, an intertextual respondent, and important for playing this very role.

To ask about importance in the first place, though, was to ask after intertextuality, for importance is a relational term. Therefore, in discussing *The Simpsons* as important, the interviewees were implicitly discussing other televisual texts, and in judging *The Simpsons* as important for teaching and mocking artifice, they were expressing considerable discontent with the artifice on other programs. This, then, explains why 'everything being a joke' might be valued – precisely because so much is seen as in *need* of ridicule. As Leo offered, '*The Simpsons* is coming at the same time as television just getting out of control [. . .] But they take the piss out of that, all the time.' Certainly, to some, the relevant part of Murdoch's quote was that *The Simpsons* is the most important thing *on television*, as some felt this was not much of a compliment, given the poor level of competition. In talking of *The Simpsons*, many of my interviewees underlined what parody itself declares – that the textual world is experiencing a crisis of sorts, a crisis that necessitates and demands ridicule, among other strategies. Hull (2000) helpfully looks at *The Simpsons*, and at the work of Matt Groening more generally, as a contemporary Foucauldian attempt to lift the rock up off all manners of discourse to reveal the worms beneath. Discourses and disciplinary institutions, though, will always exist in one form or another, hence the importance of relentless parody, and of finding the absurd and laughable in everything.

Cynicism and nihilism

That a lack of faith in the textual and social worlds would necessitate laughter, and not earnest criticism and exposition alone, would seem anathema to some communications scholars in the Habermasian tradition of a rational, sober public sphere. Similarly, to others, it may signal the death-knell of democratic discussion, given its reveling in the cynical. Many interviewees spoke glowingly of *The Simpsons* as lying in the mainstream of a contemporary ethos of media cynicism, but for us to see this as in any way positive is to buck the trend of a growing skepticism about media cynicism. Whether observed as a symptom of a postmodern malaise, or discussed in relation to a perceived ever-waning interest in the news and politics, the nature and value of cynicism are under attack. While critical pedagogy calls for the teaching of media literacy and awareness – a deliberate engendering, in other words, of media cynicism – there are many who question whether a cynical disposition can ever be positive, or whether it merely contributes to a culture of distanced apathy and removal of oneself from the public sphere into a regressive nihilism. As such, it is important that I now address this critique, and show how the opinions expressed by my interviewees point to a crudeness and incompleteness of argument on the side of those who are cynical about cynicism. Where some commentators see cynicism as static, individual, self-contained, destructive, and pessimistic or even apathetic, 'the *Simpsons* attitude' showed glimmers of an 'alternative' cynicism that is capable of being continuous, communal, discussion-forming, reconstructive, and even optimistic.

What many viewers enjoy about *The Simpsons*, I was told, is that 'everything's a joke,' and that it will criticize anyone or anything. However, Matheson (2001) sees this as the show's tragic flaw. Via a process of what Matheson calls 'hyper-irony,' *The Simpsons*' 'process of undercutting,' he says, 'runs so deeply that we cannot regard the show as merely cynical; it manages to undercut its cynicism too' (2001: 118). Yielding that *The Simpsons* 'treats nearly everything as a target,' Matheson (2001: 120) believes that all this leads to is the sad message that

> comedy can be used to attack anybody at all who thinks that he or she has any sort of handle on the answer to any major question, not to replace the object of attack with a better way of looking at things, but merely for the pleasure of attack, or perhaps for the sense of momentary superiority.
>
> (Matheson 2001: 120)

To him, therefore, the show and its audiences may well be cynical, but this cynicism is fundamentally counter-productive. In this respect, though, Matheson is by no means alone, as his conflation of cynicism with nihilism connects with many key statements on cynicism in general.

Cynicism, Giddens (1990) writes, is one of four key 'adaptive reactions' to a world replete with risk, in which we are forced to rely on endless networks of trust. We can either respond, he argues, with pragmatic acceptance, sustained optimism, radical engagement, or cynical pessimism (Giddens 1990: 134–7). Giddens is careful not to equate cynicism with apathy, but nevertheless lumps it in with a bleak, nihilistic outlook, and by setting it in opposition to these three other possible responses would also seem to preclude cynicism from engaging radically, or from being either pragmatic or optimistic. If we then turn to Eliasoph's (1998) excellent study of how Americans avoid talking about politics, the picture continues to darken. Eliasoph writes of 'cynical chic,' a distanced and distancing position whereby, wary of ulterior motives, people revel in a willful rejection of all explicit politics. Writing of a particular group of cynically chic Californians, Eliasoph (1998: 154) states 'the point of their conversation was always to convince each other that they were smart enough to know that they could not do anything about the problems.' Thus, to Eliasoph, cynicism leads to nihilistic excuses for non-action. Of the several groups she followed for two years, the cynical chic group spoke of politics the most, but to no end, instead merely retreating into a position of intellectual superiority from which nothing need be done.

Arguably, cynicism's most vociferous critics, though, have been Jeffrey Goldfarb (1991), Richard Stivers (1994), and Mark Crispin Miller (1986, 1988). Complaining of 'an easy substitution of cynical explanation and manipulation for democratic reasoning and contestation' (1991: ix), Goldfarb sees cynicism as 'a form of legitimation through disbelief' (1991: 1), whereby discontent never leads to action. Both Goldfarb (1991) and Stivers (1994) paint a picture of the United States in particular as a cynical society, where reason and deliberation have given way to complaint and a cynical disposition. 'When a citizenry does not experience democracy as a reality,' Goldfarb argues, 'it cannot be one' (1991: 177). Stivers similarly posits it as the key obstacle to forming a common culture based on an ethic of love and freedom. 'Cynicism,' he intones, 'makes things worse than they are in that it makes permanent the current condition, leaving us with no hope of transcending it' (Stivers 1994: 13). Focusing on television specifically, Mark Crispin Miller sees a pervasive cynicism that is only so much postmodern deflection, 'the hipness unto death' (1988: 16). Miller sees cynicism and ironic detachment solely as strategies to keep television viewers 'semihypnotized' (1988: 13), scared and scornful of being individuals, and, ultimately, stuck in an inertia of agency. To Miller, the cynical inability to move beyond the scorned undesirable, and to demand or create an alternative, becomes a convenient excuse for doing nothing, and for conservatism. Media cynicism, he writes, 'sustains the widespread illusion that we have all somehow recovered from a bout of vast and paralyzing gullibility' (Miller 1986: 228), and, in doing so, it 'protects itself from criticism or rejection by incorporating our very animus against the spectacle into the spectacle itself' (1986: 194).

To its critics, then, cynicism represents two great threats to democracy and informed, active citizenship. First, it is conceived of as a fundamental opting out, a frustrated and exhausted throwing up of the hands and consequent lack of faith in *any* doctrine other than that of nihilism. Thus, rather than laud these *Simpsons* viewers' cynicism, and the show's amplification of it, we could see both as blameworthy, and as a community defect, as if in the Great March Forward of Progress, the show and its viewers had decided to sit down and do nothing. Second, particularly to more Marxist critics such as Miller, cynicism is seen as the very illusion of being above the system that the system relies upon to maintain control. Or, to quote cynicism's historian and philosopher, Peter Sloterdijk (1987), cynicism is 'enlightened false consciousness.'

Sloterdijk (1987) offers a history of cynicism from antiquity to present, and in a highly exacting and encompassing study, suggests that ours is a deeply cynical age. 'We live,' he describes,

> from day to day, from vacation to vacation, from news show to news show, from problem to problem, from orgasm to orgasm, in private turbulences and medium-term affairs, tense, relaxed. With some things we feel dismay but with most things we can't really give a damn.
>
> (Sloterdijk 1987: 98–9)

There is, therefore, not only a crisis in enlightenment, 'but even a crisis in the praxis of enlightenment' (Sloterdijk 1987: 88), whereby 'When someone tries to "agitate" me in an enlightened direction, my first reaction is a cynical one: the person concerned should get his or her own shit together' (1987: 89).

> [V]alues have short lives. Being concerned, caring about people, securing peace, feeling responsible, caring about the quality of your life and about the environment – none of that really works. Just bide your time. Cynicism stands ready in the background, until the palaver has stopped and things take their course.
>
> (Sloterdijk 1987: xxvii–xxviii)

Yet amidst such cynical withdrawal and false platitudes of knowingness, the status quo and governing ideologies are free to do as they will, as Sloterdijk (1987) illustrates with the chilling example of cynical Weimar Germany.[1]

Against such charges, then, what are we to say of *Simpsons* viewers' own cynicism, and of the cynicism engendered by the show? Might critical intertextuality be leading viewers to a bleak and impotent dead end? Here, my data allow no easy or complete rebuttal. Nevertheless, the interviewees' comments point to several critical problems with this cynical view of cynicism. Similarly, critical theory on cynicism offers some rebuttals. Buckingham (2000), for instance, notes that cynicism is often wholly justifiable. Speaking of cynical reactions to politics, he argues that this response 'needs to be respected on its own terms, as a genuine and sincere assessment of the actions of politicians and of the political system' (Buckingham 2000: 203), for as he quotes a 12-year-old student, 'How can you be interested in politics when you see them saying, "I'm pretty crap myself, but he's crappier than me"?' (2000: 156). Meanwhile, Bhavnani (1991: 12) takes issue with the supposed inertia of cynicism, writing that '"Cynicism" implies some form of political analysis and therefore some level of interest,' and that justifiable cynicism has, in some cases, given birth to substantive political action, as with the Black Civil Rights and feminist movements. (Somewhat deviously, we might also note that Miller's impassioned work seems to be driven in large part by his cynicism of capitalist entertainment industry processes.) Hence, although *cynicism* is still seen here as a symptom of disenfranchisement, Buckingham (2000) and Bhavnani (1991) are keen not to write it off as a wholly negative practice.

The laughing kynic

A further, more complex response, though, is also offered by Sloterdijk himself, as he distinguishes between cynicism and 'kynicism.' Tracing kynicism back to Diogenes as the incorrigibly 'cheeky' philosopher,[2] Sloterdijk (1987) poses that where cynicism is morose, resigned, and apathetic, kynicism invokes the power of laughing and parodic/satiric ridicule, and is anything but apathetic. Kynicism, he writes, is 'a *form of dealing with knowledge*, a form of relativization, ironic treatment, application, and sublation' (Sloterdijk 1987: 292, original emphasis) that represents an 'urge of individuals to maintain themselves as fully rational living beings against the distortions and semirationalities of their societies' (1987: 217–18). Further explaining the distinction between kynics and cynics, he notes that, 'Despite all apparent lack of respect, the kynic assumes a basically serious and upright attitude toward truth and maintains a thoroughly solemn relation, satirically disguised, to it. With the cynic, this relation has given way to a thorough flabbiness and agnosticism (denial of knowledge)' (Sloterdijk 1987: 296). Thus, where cynics have lost faith in the existence of truth, and where their cynicism serves as a reaction to this loss of faith, kynics hold on to a notion of truth, but since they see it being perverted all around them, their kynicism and laughing ridicule serves as a defense and an offense to this state of affairs.

As did Bakhtin, Sloterdijk favors parody, satire, and laughter as powerful tools of criticism. And much as Bakhtin looked to the fool-philosopher as prototype of parodic power embodied, Sloterdijk (1987: 102) speaks of Diogenes as creating an 'uncivil enlightenment.' 'With Diogenes,' he notes, 'the resistance against the rigged game of "discourse" begins in European philosophy' (1987: 102), since while 'philosophy can only hypocritically live out what it says, it takes cheek to say what is lived' (1987: 102). Sloterdijk expresses considerable suspicion of philosophy as always open to hypocrisy and cooption by that which it supposedly detests. Again echoing Bakhtin, one of Sloterdijk's key accusations of contemporary philosophy is that it has become alienatingly monologic, distancing itself from lived realities to too great an extent, hence becoming cold dogma. He charges that 'It has given up its life as satire, in order to win its position in books as "theory"' (1987: 16). By contrast, Sloterdijk supports dialogic philosophy, and sees kynical satire and 'cheekiness' as pre-eminent. 'If we wanted to write a history of the kynical impulse in the field of knowledge,' he states, 'it would have to take the form of a philosophical history of satire' (1987: 290), for 'To make use of intelligence in a kynical way [. . .] means to parody rather than to propose a theory' (1987: 287).

We could paraphrase Sloterdijk's (1987) criticism of the modern age as being concerned with *complicity*. Almost all forms of knowledge are bound up with undesirable discourses of power that are themselves in need of criticism, a situation that inspires the widespread cynicism that we see today. However, Sloterdijk sees kynicism as a viable response precisely because its laughing nature and eagerness not to take itself so seriously succeeds in partially side-stepping the dangers of complicity. Kynicism is also powerful, he notes, because 'respectable thinking does not know how to deal with' it (1987: 101), and thus the content of its attacks is peculiarly resilient to counter-criticism. Ultimately, then, Sloterdijk draws an important distinction between a damaging and regressive cynicism and a challenging, forward-thinking kynicism. Sloterdijk himself feels that kynicism is dying in modern times, but I believe that it is alive and well in parodies and their accompanying interpretive communities. What I was told of *The Simpsons'* role, importance, and meaning to my interviewees bears only a passing resemblance to a wholly pessimistic, destructive, stagnant, and nihilistic postmodern cynicism. Rather, it has more in common with a dialogically infused and actively reconstructive kynicism.

To begin with, after all, my interviewees were hardly disenfranchised, embittered, and/or alienated individuals removing themselves from society. They included among them a former White House intern and senatorial campaign worker, several London School of Economics and School of Oriental and African Studies international development and politics students, a secondary school teacher with a media literacy class, and a public health student working on issues of AIDS mortality. These were not powerless, withdrawn individuals who had decided nothing could be done. In its own way, small and less important to some, more so to others, the joking around with media and politics that *The Simpsons* and their talk about it involved may even have helped them to face the realms of media and politics again with renewed vigor, optimism, and engagement. Moreover, they spoke of it glowingly, not as a weight around their ankles, dragging them and their optimism downward. As Carrie, the former White House intern, exclaimed, 'Thank God there's *The Simpsons* to give perspective to all the crap you have to deal with daily! You really do *need* that laughter, I believe'; or, as Katy, the media literacy teacher observed, 'in its own small way, it helps me do my job, I guess. Uh, not only does it show the kids what I'm talking about, but – how can I put this? – it reminds *me* exactly *what* to talk about. And, and, it lets us all have a laugh at it all, right?'

As Katy's comment here suggests, beyond regarding parody's effectiveness at an individual level, though, we must return to its sociality. For, while having a sense of humor, and being able to laugh at everything might appear to be merely a coping mechanism, if it gets people talking about issues of media and political representation, structure and address, it is powerful in and of itself. As Couldry (2000, 2003) tells us, the media's symbolic power is, in part, only as powerful as the belief in it. Rather than lead to nothing, then, and rather than plague a community, *Simpsons*-related kynicism, I was told and shown, leads to discussion and *fosters* community. Thus, where, for instance, Eliasoph (1998) found little political discussion among her subjects, *The Simpsons* proved a veritable can-opener for this rare delicacy. If my interview transcripts are in any way indicative, *The Simpsons'* parody offers an effective, easy, and safe way to introduce political or media discussion into the everyday.

Furthermore, this kynicism is far from stagnant. Morley (1999) points to the very real possibility that people may *forget* to be cynical, and several audience research projects have shown that seeing bias is not necessarily a defense against it (Buckingham 2000: 125; Jhally and Lewis 1992: 30; Morley and Brunsdon 1999: 263). Thus, the overlooking of kynical lessons is always a real possibility, and undoubtedly much of *The Simpsons'* parody will fly by many of its viewers at any given time. Nevertheless, we must also remember the *phenomenology* of cynicism. *Simpsons* cynicism, it was often stated, is powerful precisely because it keeps coming back in countless episodes, and therefore the cynicism is built upon, augmented, and fleshed out. If we 'forget' to be cynical at one point in time, we may not at another point. Especially with such a vibrant interpretive community disseminating its parodic attacks among themselves and others, 'reminders,' to this end, as well as new parodic attacks, are offered on a continual basis.

Without a doubt, different groups and individuals internalize and externalize parody and cynicism in different ways, and not all viewers will react as did these 35 viewers. Nevertheless, what is evident from my interviews and from my close textual work on the program is a different cynicism from that of Giddens (1990), Eliasoph (1998), Stivers (1994), Goldfarb (1991), or Miller's (1986, 1988) postulations. Renewing and regenerating itself, this kynicism is dialogic and hence reconstructive by nature, moving quickly to keep up with current media and political developments and players, and it may well inspire both community and agency. This kynicism craftily mixes warranted pragmatism with laughing optimism precisely to combat despairing pessimistic removal and alienation. I pose that we view this kynicism as a light of hope in media and political discussion and action, not the dark void some would have it to be.

To talk of 'lights of hope' is not to say that parody or kynicism *flood* the media world with light, and we must still be aware of parody's and kynicism's limitations. As I have already said, some viewers will not pick up on the parody, for as Peters (1999: 55) notes, if the mass media is a sower and disseminator of seeds, its practice is wasteful, for it 'lets the seeds fall where they may, not knowing in advance who will be receptive ground.' As bountiful as any crop of parody and kynicism might be, some seeds will not grow. Meanwhile, it would be a mistake to see the 'growth' of parody as always wholly positive. Parody necessarily contains an element of the conservative, I have noted, and to some consumers, this conservatism may prove its key ingredient. Buckingham (1998b), for example, writes of a film-making exercise carried out by secondary school media students. Many created parodies filled with typical media stereotypes, leading Buckingham to note the ambivalence of intent, whereby 'the notion of parody seemed to serve as a useful means of *post hoc* justification: it allowed the students to have their cake and eat it too' (1998b: 84), by joking around with sexist and homophobic stereotypes, yet labeling them as parody. We would be wise, then, to maintain a critical eye on parody, and should by no means assume it is always liberating, even to those who seemingly prove 'receptive ground.'

Furthermore, while parody may help one's resistive reading skills, to be required to resist the media with such constant efforts in the first place shows that the battle is lagging on other fronts. 'The power of viewers to reinterpret meanings,' notes Morley (1997: 125), 'is hardly equivalent to the discursive power of centralized media institutions to construct the texts which the viewer then interprets, and to imagine otherwise is simply foolish.' Or, as Silverstone (1994: 92) writes poetically, while many of us swim through the daily sea of mass media with relative skill, 'it should not be forgotten that in the processes of mass consumption we are swimming in a sea not of our own creation.' Consequently, for all our media savvy, we are still limited to the sea before us, producing a situation where, as Morley (1999) notes:

> people often express cynicism in general (so that 'not believing what you see in the media' is no more than common sense), but then in any particular case they often find themselves pushed back into reliance on the mainstream media's account of anything beyond the realm of their direct personal experience, simply for lack of any alternative perspective.
>
> (Morley 1999: 142)

Parody may help us to look through sitcoms, ads, the news, and all other forms of genre and text, but it will not replace them.

As Mittell observes of *The Simpsons*, it 'does not work to *destroy* generic codes but to *highlight* their cultural circulation and common currency among the show's media-saturated audience' (2001: 25, original emphasis). Thus, neither *The Simpsons* specifically nor parody in general rid us of a faulty media; rather, parody is only ever part of the solution. Depending upon the reader's tastes, this could be seen as a tragic flaw, or as one of its more admirable traits, for ultimately it implicates the audience and points at least one blaming finger their way for *allowing* the object of ridicule its power and existence.

Preaching to the converted

Meanwhile, another objection that could be leveled against *The Simpsons*' parody is one of scope and transformative potential. Numerous interviewees felt *The Simpsons* changed, inflected, and/or informed their reading and interpretive processes, but especially with a largely postgraduate base of subjects, one might question how much they were already highly media literate and adept questioners of discourse. Along with this, therefore, go questions of to whom *The Simpsons*' parody is truly talking, and of to what degree it is merely 'preaching to the converted.' As such, to those who felt *The Simpsons* had marked parodic skills, I passed the questions on to them and asked if they believed *The Simpsons* was just preaching to the converted.

Some viewers felt strongly that *The Simpsons* has a transformative power, so that directly due to such parody, as Sunshine glossed for example, 'there is a kind of innocence that a lot of those older sitcoms can no longer really enjoy.' Reid and Lucia even suggested that the show might work on/for them at a subconscious level, as Reid said, 'I don't think I'm realizing it at times. Sometimes I do, but I'm sure there are times [*laughs*] where I'm not, and things are going right into my head.' Lucia, meanwhile, stated that 'it always increases your awareness, I suppose, but I don't think I'm ever conscious of it being there,' suggesting that, as a result, though, 'I might watch [another] show and take it as more tongue-in-cheek, perhaps, than the authors of it intended it to be,' hence engaging in a form of do-it-yourself parody inspired by *The Simpsons*' critical intertextuality. Clearly, then, some viewers regarded *The Simpsons* as a teacher of sorts, and themselves as students of sorts.

However, others were more ambivalent about the notion of *The Simpsons* actively teaching. As might be expected (and hoped for), many claimed to be already-astute viewers, inclined to read against textual grains without *The Simpsons*' intervention. To Daphne, for instance, 'I don't assume most people watching *The Simpsons* become politically "conscientized." I think that's part of its sophistication: that those people who will recognize it, recognize it, and relate to it on that level.' Todd similarly offered that 'it's probably also true that the people who watch it already think that way,' and Whitney noted that 'I like to think of myself as already quite tuned into that sort of stuff.' Of course, we should hardly expect anyone to profess media illiteracy and utter lack of critical abilities, but all of my viewers backed up their comments elsewhere by displaying ample and impressive media literacy. We would be wise to learn from this and not assume, as do some other accounts of television and teaching (see particularly Postman 1986), that viewers are at point zero on a scale of media literacy to begin with. Media studies' and especially audience studies' catalogue of researchers who have discovered media savvy and literate viewers is large.[3] Many of these studies focus on the young, observing that these television generations, in many cases, 'have an intuitive grasp of the visual equivalent of a semicolon' (Nava and Nava 1992: 173). Are we right, then, to continue talking of 'teaching' when *The Simpsons* may be 'merely' preaching to the converted?

To answer, I want to suggest that there is nothing 'mere' about preaching to the converted. If we look at the metaphor, it describes what most preachers do all of the time. With the exception of missionaries and sidewalk evangelists, the job of most preachers is precisely to deliver sermons, lessons, and guidance to the converted, to the same people who came to church, for instance, last Sunday, and the one before that, and so on. They do so out of the concerted belief that reminders and reinforcement are necessary. Every one of us, a preacher might say, has thousands of opinions, beliefs, convictions, and ideas swimming around in our heads, but they cannot all be at the surface; hence, preaching to the converted involves grasping hold of such ideas and making them loom larger in our minds by bringing them closer to the surface. To conceive of rhetoric as the art of placing notions in others' minds is a misconception, for more often it is the art of activating what is already there. Certainly, as Mann's (1970: 425) deconstruction of how 'consensus' comes to be makes clear, many of our ideas can serve *either* side of a debate. Thus, the true talent lies in bringing ideas to the surface, more than in conversion fantasies.

Surveying research into the influence of media messages in election campaigns, Curran (1996: 146) notes that, in general, it 'reveals that people tend to derive reinforcement from elements of communication which accord with what they think.' However, as Curran points out, to say this is not to say the media has had no effect, for reinforcement is itself a potentially powerful effect (1996: 151). It may be in preaching to the converted, in other words, that the media's true power lies. It is significant, therefore, that several interviewees talked of *The Simpsons'* power as such. 'I think it might reinforce what I think anyway,' noted Niraj, while Angie stated that 'it just agrees with what I already felt. And does bolster my political belief.' Likewise, after claiming the program hardly brought new understandings to light, Leo asked himself of its parody, though, 'Do you remember? Yeah, I think so. Yeah, it's a bit of reinforcement, I think. You just remember.' Perhaps, therefore, we can look to *The Simpsons'* parody as similarly preaching to the converted with continual daily or weekly reminders, if not transformative – as some viewers still maintained it might be – and if only connecting with some viewers, at least reinforcing and, in doing so, exerting considerable influence. Moreover, through taking 'everything' as a joke, it refuses to let its position atrophy, instead revealing ever more minutia to detail what may well be the already over-riding belief in media artifice and trickery.

Avoiding hypocrisy

Ultimately, though, *The Simpsons* is definitively not a preacher, and makes no claim to stand on holy ground, and thus we must avoid carrying the metaphor too far. To illustrate this, and to elaborate upon another key element of its appeal to so many of the interviewees, let us return to Al's comment:

> everyone and everything is fair game. Including themselves. Umm, and I, I think that they're very, very clear that they don't want to [. . .] try and get too . . . a political agenda or a political sort of standing block, because it's, ultimately it's futile, because [*laughs*] who are they to say that? It's a bunch of drawn, yellow people who live in a false world, so who on Earth are they to tell us how to live our lives?

Al clearly objects to entertainment that would patronize him: he does not wish to feel like a member of the congregation being preached to in his living room pew. Moreover, he is wary of a hypocrisy that would lecture him from 'a political sort of standing block' when the speaker itself may be in need of some ridicule. It is relevant, therefore, that most interviewees appreciated, or even found it important, that *The Simpsons* regularly mocks itself. I have focused in depth on the show's parody of the sitcom, ads, and the news, but it also frequently mocks itself as textual, cultural, and political-economic product. Rather than replace and usurp authority and authoritative discourse with their own jests, wise fools always turn some jests inwards, asking for us to laugh at them too, and at their place in and complicity with the king's court. True fools implicate themselves, and here *The Simpsons* is no exception.

To begin with, as we have already seen in Chapter 2, *The Simpsons* works to discredit and fool around with its own apparent genre of sitcom. However, its de(con)struction of its environment, and of the ground upon which it stands, goes further, as both animation and television in general are mocked. 'Cartoons don't have any deep meaning,' explains Homer to Marge in 'Mr Lisa Goes to Washington,' 'They're just stupid drawings that give you a cheap laugh,' and, punctuating the point, Homer then rises from his seat with part of his butt showing, and Bart roars with laughter. Similarly, many other episodes take pot-shots at animation and at *The Simpsons'* style of animation in particular. Likewise, *The Simpsons* expresses great suspicion of television (even if playfully) and thus it couches its own criticisms, its own existence, within the context of an (a) animated (b) television (c) sitcom, all three things that it asks us not to trust. Fool-like, it would have us be suspicious of even the words it speaks.

On the level of textual self-parody, meanwhile, past episodes and constant forms and formulas are frequently placed in the cross-hairs, as illogicalities and requests for suspension of disbelief are highlighted, not covered over. In a more sustained attack, for instance, the episode 'Homer's Enemy' serves largely as metatextual commentary on the impossibility of Homer being rewarded for such blatant incompetence and stupidity. Frank Grimes, a self-made, hardworking orphan joins the nuclear power plant staff, and immediately becomes appalled by Homer's ability to come out on top. Letting us see Homer through Grimes' eyes, the episode tries to 'ground' the cult of Homer somewhat, at the same time as it playfully acknowledges the unreality of Homer's (and the family's) many adventures. Or, in a more explicit example, in the self-reflexive episode, 'Behind the Laughter,' an animated host looks back at recent episodes of *The Simpsons* and notes that they 'increasingly [have] resorted to gimicky premises and nonsensical plots,' at which point they show a clip from 'The Principal and the Pauper,' an episode that was panned by many *Simpsons* fans.

Taking metatextuality to another level, *The Simpsons* frequently comments on its role as a cultural icon. Just as 'Homer's Enemy' pokes fun at the cult of Homer, for example, 'Bart Gets Famous' plays with the cult of Bart, relying as it does on a limited repertoire of catch-phrases. Bart appears on Krusty the Clown's show, and becomes massively popular for one line ('I didn't do it'). Mimicking the fame of Bart in our world, Bart records a song, school children parrot the line, and his face is plastered everywhere. Lisa criticizes him for his repetitiveness and lack of anything else to say, but Bart simply reasons that 'I'm in television now. It's my *job* to be repetitive.' Then, inevitably, Bart's star loses its shine, and the line becomes old hat, but Lisa comforts him in a line rich with irony, saying that 'now you can go back to just being you, instead of a one-dimensional character with a silly catch-phrase.' Humor such as this often requires familiarity with the show, and is thus addressed primarily at fans, but since self-parody aims to destabilize a blind reverential following, it is largely these viewers at whom such parody *should* be aimed: lessons on a text's fallibility need only be directed at those who might consider it infallible in the first place.

At numerous moments, *The Simpsons* makes moves, albeit small, to distance itself from being yet another show-as-cultural-icon, by holding itself up to ridicule and to the criticism that 'this too shall pass.' When, in 'Bart vs. Thanksgiving,' Homer and Bart watch a huge floating Bart go by in a televised parade, and Homer comments that if 'you start building a balloon for every flash-in-the-pan cartoon character, you turn the parade into a farce,' the comment is directed as much at the audience as at *The Simpsons* itself. Likewise, when Lisa can dream, in 'Treehouse of Horror 2,' that Bart is on a poster ordering, 'Get a mammogram, man!', it would seem that *The Simpsons* is aware of itself as over-marketed, and is asking for us to pull back with knowing, ironic detachment. Signs from my audience research certainly point to a positive audience response to this, as many viewers would criticize the show, using the show's own commentary. This connection with audiences is even evident in Glynn's (1996) child audience. Glynn notes that one episode that he showed to a group of 10-year-old boys involved a merchandise-surrounded Bart, saying parodically, 'I base my entire life on Krusty's teachings,' and in the subsequent interview, in response to a question about favorite characters, one boy responded ironically, 'we base our entire lives on Bart's teachings' (Glynn 1996: 76). As such, the text inspires an ironic distance from itself, a distance that both my own and Glynn's research suggests is readily adopted by many viewers.

Being a self-parodying text, though, also involves reflecting upon producers and pay-checks. Thus, a further and favorite part of *The Simpsons*' constant preluding of itself as product is its predilection for attacking its own network. Fox is teased not only as peddling low and titillating entertainment – the tabloid program that 'covers' Homer's sexual harassment case discussed in Chapter 4 is on Fox, for instance – and as backing a pro-Republican news network, but also as being mismanaged and downright evil. In 'Lisa vs. Malibu Stacy,' Lisa forbids watching

Fox because she claims the network owns chemical weapons plants in Syria; in 'Homer the Smithers,' drag race sponsors include Duff Beer, Amalgamated Pornography, Laramie Cigarettes, Cop Stopper Exploding Bullets, and Fox; while in 'Bart Gets an Elephant,' we learn that ivory dealer Mr Blackheart's past professions include whale hunter, seal clubber, and president of the Fox Network. Even Rupert Murdoch has received his fair share of *Simpsons* scorn, depicted as unable to spell his own name when signing a contract with Homer in 'Behind the Laughter,' and introducing himself as a 'billionaire tyrant' in 'Sunday, Cruddy Sunday.' In the latter episode, too, following the closing credits, just as we see the Gracie Films logo of a woman shushing people in a theater, Murdoch yells back at the woman, 'Silence!' Here, the borders of the program are violated to portray both Murdoch's absolute control over Fox's televisual flow and his indomitable will exerted (it is suggested) over all production.

Yet *The Simpsons* is not content just to fire quips and insinuations at Fox. Indeed, one might retort that criticizing Fox for stupidity and mismanagement can merely work back into creating the image of disorganized production that allows Capital to plead innocence and lack of intention to all accusations. The suggestions of immorality (paralleling running Fox to seal-clubbing) counter any network defense of amorality, but *The Simpsons* also occasionally shows how Fox intervenes, or stands to intervene, in the running of the show. For instance, in another closing credit speech, following Homer's hearty endorsement of NBC at the end of 'Marge Simpson in "Screaming Yellow Honkers,"' we hear a gun cock, then Homer reads:

> I'd like to read the following statement, but I do so under . . . my own free will. It has come to my attention that NBC sucks. I apologize for misleading you and urge you to watch as many Fox shows as possible. So, in summary, NBC bad, Fox good.

He then sneaks in 'CBS great,' and we hear multiple shots fired. Albeit in a funny, overdone manner, this episode closes with reflection on *The Simpsons'* lack of complete freedom due to ownership.

This self-parody was greatly valued by my interviewees, and was one of the most commonly discussed aspects of the program's parody. For instance, Carrie's immediate response to me asking if the show had any targets was, 'Oh, definitely! They're always going after Fox: the network they're on.' Niraj, too, stated at the end of his tirade on mainstream television that *The Simpsons* is unique for parodying television's flaws, and for 'blatantly mak[ing] fun of television, or of their very network, Fox.' Leo laughingly offered that 'they take the piss out of everyone, including themselves,' and providing a specific example, Al noted of the 'Kamp Krusty' episode:

Krusty's whole involvement in the whole thing as this sort of corporate sponsorship nightmare who will stick his name on anything . . . which of course, at that point, *The Simpsons* were being very popular and *their* names were on all sorts of t-shirts everywhere – I think is brilliant.

More tellingly, though, was Daphne, who watched the show only occasionally. By and large, she was not a huge fan of television, and spoke at length of it being a venue for endless product endorsement, and yet she appreciated *The Simpsons*, she told me early in the interview, because 'it's self-ironic. I mean, it has, like very few other television programs, a sense of itself *as a product*, and a sense of its own irony [*laughs*].' To viewers such as Daphne, Al, and Niraj in particular, then, *The Simpsons'* self-parody was seen as part, or even the spearhead, of its attack on capitalism, consumerism, and the all-pervasive intertextuality of advertising. This self-parody was mentioned with especially high frequency when interviewees addressed how they felt the program was 'important.' Katy felt it 'important' that '*The Simpsons* often turns itself inside out, and critiques *itself*.' Similarly, attached to the already-quoted comments on how 'everything's a joke,' or on *The Simpsons'* style of comedy being important, by Laura, Carrie, Tina, Janet, Alyson, Sunshine, Daphne, Niraj, Al, Angie, and Leo were tag-ons regarding the show's proclivity to self-parody. For example, Janet said, 'I think it *is* important, because satire is important. It's important to be able to . . . laugh at yourself, and I guess it's quite important that [Murdoch]'s made fun of on the show. Nothing's sacred.'

Rupert Murdoch, it hardly bears reminding (and to put it mildly), has a poor reputation, especially among left-leaning academics, and he is perceived as avarice and cold-hearted multinationalism personified. All of my interviewees knew he owned Fox and hence *The Simpsons*, and many disliked him: as Whitney sneered upon my mention of Murdoch, 'that's a half-hour minidisc in itself.' Thus, they also knew that *The Simpsons* was 'tainted,' hardly the romantic ideal of an independent production made in someone's basement and going out on the BBC at three o'clock in the morning. *The Simpsons* may mock big business, but it is big business itself. All the more important, then, that the show be upfront about its status, and that it mock Fox, Murdoch, and itself as program, so as to avoid wearing a crown of hypocrisy. Furthermore, we should note how often 'the writers' were invoked in discussion, and how rarely the catch-all term 'the producers,' or even 'the makers,' was used, hence drawing a distinction between *The Simpsons* as aesthetic and socio-cultural entity, and *The Simpsons* as political economic product.

This is, of course, a tenuous distinction and would seem to involve a considerable amount of willful blindness. Textually, *The Simpsons* is boldly parodic, but as political-economic unit, it is a flagship not only for one of the world's largest media corporations, but also for licensing, merchandising and, hence, hypercommercialism in general. As such, draped in its fool's court-costume, it offers nothing close to pure rebellion. To some commentators, therefore, it will be seen as a failure, or worse yet a ruse, for there are some who see anything but pure revolution and radicalism as a let-down and a sign of yet more cooption into the hegemonic capitalist-corporate fold. However, such an attitude is, paradoxically, at once too optimistic and too pessimistic. The optimism lies in its belief that revolution with a substantial audience is possible on prime time, mainstream television, whereas the pessimism lies in the complete inability to see what substantial gains are made nevertheless. The notion is thus riddled with tragic flaws, and it is important that we address these flaws if we are to move beyond them and understand the value of a laughing, kynical response.

Ultimately, revolution would not play well in an entertainment show. If, as my interviewees told me, a large part of 'the *Simpsons* attitude' and ethos is that everything can be laughed at, and if the show is admired for not trying to be 'too clever,' as Al noted, or not trying 'too hard,' as Lucia stated, the teacher-like, preachy, self-righteous tone required for revolution might indeed prove revolting. Further explaining how *The Simpsons* litmus test works for her, Alyson said, 'The thing I love about [*The Simpsons*] is that it makes fun of everything, and nothing is sacred, and that's great [. . .] but it irritates the Hell out of me when people take things *too* seriously. Just chill a bit.' Give her a sanctimonious text, Alyson thereby suggests, and she will be totally uninterested. Or, as Al said with considerable approval, 'I mean, it's not sort of fighting for a revolution, it's not trying to lead any kind of revolution against anybody . . . which I think some people mistake television as being a tool for, so I think, eh, eh, it's certainly the perfect embodiment of what television is.' If the revolution will be televised, Al suggested he might not watch. So the program might be 'not entirely or fully subversive,' as Laura offered, but by keeping its messages light, it avoids the entertainment Scylla and Charybdis of patronizing hypocrisy and of simply not entertaining anyone, while simultaneously offering a degree of transparency in its self-parody.

Whither the radical?

It is a pity that, to many media and cultural studies commentators, the degree to which a program may be regarded as worthwhile and/or politically savvy is perennially marked on a scale of radicalism and revolution, where anything less than a perfect ten equates to failure. Nevertheless, since this scaling system exists, and since the show's viewers have clearly not given it a ten, in order to suggest that *The Simpsons* in particular, and parody in general, have much to offer us, we need to take apart the scale. To do so, let us start with the conundrum that whereas radicalism and revolution require numbers, and whereas entertainment programming, and particularly comedy, attract considerably more viewers than do factual programming, many viewers do not appreciate being patronized or preached to. Moreover, for most programs to reach a substantial audience these days, requires the backing at some level of commercial television,[4] a television system that is part of the problem and part of what must be revolted against. Thus, to deal with such forces involves a Faustian bargain of sorts that could only lead one's preaching of radicalism to be seen as deeply hypocritical and tainted. And this, of course, assumes that the radical show has not already been axed by angry producers and advertisers. 'Guerrilla media' groups, some Internet sites, pirate radio, and other alternative media work toward circumventing this conundrum, often with highly creative and equally successful initiatives (see Atton 2002; Downing 2001; P. M. Lewis 1989). Meanwhile, however, we are still left with a mainstream media that blankets the majority of delivery systems worldwide and, through continuous mergers and cooperative ventures (see Bagdikian 2004; Herman and McChesney 1997), is gaining in power, scope, and coverage.

With the rules of mainstream media's game prohibiting true radicalism or revolution, we must turn our critical attention to instances of the 'not entirely or fully subversive,' or to what James C. Scott (1985) has called 'everyday resistance.' Studying poor, indentured laborers among the Sedaka in Malaysia, Scott begins by noting both the ruling powers' total control and the extreme unlikelihood of revolution. 'All the more reason, then,' he argues:

> to respect, if not celebrate, the weapons of the weak. All the more reason to see in the tenacity of self-preservation – in ridicule, in truculence, in irony, in petty acts of noncompliance, in foot dragging, in dissimulation, in resistant mutuality, in the disbelief in elite homilies, in the steady, grinding efforts to hold one's own against overwhelming odds – a spirit and practice that prevents the worst and promises something better.
>
> (Scott 1985: 350)

Scott is careful not to romanticize these 'weapons of the weak,' or to regard them as ever 'enough,' but at the same time puts the case that, 'Just as peasants [. . .] do not simply vacillate between blind submission and homicidal rage, neither do they move directly from ideological complicity to strident class-consciousness' (Scott 1985: 304), and thus is keen to point out that resistance can occur in thought as well as in actions. Moreover, he points out, one can lead to the other, reasoning that, 'Acts born of intentions circle back, as it were, to influence consciousness and hence subsequent intentions and acts. Thus, acts of resistance and thoughts about (or the meaning of) resistance are in *constant* communication – in constant dialogue' (Scott 1985: 38, original emphasis). Scott, in other words, reopens the scales of radicalism, allowing that any point along the scale may be significant, and noting that what may look like low levels at one point in time, could grow to higher levels.

In media and cultural studies, Scott's work is echoed particularly by many studies of fandom. Both Jenkins (1988, 1992) and Penley (1997), for instance, examine the resistance of fan fiction writers of traditional gender roles, institutionally proscribed ways of relating to texts, and commercial media hegemony in general. Jenkins notes that:

> Nobody regards these fan activities as a magical cure for the social ills of post-industrial capitalism. They are no substitution for meaningful change, but they can be used effectively to build popular support for such change, to challenge the power of the culture industry to construct the common sense of a mass society, and to restore a much-needed excitement to the struggle against subordination.
>
> (Jenkins 1988: 104)

Grossberg (1992: 65), too, states that 'Fandom is, at least potentially, the site of optimism, invigoration and passion which are necessary conditions for any struggle to change the conditions of one's life.' In effect, these writers pose a vital point that is missed by commentary from cynics such as Philo and Miller (1998: 8), to whom unless the social structure is being radically augmented, all we are hearing is 'the gallows humor of the politically impotent.' The point is that levity, humor, and the pleasures of entertainment are necessary to many as they fight the long, uphill battle of resistance.

Critiques such as Philo and Miller (1998) also err in predetermining that when radicalism and conservatism are both present, conservatism will always win out. This is perhaps the most common complaint leveled at entertainment, comedy, and parody. Take, for instance, Comolli and Narboni's (1993) dictum that 'Economic/political and formal action have to be indissolubly wedded,' or else 'The whole thing is a closed circuit, endlessly repeating the same illusion' (1993: 47). Without explaining *how*, therefore, Comolli and Narboni (1993) determine subversion can work only if no trace element of conservatism is present. Similarly, Matheson (2001: 118) argues that '*The Simpsons* does not promote anything, because its humor works by putting forward positions only in order to undercut them.' Wallace, too, charges the show with nihilism and labels it an opiate, not a catalyst for change (2001: 251), because, ultimately, 'the traditional social order endures' (2001: 246), ensuring that 'all opposition is absorbed, and criticism is co-opted' (2001: 248). Because *The Simpsons* will, for instance, also make fun of Lisa's leftist politics at times, and thus laughs not only at high and mighty institutions, Matheson (2001) and Wallace (2001) write it off as unsuccessful.

These criticisms easily connect with the long line of criticism of carnival as serving the purposes of the dominant powers, and thus constraining and containing, not liberating, and as deflecting energies, and reifying the way things are (see Purdie

1993: 126 in particular). What this critique overlooks, though, and as Stam (1989) points out, is the pervasiveness of dialogism. As the Bakhtin school, and deconstructive critics (see Derrida 1976) have all argued in their own ways, texts can disagree with themselves, and can contain warring and contradicting discourses. Thus, I agree with Stam's (1989) assessment that 'the left badly needs analytical categories, such as those of Bakhtin, which allow for the fact that a given utterance or discourse can be progressive and regressive *at the same time*' (Stam 1989: 222, original emphasis). Parody, as Harries dubs it, can be 'conservative transgression' (2000: 120), managing conservatism and transgression concurrently, and it is a pure leap of misguided logic to assume conservatism will always win out and overpower when the two are found together. For, equally possible, as Lovell observes, is that 'The carnival may escape control' (1986: 165).

Lipsitz (1990) argues that even small shreds in otherwise overwhelmingly conservative texts may prove to be the shreds that viewers take with them. Drawing on Jameson's (1979) observation that to resolve outstanding problems, the culture industry must first open them up, hence leaving open the inherent risk of subversion, Lipsitz focuses on these gaps, or 'ruptures' as he calls them. Narrative closure, he argues, 'is not so easy to achieve. It is difficult to soothe anxieties without first aggravating them, and impossible to predict in any given case whether the emotional appeal of closure will silence the questions and criticisms' (Lipsitz 1990: 93). Lipsitz illustrates how numerous media texts 'open wounds' that viewers may possess, and he cites years of teaching experience in which students spoke again and again of how popular texts 'unleashed the memories and experiences suppressed by the dominant rhetoric of their private and public lives' (1990: xiii). Lipsitz quotes an old saying that 'You can hide the fire, but what you gonna do with the smoke?' (1990: 96).

Of course, there are no absolutes or definites in reading. Some viewers will detect no subversion (neither fire, nor smoke) and will read obliviously, or as Richard put it, 'a lot of people watch it, laugh at it, and then go back to watching repeats of *Gilligan's Island*.' The other side of preaching to the converted is that perhaps only the congregation hear what is being said. I cannot say for certain how universal or peculiar these readings of *The Simpsons* are. Undoubtedly, though, other viewers and other interpretive communities are reading *The Simpsons* in other ways. Even though the text often screams its parody, some of these ways will be in no or little way parodic; similarly, while the text makes staunchly conservative readings difficult, some of these interpretive communities may even be more powerfully hegemonic and conservative. However, I have no pretensions to speak the universal, or to use this audience research to propose a grand, all-encompassing conclusion. As Buckingham states:

> Qualitative research [. . .] does not always lead to neat conclusions. In some
> respects, this is not its aim. In attempting to represent and analyse the

> complexity of audience engagements with the media, such research often seeks
> precisely to challenge the easy generalisations that are sometimes seen to
> constitute research 'findings.'
>
> (Buckingham 2000: 201)

If my audience research challenges an easy generalization, it is that subversion always drowns in the commercial media.

I have characterized parody as 'fool-like,' and both the close textual work of Part II, and the ways in which many of my interviewees described *The Simpsons*, fits this picture. Of the king's court, *The Simpsons* as fool lives in the realm of King Murdoch. There, it continually mocks the pomp and artifice it sees around it, and yet it is never completely subversive, for to be so would be to risk either termination, and/or charges of patronization and/or hypocrisy. Ultimately, then, it does not deal in complete answers or solutions. Nor does it deal in dubious claims to being an authority itself; instead, it stands at once inside and outside power, using, as Hutcheon (1988: 20) notes of successful parody, 'the invasive culture industry to challenge its own commodification processes from within,' and if it is to work, it counts on its audience. As fool, it must entertain, and leave active resistance to its listeners, for while it is willing, at times caustically, at times gently, to point with derisive laughter at illogicalities, if it is to stay relevant, funny, and in the king's court, it must rely on the audience to carry that resistance further. And the fool is loved because it is funny but smart, smart but funny, and although 'To include irony and play is *never* necessarily to exclude seriousness and purpose' (Hutcheon 1988: 27, original emphasis), it tries to avoid being too serious, and is a laughing teacher and critic of our media surroundings.

CONCLUSION

THROUGH USING THE EXAMPLE OF *THE SIMPSONS*, I have shown how, as a critical intertextuality, parody employs a joking, laughing, and hence 'irrational' language and tone, but in doing so, still manages to foster a public sphere. The talk that surrounds shows such as *The Simpsons* includes mockery and discussion of prevalent media genres and of their role in our lives. This at times implicitly acknowledges that much of the media is failing to create a public sphere, but the talk *about* that failure builds its own public sphere. Albeit in a small, unfinished, and often conflicted form, parody can therefore contribute to that which political economists claim is dying or dead on serious television. The fact that it is not purely rational, following what has been said of kynicism, may actually prove a positive, redeeming, and empowering aspect of parody, rather than a damning one. Comedy, as Bakhtin (1981, 1984, 1986) argues, helps make its targets less distant and less intimidating, and as Richard Dyer (1992: 2) states, in general, part of entertainment's 'meaning is anti-seriousness, against coming on heavy about things.' A humorless, totally rational existence may appeal to some, but to many, rationality can often tax too heavily, and parody finds a way to maintain critique while staying 'light.' 'Our established models of the public sphere are deeply rooted in a commitment to rational argument,' notes Graham Murdock (1999: 14), 'But images do not walk in straight lines. They do not wait to take turns. They work by association, detonating a collision of connotations. They argue by simultaneity, not sequence.' To some, this might suggest the inappropriateness of television to fostering a public sphere, but we should instead see it as signalling the irrelevance of Habermas' rationality stipulation. Moreover, since parody works in ways that serious programming cannot, it is not only a viable alternative or 'substitute': rather, it also complements serious programming.

Hartley (1999: 119) notes a tradition within television studies that is deeply pessimistic about the political potential of the popular media, often sneeringly reducing 'popularity' to 'populism,' but it is time that we move beyond this unhelpful barrier. We have lost too many years of research, and our discussion of the public sphere has progressed too sluggishly, due to a dogged refusal by some to look toward entertainment and comedy as public spheres. Certainly, if the news is failing as spectacularly as many critics tell us it is at teaching and extending citizenship, surely we should be looking to other genres that might be stemming the tide. Moreover, since parody is an inherently intertextual form, working on and through its targets, and bringing other genres into a public forum of sorts, its criticisms hold great potential to inflect and infect the ways in which we use, make sense of, and interpret television as a whole, and its many genres. Instead, then, of following Bourdieu (1998: 10) by seeing television wholly as 'a serious danger for all the various areas of cultural production – for art, for literature, for science, for philosophy, and for law [. . .] and no less of a threat to political life and democracy itself,' we should also look to the parts of it that are trying to teach of, to help us defend against, and to *rehabilitate* cultural production, political life, and democracy.

Parody's and television's development of kynicism, public pedagogy and the public sphere is, admittedly, a best case scenario. The success of critical intertextuality is never automatic, for not only must its critique actually be probing and insightful, but also, if it is to tap into its full potential, it requires a supportive interpretive community to carry on its work. Thus, to talk of parody and television as capable of such subversion or transgression is, to a certain degree, to adopt an optimistic view. However, as I have shown, this is neither blind nor naive optimism, and if it seems so, this is in large part because television studies can often work with an overwhelming pessimism that makes any lights of hope offend the critic's eyes. Gitlin's (1994) *Inside Prime Time* is illustrative here, as he allows of network television that 'the system that cranks out mind candy occasionally proves hospitable to something else, while at the same time betraying its limits,' with 'the exceptions reveal[ing] the rules' and only at 'the end of a chain of *ifs*' (1994: 273, original emphasis). To Gitlin, any good show only proves how bad everything else – and television in general – is. Ultimately, though, such reasoning and pessimism runs up against the obstacle of intertextuality.

If texts never talked to one another, and went about their business by themselves; if we consumed them as solitary units; and if our discussion of texts never brought them together, then the lone existence of a few critical exceptions to the rule of televisual hegemonic status quo would indeed be an altogether depressing sight. However, this is a chain of impossible ifs, for texts *do* talk to each other, for the very nature of textuality is intertextuality, while any one text is always a plethora of other texts in action. Textual meanings congregate, bump into, and overrule one another, disagreeing, agreeing, and jostling for power. Amidst this general chaos of textual interaction, we can trace the trajectories of critical intertextuality, of texts that shoot at and through other texts, deliberately trying to offset other meanings. Much then, as the one child with chickenpox in a room of five hundred is cause for concern, parody as a critical intertextuality can play a powerful role as 'infector.' To make sense of parody, therefore, we need to look not only to the vast room full of conservative texts, but also to parody's intertextual potential. Reading through intertextuality, what becomes important are the passages of our journey, not so much the individual texts stopped at along the way.

It may seem peculiarly suspicious that a conservative media mainstream would *allow* such textual disturbances to exist. First, though, the media system is nowhere near as totally organized, coherent, and unified in either belief or action as some crude accounts of 'The Media' suggest. Second, because hegemony works by suggestion, not outright coercion, its level of control of the world of semiosis is always loose enough to allow counter-hegemonic discourse. Third, since parody's challenges and criticisms are semiotic and hence indirect, not structural and direct, network heads are quite likely to arrogantly underestimate their effects, regarding semiotic and intertextual criticism as inconsequential (as do some media scholars). Fourth, good parody can ultimately use the structure of commercial television against itself. Network heads play what sells, and thus, over time, they can become beholden to texts and artists that bring in audiences, regardless of their messages. Here, *The Simpsons* is an excellent example, as not only did producer James Brooks manage to parlay his name currency in the industry into a 'no notes' policy in the show's contract with Fox, but also, as the show has aged, and realized Fox's reliance on the money and cultural caché it brings in, it has been able to push more boundaries in terms of ridiculing Fox and television generally.

At the end of season eleven's 'Missionary Impossible,' Rupert Murdoch is depicted soliciting donations in a telethon to keep Fox afloat, even though, we are told, 'Fox makes a fortune from advertising.' Bart calls to donate $10,000, and, overjoyed, Murdoch exclaims that Bart has 'saved' his network, to which Bart responds, 'Wouldn't be the first time.' Here, *The Simpsons*' writers express a confidence in their security within the Murdoch empire. The staff prove themselves willing *and able* to criticize the network, as is also evident in Bart's blackboard line in 'The Trouble with Trillions' – aired when the cast were engaged in a much-publicized battle for higher pay – that 'I will not demand what I'm worth.' Much established wisdom and empirical work may therefore correctly state that a sitcom writer is often reduced to 'a jobbing writer rather than an inspired creative talent'

(P. Taylor 1988: 185–6), with his or her scripts pruned and watered down by producers (see Gitlin 1994; Mayerle 1994; Taylor 1988), and Feuer (2001: 70) points out that US sitcoms often weaken ideologically from initially strong first seasons, but *The Simpsons'* writers and itself as a show have *gained* power with time. Clearly, this power is contingent upon initial success, and thus this is a privilege that is never assured, and that must be worked toward, but it illustrates that fools can use their kings as much as kings use their fools.

However, if *The Simpsons* is often successful in realizing parody's potential, questions still linger with regards to how successful *other* parodies have been. Certainly, while writing this book, I have often been challenged to rethink its premise when faced with some of television's more spectacularly poor parody. *The Simpsons*, though, is still in good company, and while many of my interviewees ranked it in the upper echelons of parody, most expressed great affection and respect for numerous other parodies, including *King of the Hill*, *Kids in the Hall*, *Malcolm in the Middle*, *The Larry Sanders Show*, *Family Guy*, *The Day Today*, *Brasseye*, *The Dave Letterman Show*, *Buffy the Vampire Slayer*, *South Park*, *Ally McBeal*, *Seinfeld*, *Roseanne*, *Futurama*, and *Monty Python's Flying Circus*. Several interviewees, too, saw Chris Morris' fantastic British news parodies, *The Day Today* and *Brasseye*, or the increasingly edgy *South Park*, as outclassing *The Simpsons*.

Moreover, while my interviews were conducted before the meteoric ascendency in the United States of *The Daily Show with Jon Stewart*, news parody has rarely come better than Comedy Central's nightly show, and the supportive interpretive community and fan following that *The Daily Show* has attracted, particularly in the run-up to the United States' 2004 Presidential Election, arguably eclipses anything *The Simpsons* has mustered. For a while, much discussion of the news in several pockets of American society was often introduced by, 'Did you see on *The Daily Show* last night, . . . ?' But, as host Jon Stewart told *Entertainment Weekly*:

> I think a lot of the response to our show is people sending messages. You know, we won the TV Critics' Association award for Outstanding Achievement in News and Information. That was far more about saying "f___ you" to [other news programs] than about praising us.
>
> (*Entertainment Weekly* 2004: 48)

In other words, while some viewers have learnt to watch sitcoms, ads, and the news with *The Simpsons*, many viewers also watch the news with Jon Stewart. As Stewart notes in his reflection upon his show's critical acclaim, watching parody and talking about it are ways of watching and talking about television more generally. Stewart has been explicit, both on and off *The Daily Show*, about his utter disappointment with American media, and in good parodic fashion, his show has inspired considerable public discussion, analysis, and critique of this media. In doing so, it has also shown the powers of parody to popularize media critique, and hence it shows that *The Simpsons* is by no means alone as parodic fool.

Television is open to attack, and while the nature of parody's ensuing attacks may at times seem wholly good-natured and inconsequential, successful parody can channel the powers of intertextuality to inspire a wholesale reassessment and reinterpretation of any of television's genres and their accompanying ideologies. While this should therefore change the ways in which we regard parody, comedy, and entertainment as contributing to a public sphere, and as both broadcasting and provoking critical discussion of television's construction of reality, it also demands a reappraisal of the role and nature of textuality. Texts do not just work by themselves, in a vacuum, conducting a solitary discussion with their audiences. Rather, texts and texts, texts and audiences, are constantly in dialogue, responding to, predicting, interrupting, ridiculing, supporting, or undercutting each other's messages. Therefore, to continue to examine texts and their effects, power, or other qualities, particularly in the hyper-intertextual environment of television, more effort is required to study the intertextual passages between texts, other texts, and audiences, so that our analysis can include an understanding not only of what or how we are watching, but also of what we watch *with*.

APPENDIX: INTERVIEWEE INFORMATION

Pseudonym	Gender	Age	Nationality	Education*
Al	Male	28	English-Canadian	Masters
Alyson	Female	27	American	Masters student
Angie	Female	27	Danish-Canadian	Masters student
Carrie	Female	26	American	Masters student
Charlie	Male	27	Canadian	Bachelors
and Sunshine	Female	26	Canadian	Bachelors
Cleo	Female	31	Greek-Canadian	Masters
Daphne	Female	33	South African	PhD student
Eric	Male	33	Australian	PhD
Harold	Male	35	American	PhD student
Janet	Female	22	Australian	Bachelors
and Ryan	Male	29	Scottish	Masters
Jesse	Male	26	Australian	PhD student
and Susan	Female	27	Australian	Masters student
Joanne	Female	26	Canadian	Bachelors
Judy	Female	30	South African	PhD student
Katy	Female	38	Canadian	Masters student
Laura	Female	27	Canadian	PhD student
Leo	Male	29	Australian	Masters
Ling	Female	22	Canadian	Masters student
Lucia	Female	23	American	Masters student
Mary	Female	26	Canadian	Masters student

Niraj	Male	28	American	Masters student
Reid	Male	28	Canadian	Bachelors
Rhys	Male	25	Canadian	PhD student
Richard	Male	28	Australian	PhD student
Sonia	Female	26	Canadian	Masters student
Sujata	Female	27	Canadian	Masters student
Thanos	Male	31	Greek	PhD student
and Vivi	Female	33	Greek	PhD student
Tina	Female	23	American	Masters student
Todd	Male	27	Australian	PhD student
Wei	Female	29	Singaporean	PhD student
Whitney	Male	25	English	Masters
Zach	Male	27	South African	Masters

Note: * Highest degree earned, or stage of education.

NOTES

Introduction

1   The obvious English exception is *The Royle Family*, a show in which *all* the family do is watch television.

1 Intertextuality and the study of texts

1   Bakhtin scholars have long argued over whether Volosinov and Medvedev were no more than Bakhtinian pen-names. I do not wish to join the debate here. However, based on the arguments put forward by Hirschkop (1999) to suggest particularly Volosinov was a real, publishing person, I will refer to Bakhtin, Volosinov, and Medvedev separately, or together as the Bakhtin circle, with the proviso that I may be writing of the one man.
2   Taking a different approach, based on the study of metaphor, linguists Lakoff and Johnson (1980) also suggest that the foundation of understanding is the metaphor or analogy, and that any object or concept is only conceived of in relation to other already-known objects or concepts.
3   Lotman (1977) conceives of this process as a 'creolization,' suggesting that 'in the process of assimilation the author's language is more often distorted and creolized with languages already in the arsenal of the reader's consciousness' (1977: 25).
4   Bennett and Woollacott (1987) propose the hyphenated form for 'inter-textuality', for:

> whereas Kristeva's concept of *intertextuality* refers to the system of references to other texts which can be discerned within the internal composition of a specific individual text, we intend the concept of *inter-textuality* to refer to the social organisation of the relations between texts within specific conditions of reading.
>
> (Bennett and Woollacott 1987: 44–5, original emphasis)

However, as both definitions are largely commensurate with each other, and as Kristeva herself often uses 'intertextuality' to refer to what Bennett and Woollacott dub 'inter-textuality,' I will continue to use the unhyphenated form.

5 Bakhtin (1981: 46) even saw this dialogism thrive *within* the text, as author and characters talk to each other.

6 For a comprehensive overview of this history and its assumptions, see Altman (1999).

7 Indeed, Hermes' (1995) *Reading Women's Magazines* has proven that genres can be studied through their readers (see also Lindlof et al. 1998), without necessarily engaging in any content or textual analysis.

8 As Rebecca Tushnet (1997) argues, there are enough grounds to declare that texts and their characters become the property of their consumers, even in a legal sense.

2 Domesticom parody, genre, and critical intertextuality

1 Between 1984–5 and 1994–5, for instance, 70 of the 102 Nielsen top 10 programs were sitcoms (Staiger 2000: 26).

2 See, for instance, Carter (1995), Feuer (1987), Haralovich (1988), Holbert et al. (2003), Lipsitz (1988), Rowe (1994), and Weispfenning (2003).

3 Perhaps best illustrated by English sitcom *The Royle Family*, in which the television and camera offer themselves as mirror, reflecting one side (audience) in the other (characters sitting in front of the television).

4 Television is not *just* domestic, though, as McCarthy's (2001) study of 'ambient television' renders clear.

5 Both Jhally and Lewis' (1992) and Means Coleman's (2000) studies of *Cosby* audiences suggest that many black viewers (and, no doubt, some white) saw the show as radical and progressive, but with Jhally and Lewis also illustrating how many white audiences saw the show as validating the supposed fairness and color-blindness of the American Dream, and with M.C. Miller's (1988) discussion of the show's hypercommercialism, it is hard to see the show as more than a neoconservative idyll with a radical, progressive subculture attached.

6 For a British variant, see Saffron as parental child in *Absolutely Fabulous*.

7 *Married . . . with Children* attacked notions of the perfectly happy suburban nuclear family, but the show also actively reveled in a misogyny that can in no way be regarded as dissenting against the sitcom's sexist history.

8 *The Simpsons* has provoked the ire of several governments and nationals in its time, most notably from the Australian government following 'Bart vs. Australia' (see Beard 2004), and, more recently, from the city of Rio in the form of a lawsuit for lost tourist revenue following 'Blame it on Lisa' (see Bellos 2002). Nevertheless, equally yet oppositely, my lone Scottish interviewee's favorite character was Groundskeeper Willie; Indian-Canadian interviewee Sujata loved Apu, the Indian storekeeper; and several Australian interviewees listed the Australia episode as their favorite.

9 Harry Shearer and Hank Azaria, for example, each voice over 40 characters.

3 The logic of television and ad parody

1 See, for instance, Berger (2004), Bordo (1993), G. Dyer (1982), Ewen (1976), Jhally (1987), Kilbourne (1999), Klein (2002), McAllister (1996), Myers (1986), Nava et al. (1997), Preston (1994), and Williamson (1978).

2 For more on what high-level involvement entails, see Barker and Brooks (1998) on 'high investors' and Harrington and Bielby (1996) and Hills (2002) on fan cultures.

3 See Bellamy and Walker (1996) and Perse (1998) for statistics and analysis of remote control use, and its effects on television viewing.

4 News parody and the public sphere

1 See Buckingham (2000), Curran (1991), Dahlgren (1995), Fraser (1987), Habermas (1997), Hartley (1996), Peters (1993), Schudson (1992), Serra (2000), and Stallybrass and White (1986).
2 See particularly Altheide and Snow (1991), Bagdikian (2004), W. L. Bennett (1988), Diamond (1982), Downie and Kaiser (2002), Herman and Chomsky (1988), McChesney (2004), McManus (1994), and Postman and Powers (1992).
3 Indeed, in his prologue to Bakhtin's (1984) *Rabelais and his World*, Michael Holquist recounts how the Soviet Union's Commissar of Enlightenment until 1933, Anatoly Lunacharsky, set up a commission to study satiric and parodic genres, and deemed them 'safe' to the state, due to the 'wine barrel' argument (Bakhtin 1984: xviii). For other post-1444 versions of this argument, see particularly Eco (1984), Linstead (1988), and Purdie (1993).

5 Parody and/as interpretive community

1 For further information on interviewees, see Appendix.
2 Although, as Bhavnani argues, changing names runs the risk of stereotyping by name or origin of name (1991: 94–5), I found the alternative of numbering or coding interviewees rather dehumanizing and awkward to read.
3 The interviewees' critical capacities and vocabulary simultaneously proved a boon to the interviews, ensuring that in many cases, they and I spoke the same language. Much sociological research requires considerable translation out of academic-speak in the interview, and translation into academic-speak in the writing up. By contrast, I felt little need to translate and could instead be fairly direct. Translation pulls words away from their speaker and toward their translator, and while, as editor and commentator, I am still a translator of sorts (Clifford and Marcus 1986), my interviewees' use of an 'academicized' register has allowed me to bend, augment, and possess their accounts less than if we had spoken 'different' languages. It also allowed them more power in the interview, for they were on closer par with me.

6 'The *Simpsons* attitude'

1 Sloterdijk (1987) makes a strong case that the rise to power and the extremes of National Socialism and Adolf Hitler were enabled by a pervasive cynicism in post-World War I Germany.
2 According to legend, for instance, Diogenes was once sought out by Alexander of Macedonia on a sunny day. Attempting an act of magnanimity, Alexander offered to grant any wish of Diogenes. The philosopher replied simply but angrily, 'Stop blocking my sun!' (Sloterdijk 1987: 160).
3 See, for instance, Barnhurst (1998), Buckingham (1987, 1998b, 2000), Fiske (1989c), Gillespie (1995), Lembo (2000), McRobbie (1996), Nava and Nava (1992), Schrøder (1997), Seiter (1993), and Willis (1990).
4 Public broadcasting occasionally presents a viable alternative, but as Ang (1991) argues, all-too-often it suffers either from adopting wholesale the values of commercial television and thus being an alternative only in name and ownership, or from addressing its viewers with a patronizing tone that loses many of them (Ang 1996: 31). Also, while *The Simpsons* is broadcast on public broadcasting channels in many countries, the coffers of commercial television are still responsible for its existence and availability for international sale.

BIBLIOGRAPHY

Abercrombie, Nicholas and Longhurst, Brian (1998) *Audiences: A Sociological Theory of Performance and Imagination*, London: Sage.

Adorno, Theodor (1991) *The Culture Industry: Selected Essays on Mass Culture*, ed. J. M. Bernstein, London: Routledge.

Alasuutari, Pertti (1999) 'Introduction: Three Phases of Reception Studies,' in Alasuutari (ed.) *Rethinking the Media Audience: The New Agenda*, London: Sage, 1–21.

Alberti, John (ed.) (2004) *Leaving Springfield: The Simpsons and the Possibility of Oppositional Culture*, Detroit, MI: Wayne State University Press.

Allen, Irving Lewis (1982) 'Talking about Media Experiences: Everyday Life as Popular Culture,' *Journal of Popular Culture* 16.3, 106–15.

Alters, Diane (2003) '"We Hardly Watch that Rude, Crude Show": Class and Taste in *The Simpsons*,' in Carol A. Stabile and Mark Harrison (eds) *Prime Time Animation: Television Animation and American Culture*, London: Routledge, 165–84.

Altheide, David and Snow, Robert (1991) *Media Worlds in the Postjournalism Era*, New York: Aldine de Gruyter.

Althusser, Louis (1971) 'Ideology and Ideological State Apparatuses,' in *Lenin and Philosophy and Other Essays*, trans. Ben Brewster, New York: Monthly Review, 127–86.

Altman, Rick (1986) 'Television/Sound,' in Tania Modleski (ed.) *Studies in Entertainment: Critical Approaches to Mass Culture*, Bloomington, IN: Indiana University Press, 39–54.

—— (1999) *Film/Genre*, London: British Film Institute (BFI).

Ang, Ien (1985) *Watching Dallas: Soap Opera and the Melodramatic Imagination*, trans. Della Couling, London: Methuen.

—— (1991) *Desperately Seeking the Audience*, London: Routledge.

—— (1994) 'In the Realm of Uncertainty: The Global Village and Capitalist Postmodernity,' in

David Crowley and David Mitchell (eds) *Communication Theory Today*, Cambridge: Polity, 193–213.

—— (1996) *Living Room Wars: Rethinking Media Audiences for a Postmodern World*, London: Routledge.

Appadurai, Arjun (1995) 'Disjuncture and Difference in the Global Cultural Economy,' in Mike Featherstone (ed.) *Global Culture: Nationalism, Globalization and Modernity*, London: Sage, 295–310.

Arnold, David L. G. (2001) '"And the Rest Writes Itself": Roland Barthes Watches *The Simpsons*,' in William Irwin, Mark T. Conard, and Aeon J. Skoble (eds) *The Simpsons and Philosophy: The D'Oh! of Homer*, Chicago: Open Court, 252–68.

—— (2004) '"Use a Pen, Sideshow Bob": *The Simpsons* and the Threat of High Culture,' in John Alberti (ed.) *Leaving Springfield: The Simpsons and the Possibility of Oppositional Culture*, Detroit, MI: Wayne State University Press, 1–28.

Arnold, Matthew (1978) 'Culture and Anarchy,' in *Selected Poems and Prose*, London: J. M. Dent and Sons, 212–26.

Attallah, Paul (1984) 'The Unworthy Discourse: Situation Comedy in Television,' in Willard D. Rowland, Jr. and Bruce Watkins (eds) *Interpreting Television: Current Research Perspectives*, London: Sage, 222–49.

Atton, Chris (2002) *Alternative Media*, London: Sage.

Bagdikian, Ben (2004) *The New Media Monopoly*, Boston, MA: Beacon Press.

Bakhtin, Mikhail Mikhailovich (1981) *The Dialogic Imagination*, trans. Caryl Emerson and Michael Holquist, ed. Michael Holquist, Austin, TX: University of Texas Press.

—— (1984) *Rabelais and his World*, trans. Hélène Iswolsky, Cambridge, MA: MIT Press.

—— (1986) *Speech Genres and Other Late Essays*, trans. Vern W. McGee, eds Caryl Emerson and Michael Holquist, Austin, TX: University of Texas Press.

Balnaves, Mark, Donald, James, and Donald, Stephanie Hemelryk (2001) *The Penguin Atlas of Media and Information*, Harmondsworth: Penguin.

Bandura, Albert (1971) 'Influence of Models' Reinforcement Contingencies on the Acquisition of Imitative Responses,' in Bandura (ed.) *Psychological Modeling: Conflicting Theories*, Aldine Atherton: New York, 112–27.

Barker, Martin (2000) *From Antz to Titanic: Reinventing Film Analysis*, London: Pluto.

Barker, Martin and Brooks, Kate (1998) *Knowing Audiences: Judge Dredd, its Friends, Fans and Foes*, Luton: University of Luton Press.

Barker, Martin, Arthurs, Jane, and Harindranath, Ramaswami (2001) *The Crash Controversy: Censorship Campaigns and Film Reception*, London: Wallflower.

Barnhurst, Kevin G. (1998) 'Politics in the Fine Meshes: Young Citizens, Power and Media,' *Media, Culture and Society* 20.2, 201–18.

Barthes, Roland (1973) *Mythologies*, trans. Annette Lavers, St. Albans: Paladin.

—— (1990) *S/Z*, trans. Richard Miller, Oxford: Basil Blackwell.

—— (1995) *The Pleasure of the Text*, trans. Richard Miller, New York: Hill and Wang.

Baudrillard, Jean (1983a) *In the Shadow of the Silent Majorities or, The End of the Social and Other Essays*, trans. Paul Foss, John Johnston, and Paul Patton, New York: Semiotext(e).

—— (1983b) *Simulations*, trans. Paul Foss, Paul Patton, and Philip Beitchman, New York: Semiotext(e).

Bausinger, Herman (1984) 'Media, Technology and Everyday Life,' *Media, Culture and Society* 6.4, 343–51.

Bazalgette, Carey (1997) 'An Agenda for the Second Phase of Media Literacy Development,' in Robert Kubey (ed.) *Media Literacy in the Information Age: Current Perspectives*, New Brunswick, NJ: Transaction, 69–78.

BBC (2004) 'Archbishop "May Star in Simpsons,"' June 20. Available: <http://news.bbc.co.uk/1/hi/entertainment/tv_and_radio/3823541.stm> (accessed November 17, 2004).

Beard, Duncan Stuart (2004) 'Local Satire with a Global Reach: Ethnic Stereotyping and Cross-Cultural Conflicts in *The Simpsons*,' in John Alberti (ed.) *Leaving Springfield: The Simpsons and the Possibility of Oppositional Culture*, Detroit, MI: Wayne State University Press, 273–91.

Bell, Diane (1983) *Daughters of the Dreaming*, North Sydney: McPhee Gribble / George Allen and Unwin.

Bellamy, R. V., Jr. and Walker, J. R. (eds) (1996) *Television and the Remote Control: Grazing on a Vast Wasteland*, New York: Guilford.

Bellos, Alex (2002) 'Doh! Rio Blames it on The Simpsons,' *Guardian*, September 4, 2.

Bennett, Tony (1979) *Formalism and Marxism*, London: Routledge.

—— (1991) 'Holy Shifting Signifiers: Forward,' in Roberta E. Pearson and William Uricchio (eds) *The Many Lives of the Batman: Critical Approaches to a Superhero and his Media*, London: BFI, vii–ix.

Bennett, Tony and Woollacott, Janet (1987) *Bond and Beyond: The Political Career of a Popular Hero*, London: Macmillan.

Bennett, W. L. (1988) *News: The Politics of Illusion*, New York: Longman.

Berger, Arthur Asa (2004) *Ads, Fads, and Consumer Culture*, New York: Rowman and Littlefield.

Bergson, Henri (1935) *Laughter: An Essay on the Meaning of the Comic*, trans. Cloudesley Brereton and Fred Rothwell, London: Macmillan.

Bhavnani, Kum-Kum (1991) *Talking Politics: A Psychological Framing for Views from Youth in Britain*, Cambridge: Cambridge University Press.

Bird, S. Elizabeth (2003) *The Audience in Everyday Life: Living in a Media World*, London: Routledge.

Blackman, Lisa and Walkerdine, Valerie (2001) *Mass Hysteria: Critical Psychology and Media Studies*, London: Palgrave.

Bloch, Maurice E. F. (1998) 'Time, Narratives and the Multiplicity of Representations of the Past,' in *How We Think They Think: Anthropological Approaches to Cognition, Memory and Literacy*, Boulder, CO: Westview.

Bloom, Harold (1973) *The Anxiety of Influence: A Theory of Poetry*, London: Oxford University Press.

—— (1975) *Kabbalah and Criticism*, New York: Seabury.

Bolin, Göran (2000) 'Film Swapping in the Public Sphere: Youth Audiences and Alternative Cultural Publicities,' *Javnost: The Public* 7.2, 57–74.

Bonné, John (2003) '"Simpsons" Evolves as an Industry,' *MSNBC* November 7. Available: <http://www.msnbc.com/id/3403870/> (accessed November 17, 2004).

Bordo, Susan (1993) *Weight: Feminism, Western Culture, and the Body*, Berkeley, CA: University of California Press.

Bourdieu, Pierre (1984) *Distinction: A Social Critique of the Judgement of Taste*, trans. Richard Nice, London: Routledge and Kegan Paul.

—— (1991) *Language and Symbolic Power*, trans. Gino Raymond and Matthew Adamson, ed. John B. Thompson, Oxford: Polity.

—— (1998) *On Television and Journalism*, trans. Priscilla Parkhurst Ferguson, London: Pluto.

British Film Institute (BFI) (1982) *Television Sitcom*, Dossier 17, London: BFI.

Brooker, Will (2001) 'Living on *Dawson's Creek*: Teen Viewers, Cultural Convergence and Television Overflow,' *International Journal of Cultural Studies* 4.4, 456–72.

—— (2002) *Using the Force: Creativity, Community and Star Wars Fans*, London: Continuum.

Brooks, Cleanth (1949) *The Well Wrought Urn: Studies in the Structure of Poetry*, London: Dobson.

Brooks, Tim and Marsh, Earle (1999) *The Complete Directory to Prime Time Network and Cable TV Shows 1946–Present*, New York: Ballantine.

Brunsdon, Charlotte (1981) '*Crossroads*: Notes on a Soap Opera,' *Screen* 22.4, 32–7.

—— (1997) *Screen Tastes: Soap Operas and Satellite Dishes*, London: Routledge.

Brunsdon, Charlotte and Morley, David (1978) *Everyday Television: Nationwide*, London: BFI.

Buckingham, David (1987) *Public Secrets: EastEnders and its Audience*, London: BFI.

—— (ed.) (1998a) *Teaching Popular Culture: Beyond Radical Pedagogy*, London: UCL Press.

—— (1998b) 'Pedagogy, Parody and Political Correctness,' in Buckingham (ed.) *Teaching Popular Culture: Beyond Radical Pedagogy*, London: UCL Press, 63–87.

—— (2000) *The Making of Citizens: Young People, News and Politics*, London: Routledge.

Caldwell, John Thornton (1995) *Televisuality: Style, Crisis, and Authority in American Television*, New Brunswick, NJ: Rutgers University Press.

Cantor, Paul A. (1999) '*The Simpsons*: Atomistic Politics and the Nuclear Family,' *Political Theory* 27.6, 734–49.

Cardiff, David and Scannell, Paddy (1987) 'Broadcasting and National Identity,' in James Curran, Anthony Smith and Pauline Wingate (eds) *Impacts and Influences: Essays on Media Power*, London: Methuen, 157–73.

Carter, Cynthia (1995) 'Nuclear Family Fall-Out: Postmodern Family Culture and the Media,' in Barbara Adam and Stuart Allan (eds) *Theorizing Culture: An Interdisciplinary Technique after Postmodernism*, London: UCL Press, 186–200.

Cassy, John and Brown, Maggie (2003) 'Homer is Where the Heart Is,' *Guardian*, February 10. Available: <http://www.media.guardian.co.uk> (accessed November 17, 2004).

Caughie, John (1990) 'Playing at Being American: Games and Tactics,' in Patricia Mellancamp (ed.) *Logics of Television: Essays in Cultural Criticism*, London: BFI, 44–58.

—— (1991) 'Adorno's Reproach: Repetition, Difference and Television Genre,' *Screen* 32.2, 127–53.

Chaney, David C. (2001) 'From Ways of Life to Lifestyle: Rethinking Culture as Ideology and Sensibility,' in James Lull (ed.) *Culture in the Communication Age*, London: Routledge, 78–88.

Chin, Bertha and Gray, Jonathan (2001) '"One Ring to Rule Them All": Pre-Viewers and Pre-Texts of the *Lord of the Rings* Films,' *Intensities* 2 (http://www.cult-media.com/issue2/Achingray.htm).

Chocano, Carina (2001) 'Matt Groening,' *Salon*. Available: <http://www.salon.com/people/bc/2001/01/30/groening/print.html> (accessed November 17, 2004).

Clark, Katerina and Holquist, Michael (1984) *Mikhail Bakhtin*, London: Harvard University Press.

Clayton, Jay and Rothstein, Eric (1991) 'Figures in the Corpus: Theories of Influence and Intertextuality,' in Clayton and Rothstein (eds) *Influence and Intertextuality in Literary History*, London: University of Wisconsin Press, 3–36.

Clifford, James (1992) 'Traveling Cultures,' in Lawrence Grossberg, Cary Nelson and Paula A. Treichler (eds) *Cultural Studies*, London: Routledge, 96–112.

Clifford, James and Marcus, George E. (eds) (1986) *Writing Culture: The Poetics and Politics of Ethnography*, London: University of California Press.

Cohen, Ralph (1986) 'History and Genre,' *New Literary History* 17.2, 203–18.

Coleridge, Samuel Taylor (1991) *Biographia Literaria*, in Charles Kaplan and William Anderson (eds) *Criticism: Major Statements*, 3rd edn, New York: St. Martin's, 276–99.

Collet, P. and Lamb, R. (1986) 'Watching People Watching Television,' report presented to the Independent Broadcasting Authority, London.

Collins, Jim (1992) 'Television and Postmodernism,' in Robert C. Allen (ed.) *Channels of Discourse, Reassembled: Television and Contemporary Criticism*, London: Routledge, 327–53.

Comolli, Jean-Louis and Narboni, Jean (1993) 'Cinema/Ideology/Criticism (1),' in Anthony Easthope (ed.) *Contemporary Film Theory*, London: Longman, 43–52.

Corner, John (1980) 'Codes and Cultural Analysis,' *Media, Culture and Society* 2, 73–86.

—— (1995) *Television Form and Public Address*, London: Edward Arnold.

—— (1996) 'Reappraising Reception: Aims, Concepts and Methods,' in James Curran and Michael Gurevitch (eds) *Mass Media and Society*, 2nd edn, London: Edward Arnold, 280–304.

Couldry, Nick (2000) *In the Place of Media Power: Pilgrims and Witnesses of the Media Age*, London: Routledge.

—— (2003) *Media Rituals: A Critical Approach*, London: Routledge.

Crosman, Robert (1980) 'Do Readers Make Meaning?', in Susan R. Suleiman and Inge Crosman (eds) *The Reader in the Text: Essays on Audience and Interpretation*, Princeton, NJ: Princeton University Press, 149–64.

Culler, Jonathan (1981) *The Pursuit of Signs: Semiotics, Literature, Deconstruction*, London: Routledge and Kegan Paul.

Curran, James (1991) 'Rethinking the Media as a Public Sphere,' in Peter Dahlgren and Colin Sparks (eds) *Communication and Citizenship: Journalism and the Public Sphere in the New Media Age*, London: Routledge, 27–57.

—— (1996) 'Rethinking Mass Communications,' in Curran, David Morley, and Valerie Walkerdine (eds) *Cultural Studies and Communications*, London: Edward Arnold, 119–65.

Dahlgren, Peter (1981) 'TV News and the Suppression of Reflexivity,' in Elihu Katz and Tamas Szecsko (eds) *Mass Media and Social Change*, London: Sage, 101–13.

—— (1995) *Television and the Public Sphere: Citizenship, Democracy and the Media*, London: Sage.

Dayan, Daniel and Katz, Elihu (1994) *Media Events: The Live Broadcasting in History*, London: Harvard University Press.

Debord, Guy (1995) *The Society of the Spectacle*, trans. Donald Nicholson-Smith, New York: Zone.

de Certeau, Michel (1984) *The Practice of Everyday Life*, trans. Steven F. Rendall, London: University of California Press.

Deleuze, Gilles and Guattari, Felix (1988) *A Thousand Plateaus: Capitalism and Schizophrenia*, trans. Brian Massumi, London: Athlone.

DeLillo, Don (1999) *White Noise*, London: Picador.

Derrida, Jacques (1976) *Of Grammatology*, trans. Gayatri Chakravorty Spivak, London: Johns Hopkins University Press.

—— (1978) 'Force and Signification,' in *Writing and Difference*, trans. Alan Bass, London: Routledge, 3–30.

Diamond, Edwin (1982) *The Tin Kazoo: Television, Politics, and the News*, Cambridge, MA: MIT Press.

Doherty, Brian (1999) 'Matt Groening,' *Mother Jones*. Available: <http://www.motherjones.com/arts/qa/1999/03/groening.html> (accessed November 17, 2004).

Downie, Leonard Jr. and Kaiser, Robert G. (2002) *The News about the News: American Journalism in Peril*, New York: Vintage.

Downing, John D. H. (2001) *Radical Media: Rebellious Communication and Social Movements*, Thousand Oaks, CA: Sage.

Dyer, Gillian (1982) *Advertising as Communication*, London: Routledge.

Dyer, Richard (1992) *Only Entertainment*, London: Routledge.

Eaton, Mick (1978) 'Television Situation Comedy,' *Screen* 19.4, 61–89.

Eco, Umberto (1979) 'Can Television Teach?' *Screen Education* 31, 15–24.

—— (1984) 'The Frames of Comic "Freedom,"' in Thomas A. Sebeok (ed.) *Carnival!*, New York: Mouton, 1–9.

The Economist (2002) 'Power in your Hand: A Survey of Television,' April 13, special insert.

Eisenstein, Sergei (1998) *The Eisenstein Reader*, trans. Richard Taylor and William Powell, ed. Richard Taylor, London: BFI.

Eliasoph, Nina (1998) *Avoiding Politics: How Americans Produce Apathy in Everyday Life*, Cambridge: Cambridge University Press.

Ellis, John (1993) *Visible Fictions: Cinema: Television: Video*, London: Routledge.

—— (1999) 'Television as Working-Through,' in Jostein Gripsrud (ed.) *Television and Common Knowledge*, London: Routledge, 55–70.

—— (2000) *Seeing Things: Television in the Age of Uncertainty*, London: I. B. Tauris.

Engelhardt, Tom (1986) 'The Shortcake Strategy,' in Todd Gitlin (ed.) *Watching Television*, New York: Pantheon, 68–110.

Entertainment Weekly (2004) 'Jon Stewart,' 799–800, December 31, 2004 / January 7, 2005, 44–8.

Ewen, Stuart (1976) *Captains of Consciousness: Advertising and the Social Roots of the Consumer Culture*, New York: McGraw-Hill.

Fetterley, Judith (1978) *The Resisting Reader: A Feminist Approach to American Fiction*, London: Indiana University Press.

Feuer, Jane (1987) 'Genre Study and Television,' in Robert C. Allen (ed.) *Channels of Discourse: Television and Contemporary Criticism*, London: Routledge, 113–33.

—— (2001) 'Situation Comedy, Part 2,' in Glen Creeber (ed.) *The Television Genre Book*, London: BFI, 67–70.

Fish, Stanley (1980a) *Is There a Text in this Class? The Authority of Interpretive Communities*, London: Harvard University Press.

—— (1980b) 'Literature in the Reader: Affective Stylistics,' in Jane Tompkins (ed.) *Reader-Response Criticism: From Formalism to Post-Structuralism*, London: Johns Hopkins University Press, 70–100.

Fiske, John (1989a) 'Moments of Television: Neither the Text nor the Audience,' in Ellen Seiter, Hans Borchers, Gabrielle Keutzner and Eva-Maria Warth (eds) *Remote Control: Television, Audiences, and Cultural Power*, London: Routledge, 56–78.

—— (1989b) *Reading the Popular*, London: Unwin Hyman.

—— (1989c) *Understanding Popular Culture*, London: Unwin Hyman.

—— (1992) 'The Cultural Economy of Fandom,' in Lisa A. Lewis (ed.) *The Adoring Audience: Fan Culture and Popular Media*, London: Routledge, 30–49.

Fleming, Dan (1996) *Powerplay: Toys as Popular Culture*, Manchester: Manchester University Press.

Fog-Olwig, Karen (1998) 'Epilogue: Contested Homes: Home-Making and the Making of Anthropology,' in Nigel Rapport and Andrew Dawson (eds) *Migrants of Identity: Perceptions of Home in a World of Movement*, Oxford: Berg, 225–36.

Fornäs, Johan (1995) *Cultural Theory and Late Modernity*, London: Sage.

—— (2000) 'The Crucial in Between: The Centrality of Mediation in Cultural Studies,' *European Journal of Cultural Studies* 3.1, 45–65.

Foucault, Michel (1972) *The Archaeology of Knowledge*, trans. A. M. Sheridan Smith, London: Tavistock.

—— (1977) *Discipline and Punish*, New York: Pantheon.

—— (1981) 'The Order of Discourse', trans. Ian McLeod, in Robert Young (ed.) *Untying the Text: A Post-Structuralist Reader*, London: Routledge and Kegan Paul, 48–78.

Fraser, Nancy (1987) 'What's Critical about Critical Theory? The Case of Habermas and Gender,' in Seyla Benhabib and Drucilla Cornell (eds) *Feminism as Critique: The Politics of Gender*, Minneapolis, MN: University of Minnesota Press.

Freud, Sigmund (1960) *Jokes and their Relation to the Unconscious*, trans. James Strachey, London: Hogarth.

Frow, John (1990) 'Intertextuality and Ontology,' in Michael Worton and Judith Still (eds) *Intertextuality: Theories and Practices*, Manchester: Manchester University Press, 45–55.

Galician, Mary-Lou (2003) *Sex, Love, and Romance in the Mass Media: Analysis and Criticism of Unrealistic Portrayals and their Influence*, Mahwah, NJ: Lawrence Erlbuam.

Garrett, Jade (2001) '*Simpsons*' Actors Win Fight for More Doh!', *The Independent*, May 2, 7.

Gauntlett, David and Hill, Annette (1999) *TV Living: Television, Culture and Everyday Life*, London: BFI/Routledge.

Geertz, Clifford (1993) *The Interpretation of Cultures*, London: Fontana.

Genette, Gerard (1997) *Paratexts: Thresholds of Interpretation*, trans. Jane E. Lewin, Cambridge: Cambridge University Press.

Geraghty, Christine (1998) 'Audiences and "Ethnography": Questions of Practice,' in Geraghty and David Lusted (eds) *The Television Studies Book*, London: Edward Arnold, 141–57.

Gerbner, George, Gross, Larry, Morgan, Michael, and Signorielli, Nancy (1994) 'Growing Up with Television: The Cultivation Perspective,' in J. Bryant and D. Zillman (eds) *Media Effects: Advances in Theory and Research*, Mahwah, NJ: Lawrence Erlbaum, 17–41.

Giddens, Anthony (1990) *The Consequences of Modernity*, Cambridge: Polity.

Gillespie, Marie (1995) *Television, Ethnicity and Cultural Change*, London: Routledge.

Giroux, Henry A. (1994) *Disturbing Pleasures: Learning Popular Culture*, London: Routledge.

—— (1997) 'Is There a Place for Cultural Studies in Colleges of Education?', in Giroux with Patrick Shannon (eds) *Education and Cultural Studies: Toward a Performative Practice*, London: Routledge, 232–47.

Gitlin, Todd (1988) 'Hip Deep in Post-Modernism,' *New York Times Book Review*, November 6, 35–6.

—— (1994) *Inside Prime Time*, revised edn, London: Routledge.

Glynn, Kevin (1996) 'Bartmania: The Social Reception of an Unruly Image,' *Camera Obscura: Feminism, Culture, and Media Studies* 38, 61–91.

—— (2000) *Tabloid Culture: Trash Taste, Popular Power, and the Transformation of American Television*, London: Duke University Press.

Goldfarb, Jeffrey C. (1991) *The Cynical Society: The Culture of Politics and the Politics of Culture in American Life*, London: University of Chicago Press.

Goldsack, Laura (1999) 'A Haven in a Heartless World? Women and Domestic Violence,' in Tony Chapman and Jenny Hockey (eds) *Ideal Homes? Social Change and Domestic Life*, London: Routledge, 121–32.

Gray, Ann (1987) 'Behind Closed Doors: Video Recorders in the Home,' in Helen Baehr and Gillian Dyer (eds) *Boxed In: Women and Television*, London: Pandora, 38–53.

Gray, Jonathan (2003a) 'Imagining America: *The Simpsons* and the Anti-Suburb Global,' paper presented at International Communication Association conference, May 27–31.

—— (2003b) 'New Audiences, New Textualities: Anti-Fans and Non-Fans,' *International Journal of Cultural Studies* 6.1, 65–82.

—— (2005a) 'Antifandom and the Moral Text: Television without Pity and Textual Dislike,' *American Behavioral Scientist* 48.7, 840–858.

—— (2005b) 'Bonus Material: The DVD Layering of *Two Towers*,' in Ernest Mathijs (ed.) *The Lord of the Rings: Public Presence and Commercial Contexts*, London: Wallflower.

—— (2005c) 'Television Teaching: Parody, *The Simpsons*, and Media Literacy Education,' *Critical Studies in Media Communication*, 22.3, 223–38.

Gripsrud, Jostein (1989) '"High Culture" Revisited,' *Cultural Studies* 3.2, 194–207.

Groombridge, Brian (1972) *Television and the People*, Harmondsworth: Penguin.

Grossberg, Lawrence (1992) 'Is There a Fan in the House?: The Affective Sensibility of Fandom,' in Lisa A. Lewis (ed.) *The Adoring Audience: Fan Culture and Popular Media*, London: Routledge, 50–65.

Grote, David (1983) *The End of Comedy: The Sit-Com and the Comedic Tradition*, Hamden, CN: Archon.

Habermas, Jürgen (1989) *The Structural Transformation of the Public Sphere: An Inquiry into a Category of Bourgeois Society*, trans. Thomas Burger, Cambridge: Polity.

—— (1997) *Between Facts and Norms: Contributions to a Discourse Theory of Law and Democracy*, trans. W. Rehg, Cambridge: Polity.

Hagen, Ingunn (1994) 'The Ambivalences of TV News Viewing: Between Ideals and Everyday Practices,' *European Journal of Communication* 9.2, 193–220.

Hall, Stuart (1980) 'Encoding, Decoding,' in Hall, Dorothy Hobson, Andrew Lowe, and Paul Willis (eds) *Culture, Media, Language: Working Papers in Cultural Studies, 1972–1979*, London: Unwin Hyman, 128–38.

Hallin, Daniel (1994) *We Keep American on Top of the World: Television, Journalism, and the Public Sphere*, London: Routledge.

Hammersley, Martyn and Atkinson, Paul (1983) *Ethnography: Principles in Practice*, London: Tavistock.

Handelman, Don (1998) *Models and Mirrors: Towards an Anthropology of Public Events*, Oxford: Berghahn.

Haralovich, Mary Beth (1988) 'Suburban Family Sitcoms and Consumer Product Design: Addressing the Social Subjectivity of Homemakers in the 1950s,' in Phillip Drummond and Richard Paterson (eds) *Television and its Audience: International Research Perspectives*, London: BFI, 38–60.

Harries, Dan (2000) *Film Parody*, London: BFI.

Harrington, C. Lee and Bielby, Denise (1996) *Soap Fans: Pursuing Pleasure and Making Meaning in Everyday Life*, Philadelphia, PA: Temple University Press.

Hartley, John (1982) *Understanding News*, London: Routledge.

—— (1987) 'Invisible Fictions: Television Audiences, Paedocracy, Pleasure,' *Textual Practice* 1.2, 121–38.

—— (1996) *Popular Reality: Journalism, Modernity, Popular Culture*, London: Edward Arnold.

—— (1999) *The Uses of Television*, London: Routledge.

—— (2001) 'Situation Comedy, Part 1,' in Glen Creeber (ed.) *The Television Genre Book*, London: BFI, 65–7.

Hebdige, Dick (1979) *Subculture: The Meaning of Style*, London: Methuen.

Henry, Matthew (1994) 'The Triumph of Popular Culture, Situation Comedy, Postmodernism, and *The Simpsons*,' *Studies in Popular Culture* 17.1, 85–99.

Herman, Edward S. and Chomsky, Noam (1988) *Manufacturing Consent: The Political Economy of the Mass Media*, New York: Pantheon.

Herman, Edward S. and McChesney, Robert W. (1997) *The Global Media: The New Missionaries of Global Capitalism*, London: Cassell.

Hermes, Joke (1995) *Reading Women's Magazines: An Analysis of Everyday Media Use*, Oxford: Polity.

—— (1999) 'Media Figures in Identity Construction,' in Pertti Alasuutari (ed.) *Rethinking the Media Audience: The New Agenda*, London: Sage, 69–85.

Hesmondhalgh, David (2002) *The Cultural Industries*, London: Sage.

Hills, Matt (2002) *Fan Cultures*, London: Routledge.

Hirschkop, Ken (1999) *Mikhail Bakhtin: An Aesthetic for Democracy*, Oxford: Oxford University Press.

Hobbs, Renee (1998) 'The Simpsons Meet Mark Twain: Analyzing Popular Texts in the Classroom,' *English Journal* 87.1, 49–51.

Hobson, Dorothy (1987) 'Housewives and the Mass Media,' in S. Hall, D. Hobson, A. Lowe, and P. Willis (eds) *Culture, Media, Language: Working Papers in Cultural Studies, 1972–1979*, London: Hutchinson, 105–14.

Hoggart, Richard (1957) *The Uses of Literacy*, London: Chatto and Windus.

Holbert, R. Lance, Shah, Dhavan V., and Kwak, Nojin (2003) 'Political Implications of Prime-Time Drama and Sitcom Use: Genres of Representation and Opinions Concerning Women's Rights,' *Journal of Communication* 53.1, 45–60.

Hull, Margaret Betz (2000) 'Postmodern Philosophy Meets Pop Cartoon: Michel Foucault and Matt Groening,' *Journal of Popular Culture* 34.2, 57–67.

Hutcheon, Linda (1985) *A Theory of Parody: The Teachings of Twentieth-Century Art Forms*, London: Routledge.

—— (1988) *A Poetics of Postmodernism: History, Theory, Fiction*, London: Routledge.

Iampolski, Mikhail (1998) *The Memory of Tiresias: Intertextuality and Film*, trans. Harsha Ram, London: University of California Press.

Illich, Ivan D. (1971) *Deschooling Society*, London: Calder and Boyars.

Irwin, William, Conard, Mark T., and Skoble, Aeon J. (eds) (2001) *The Simpsons and Philosophy: The D'Oh! of Homer*, Chicago: Open Court.

Iser, Wolfgang (1978) *The Act of Reading: A Theory of Aesthetic Response*, London: Routledge and Kegan Paul.

—— (1980) 'The Reading Process: A Phenomenological Approach,' in Jane Tompkins (ed.) *Reader-Response Criticism: From Formalism to Post-Structuralism*, London: Johns Hopkins University Press, 50–69.

Jackson, H. J. (2001) *Marginalia: Readers Writing in Books*, London: Yale University Press.

Jameson, Fredric (1979) 'Reification and Utopia in Mass Culture,' *Social Text* 1.1, 7–39.

—— (1984) 'Postmodernism, or the Cultural Logic of Late Capitalism,' *New Left Review* 146, 53–92.

Jenkins, Henry (1988) '*Star Trek* Rerun, Reread, Rewritten: Fan Writing as Textual Poaching,' *Critical Studies in Mass Communiation* 5.2, 85–107.

—— (1992) *Textual Poachers: Television Fans and Participating Culture*, London: Routledge.

Jenny, Laurent (1982) 'The Strategy of Form', trans. R. Carter, in Tzvetan Todorov (ed.) *French Literary Theory Today: A Reader*, Cambridge: Cambridge University Press, 34–63.

Jhally, Sut (1987) *The Codes of Advertising: Fetishism and the Political Economy of Meaning in the Consumer Society*, London: Routledge.

Jhally, Sut and Lewis, Justin (1992) *Enlightened Racism: The Cosby Show, Audiences, and the Myth of the American Dream*, Oxford: Westview.

Jones, Gerard (1992) *Honey, I'm Home! Sitcoms: Selling the American Dream*, New York: Grove Weidenfeld.

Kellert, Stephen H. (1993) *In the Wake of Chaos*, Chicago: University of Chicago Press.

Kilbourne, Jean (1999) *Can't Buy Me Love: How Advertising Changes the Way We Feel*, New York: Touchstone.

Klein, Naomi (2002) *No Logo*, New York: Picador.

Kline, Stephen (1993) *Out of the Garden: Toys and Children's Culture in the Age of TV Marketing*, London: Verso.

Klinger, Barbara (1989) 'Digressions at the Cinema: Reception and Mass Culture,' *Cinema Journal* 28.4, 3–19.

Kress, Gunther (2000) 'Text as the Punctuation of Semiosis: Pulling at Some Threads,' in Ulrike H. Meinhof and Jonathan Smith (eds) *Intertextuality and the Media: From Genre to Everyday Life*, Manchester: Manchester University Press, 132–54.

Kristeva, Julia (1980a) *Desire in Language: A Semiotic Approach to Literature and Art*, trans. Thomas Gora, Alice Jardine, and Leon S. Roudiez, ed. Leon Roudiez, Oxford: Basil Blackwell.

—— (1980b) *Revolution in Poetic Language*, trans. Margaret Waller, New York: Columbia University Press.

Kubey, Robert (1998) 'Obstacles to the Development of Media Education in the United States,' *Journal of Communication* 48.1, 58–69.

Kuhn, Annette (1999) '"That Day *Did* Last Me All My Life": Cinema Memory and Enduring

Fandom,' in Melvyn Stokes and Richard Maltby (eds) *Identifying Hollywood's Audiences: Cultural Identity and the Movies*, London: BFI, 135–46.

Kuhn, Thomas S. (1970) *The Structure of Scientific Revolutions*, London: University of Chicago Press.

Lakoff, George and Johnson, Mark (1980) *Metaphors We Live By*, London: University of Chicago Press.

Langer, John (1998) *Tabloid Television: Popular Television and the 'Other News'*, London: Routledge.

Lavery, David (ed.) (2002) *This Thing of Ours: Investigating The Sopranos*, New York: Columbia University Press.

Leavis, F. R. (1962) *The Common Pursuit*, London: Chatto and Windus.

Lembo, Ron (2000) *Thinking through Television*, Cambridge: Cambridge University Press.

Levinson, Paul (1997) *The Soft Edge: A Natural History and Future of the Information Revolution*, London: Routledge.

Lewis, Justin (1983) 'The Encoding/Decoding Model: Criticisms and Redevelopments for Research on Decoding,' *Media, Culture and Society* 5, 179–97.

—— (1986) 'Decoding Television News,' in Phillip Drummond and Richard Paterson (eds) *Television in Transition: Papers from the First International Television Studies Conference*, London: BFI, 205–34.

—— (1991) *The Ideological Octopus: An Exploration of Television and its Audience*, London: Routledge.

Lewis, Lisa A. (ed.) (1992) *The Adoring Audience: Fan Culture and Popular Media*, London: Routledge.

Lewis, Peter M. (1989) *The Invisible Medium: Public, Commercial and Community Radio*, London: Macmillan.

Lindlof, Thomas R. (1988) 'Media Audiences as Interpretive Communities,' in James A. Anderson (ed.) *Communication Yearbook 11*, 81–107.

Lindlof, Thomas R., Coyle, Kelly, and Grodin, Debra (1998) 'Is There a Text in This Audience? Science Fiction and Interpretive Schism,' in Cheryl Harris and Alison Alexander (eds) *Theorizing Fandom: Fans, Subculture and Identity*, Cresskill, NJ: Hampton, 219–47.

Linstead, Steve (1988) '"Jokers Wild": Humour in Organisational Culture,' in Chris Powell and George E. C. Paton (eds) *Humour in Society: Resistance and Control*, New York: St. Martins, 123–48.

Lipsitz, George (1988) 'The Meaning of Memory: Family, Class, and Ethnicity in Early Network Television Programs,' *Camera Obscura: Journal of Feminism and Film Theory* 16, 79–116.

—— (1990) *Time Passages: Collective Memory and American Popular Culture*, London: University of Minnesota Press.

Livingstone, Sonia and Lunt, Peter (1994) *Talk on Television*, London: Routledge.

Loaded (1996) 'And on the Seventh Day Matt Created Bart,' in *The Simpsons Archive*. Available: <http://www.snpp.com/other/interviews/groening96.html> (accessed November 17, 2004).

Lorenz, Edward (1995) *The Essence of Chaos*, London: UCL Press.

Lotman, Jurij (1977) *The Structure of the Artistic Text*, trans. Gail Lenhoff and Ronald Vroon, Ann Arbor, MI: University of Michigan Press.

Lovell, Terry (1986) 'Television Situation Comedy,' in David Punter (ed.) *Introduction to Contemporary Cultural Studies*, London: Longman, 149–67.

Lull, James (1990) *Inside Family Viewing: Ethnographic Research on Television's Audiences*, London: Routledge.

—— (2001) 'Superculture for the Communication Age,' in Lull (ed.) *Culture in the Communication Age*, London: Routledge, 132–63.

Lury, Karen (2001) *British Youth Television: Cynicism and Enchantment*, Oxford: Clarendon.

McAllister, Matthew (1996) *The Commercialization of American Culture: New Advertising, Control, and Democracy*, London: Sage.

—— (2004) 'From Lard Lad to Butterfinger: Contradictions of *The Simpsons* in Promotional and Commercial Culture,' paper presented at International Communication Association conference, May 27–31.

McCarthy, Anna (2001) *Ambient Television: Visual Culture and Public Space*, London: Duke University Press.

McChesney, Robert W. (2004) *The Problem of the Media: US Communication Politics in the Twenty-First Century*, New York: Monthly Review.

McLuhan, Marshall (1995) *Essential McLuhan*, eds Eric McLuhan and Frank Zingrone, Concord, ON: Anansi.

—— (1997) *Understanding Media: The Extensions of Man*, London: MIT Press.

McLuhan, Marshall with Watson, Wilfred (1971) *From Cliché to Archetype*, New York: Pocket Books.

McManus, John H. (1994) *Market-Driven Journalism: Let the Citizen Beware*, London: Sage.

McRobbie, Angela (1996) '*More!*: New Sexualities in Girls' and Women's Magazines,' in James Curran, David Morley, and Valerie Walkerdine (eds) *Cultural Studies and Communications*, London: Edward Arnold, 172–94.

Mai, Hans-Peter (1991) 'Bypassing Intertextuality: Hermeneutics, Textual Practice, Hypertext,' in Heinrich Plett (ed.) *Intertextuality*, New York: Walter de Gruyter, 30–59.

Maigret, Eric (1999) '"Strange" Grew Up with Me: Sentimentality and Masculinity in Readers of Superhero Comics,' *Reseaux, The French Journal of Communication* 7.1, 5–27.

Mander, Jerry (1977) *Four Arguments for the Elimination of Television*, New York: Quill.

Mann, Michael (1970) 'The Social Cohesion of Liberal Democracy,' *American Sociological Review* 35.3, 423–39.

Marc, David (1989) *Comic Visions: Television Comedy and American Culture*, London: Unwin Hyman.

Massey, Doreen (1994) 'The Political Place of Locality Studies,' *Space, Place and Gender*, Oxford: Polity, 125–45.

Masterman, Len (1997) 'A Rationale for Media Education,' in Robert Kubey (ed.) *Media Literacy in the Information Age: Current Perspectives*, New Brunswick, NJ: Transaction, 15–68.

Matheson, Carl (2001) '*The Simpsons*, Hyper-Irony, and the Meaning of Life,' in William Irwin, Mark T. Conard, and Aeon J. Skoble (eds) *The Simpsons and Philosophy: The D'Oh! of Homer*, Chicago: Open Court, 108–25.

Mayerle, Judith (1994) 'Roseanne – How Did You Get Inside My House? A Case Study of a Hit Blue-Collar Situation Comedy,' in Horace Newcomb (ed.) *Television: The Critical View*, 5th edn, Oxford: Oxford University Press, 202–11.

Means Coleman, Robin (2000) *African American Viewers and the Black Situation Comedy: Situating Racial Humor*, New York: Garland.

Medrich, Elliott A. (1979) 'Constant Television: A Background to Everyday Life,' *Journal of Communication* 29.3, 171–6.

Meehan, Eileen (1991) '"Holy Commodity Fetish, Batman!": The Political Economy of a Commercial Intertext,' in Roberta E. Pearson and William Uricchio (eds) *The Many Lives of the Batman: Critical Approaches to a Superhero and his Media*, London: BFI, 47–65.

Meijer, Irene Costera (1998) 'Advertising Citizenship: An Essay on the Performative Power of Consumer Culture,' *Media, Culture and Society* 20.2, 235–249.

Meinhof, Ulrike H. and Smith, Jonathan (2000) '*Spitting Image*: TV Genre and Intertextuality,' in Meinhof and Smith (eds) *Intertextuality and the Media: From Genre to Everyday Life*, Manchester: Manchester University Press, 43–60.

Mellancamp, Patricia (2003) 'Situation Comedy, Feminism, and Freud: Discourses of Gracie and Lucy,' in Joanne Morreale (ed.) *Critiquing the Sitcom*, Syracuse, NY: Syracuse University Press.

Meyrowitz, Joshua (1985) *No Sense of Place: The Impact of Electronic Media on Social Behavior*, Oxford: Oxford University Press.

Miller, Mark Crispin (1986) 'Deride and Conquer,' in Todd Gitlin (ed.) *Watching Television*, New York: Pantheon, 183–228.

—— (1988) *Boxed In: The Culture of TV*, Evanston, IL: Northwestern University Press.

Miller, Toby (1997) *The Avengers*, London: BFI.

Mittell, Jason (2001) 'Cartoon Realism: Genre Mixing and the Cultural Life of *The Simpsons*,' *Velvet Light Trap: A Critical Journal of Film and Television* 47, 15–28.

—— (2004) *Genre and Television: From Cop Shows to Cartoons in American Culture*, London: Routledge.

Moeller, Susan D. (1999) *Compassion Fatigue: How the Media Sell Disease, Famine, War and Death*, London: Routledge.

Morey, John (1981) *The Space between Programmes: TV Continuity*, London: Comedia.

Morgan, Michael (1998) 'Provocations for a Media Education in Small Letters,' in David Buckingham (ed.) *Teaching Popular Culture: Beyond Radical Pedagogy*, London: UCL Press, 107–31.

Morley, David (1980) *The Nationwide Audience*, London: BFI.

—— (1986) *Family Television*, London: Comedia.

—— (1992) *Television, Audiences and Cultural Studies*, London: Routledge.

—— (1997) 'Theoretical Orthodoxies: Textualism, Constructivism and the "New Ethnography" in Cultural Studies,' in Marjorie Ferguson and Peter Golding (eds) *Cultural Studies in Question*, London: Sage, 121–37.

—— (1999) 'Finding Out about the World from Television News: Some Difficulties,' in Jostein Gripsrud (ed.) *Television and Common Knowledge*, London: Routledge, 136–58.

—— (2000) *Home Territories: Media, Mobility and Identity*, London: Routledge.

Morley, David and Brunsdon, Charlotte (1999) *The Nationwide Television Studies*, London: Routledge.

Morreale, Joanne (ed.) (2003) *Critiquing the Sitcom*, Syracuse, NY: Syracuse University Press.

Morse, Margaret (1990) 'An Ontology of Everyday Distraction: The Freeway, the Mall, and Television,' in Patricia Mellencamp (ed.) *Logics of Television: Essays in Cultural Criticism*, London: BFI, 193–221.

Mulvey, Laura (1975) 'Visual Pleasure and Narrative Cinema,' *Screen* 16.3, 6–18.

Murdock, Graham (1999) 'Rights and Representations: Public Discourse and Cultural Citizenship,' in Jostein Gripsrud (ed.) *Television and Common Knowledge*, London: Routledge, 7–17.

Myers, Kathy (1986) *Understains: The Sense and Seduction of Advertising*, London: Comedia.

Naficy, Hamid (1989) 'Television Intertextuality and the Discourse of the Nuclear Family,' *Journal of Film and Video* 41.4, 38–52.

Nava, Mica and Nava, Orson (1992) 'Discriminating or Duped? Young People as Consumers of Advertising/Art,' in Mica Nava (ed.) *Changing Cultures: Feminism, Youth and Consumerism*, London: Sage, 171–84.

Nava, Mica, Blake, Andrew, MacRury, Iain, and Richards, Barry (eds) (1997) *Buy This Book: Studies in Advertising and Consumption*, London: Routledge.

Neale, Stephen (1980) *Genre*, London: BFI.

—— (2000) *Genre and Hollywood*, London: Routledge.

Neale, Stephen and Krutnik, Frank (1990) *Popular Film and Television Comedy*, London: Routledge.

Nelson, Jenny L. (1990) 'The Dislocation of Time: A Phenomenology of Television Reruns,' *Quarterly Review of Film and Video* 12.3, 79–92.

Newcomb, Horace M. and Hirsch, Paul M. (1984) 'Television as a Cultural Forum: Implications for Research,' in Willard D. Rowland, Jr. and Bruce Watkins (eds) *Interpreting Television: Current Research Perspectives*, London: Sage, 58–73.

Nielsen, Aldon L. (1994) *Writing Between the Lines: Race and Intertextuality*, London: University of Georgia Press.

Norrick, Neal R. (1989) 'Intertextuality in Humor,' *Humor* 2.2, 117–39.

Oakley, Ann (1976) *Housewife*, Harmondsworth: Penguin.

Ott, Brian and Walter, Cameron (2000) 'Intertextuality: Interpretive Practice and Textual Strategy,' *Critical Studies in Mass Communication* 17.4, 429–42.

Owen, David (2000) 'Taking Humor Seriously,' *New Yorker*, March 13, 64–75.

Palmer, Jerry (1987) *The Logic of the Absurd: On Film and Television Comedy*, London: BFI.

Palmer, Patricia (1988) 'The Social Nature of Children's Television Viewing,' in Phillip Drummond and Richard Paterson (eds) *Television and its Audience: International Research Perspectives*, London: BFI, 139–53.

Parisi, Peter (1993) '"Black Bart" Simpson: Appropriation and Revitalization in Commodity Culture,' *Journal of Popular Culture* 27.1, 125–42.

Paterson, Richard (1980) 'Planning the Family: The Art of the Television Schedule,' *Screen Education* 35, 79–85.

Pearson, Roberta E. and Uricchio, William (eds) (1991) *The Many Lives of the Batman: Critical Approaches to a Superhero and his Media*, London: BFI.

Penley, Constance (1997) *NASA/TREK: Popular Science and Sex in America*, London: Verso.

Perse, Elizabeth M. (1998) 'Implications of Cognitive and Affective Involvement for Channel Changing,' *Journal of Communication* 48.3, 49–68.

Peters, John Durham (1993) 'Distrust of Representation: Habermas on the Public Sphere,' *Media, Culture and Society* 15, 541–71.

—— (1999) *Speaking into the Air: A History of the Idea of Communication*, London: University of Chicago Press.

Philo, Greg and Miller, David (1998) *Cultural Compliance*, Glasgow: Glasgow Media Group.

Pinsky, Mark I. (2001) *The Gospel According to the Simpsons: The Spiritual Life of the World's Most Animated Family*, Louisville, KY: Westminster John Knox.

Postman, Neil (1986) *Amusing Ourselves to Death: Public Discourse in the Age of Show Business*, London: Penguin.

Postman, Neil and Powers, Steve (1992) *How to Watch TV News*, London: Penguin.

Powell, Chris (1988) 'A Phenomenological Analysis of Humour in Society,' in Chris Powell and George E. C. Paton (eds) *Humour in Society: Resistance and Control*, New York: St. Martins, 86–105.

Pratt, Mary Louise (1986) 'Interpretive Strategies / Strategic Interpretations: On Anglo-American Reader-Response Criticism,' in Jonathan Arac (ed.) *Postmodernism and Politics*, Minneapolis, MN: University of Minnesota Press, 26–54.

Preston, Ivan L. (1994) *The Tangled Web They Weave: Truth, Falsity, and Advertisers*, Madison, WI: University of Wisconsin Press.

Propp, Vladimir (1990) *Morphology of the Folktale*, trans. Laurence Scott, Austin, TX: University of Texas Press.

Purdie, Susan (1993) *Comedy: The Mastery of Discourse*, London: Harvester Wheatsheaf.

Radway, Janice (1987) *Reading the Romance: Women, Patriarchy, and Popular Literature*, London: Verso.

—— (1988) 'Reception Study: Ethnography and the Problems of Dispersed Audiences and Nomadic Subjects,' *Cultural Studies* 2.3, 359–76.

Ransom, John Crowe (1979) *The New Criticism*, Westport, CT: Greenwood.

Ray, William (1984) *Literary Interpretation: From Phenomenology to Deconstruction*, Oxford: Blackwell.

Richards, I. A. (1978) *Practical Criticism: A Study of Literary Judgement*, London: Routledge and Kegan Paul.

Richards, Jeffrey (1997) *Films and British National Identity: From Dickens to Dad's Army*, Manchester: Manchester University Press.

Richardson, Kay (2000) 'Intertextuality and the Discursive Construction of Knowledge: The Case of Economic Understanding,' in Ulrike Meinhof and Jonathan Smith (eds) *Intertextuality and the Media: From Genre to Everyday Life*, Manchester: Manchester University Press, 76–97.

Riffaterre, Michael (1990) 'Compulsory Reader Response: The Intertextual Drive,' in Michael Worton and Judith Still (eds) *Intertextuality: Theories and Practices*, Manchester: Manchester University Press, 56–78.

Rose, Margaret A. (1993) *Parody: Ancient, Modern, and Post-Modern*, Cambridge: Cambridge University Press.

Rowe, Kathleen K. (1994) '*Roseanne* – Unruly Woman as Domestic Goddess,' in Horace Newcomb (ed.) *Television: The Critical View*, 5th edn, Oxford: Oxford University Press, 101–16.

Rushkoff, Douglas (2004) 'Bart Simpson: Prince of Irreverence,' in John Alberti (ed.) *Leaving Springfield: The Simpsons and the Possibility of Oppositional Culture*, Detroit, MI: Wayne State University Press, 292–301.

Ryan, Michael and Kellner, Douglas (1988) *Camera Politica: The Politics and Ideology of Contemporary Hollywood Film*, Bloomington, IN: Indiana University Press.

Saussure, Ferdinand de (1983) *Course in General Linguistics*, trans. Wade Baskin, eds Charles Bally and Albert Sechehaye, London: McGraw-Hill.

Scanlan, Stephen J. and Feinberg, Seth L. (2000) 'The Cartoon Society: Using *The Simpsons* to Teach and Learn Sociology,' *Teaching Sociology* 28.2, 127–39.

Schatz, Thomas (1981) *Hollywood Genres: Formulas, Filmmaking, and the Studio System*, New York: Random House.

Schlesinger, P., Dobash, R. E., Dobash, R. P., and Weaver, C. K. (1992) *Women Viewing Violence*, London: BFI.

Scholes, Robert (1985) *Textual Power: Literary Theory and the Teaching of English*, London: Yale University Press.

Schrøder, Kim Christian (1997) 'Cynicism and Ambiguity: British Corporate Responsibility Advertisements and their Readers in the 1990s,' in M. Nava, A. Blake, I. MacRury, and B. Richards (eds) *Buy This Book: Studies in Advertising and Consumption*, London: Routledge, 276–90.

Schudson, Michael (1992) 'Was There Ever a Public Sphere? If So, When? Reflections on the American Case,' in Craig Calhoun (ed.) *Habermas and the Public Sphere*, Cambridge, MA: MIT Press, 143–63.

Scott, James C. (1985) *Weapons of the Weak: Everyday Forms of Peasant Resistance*, London: Yale University Press.

Seib, Philip (2002) *The Global Journalist: News and Conscience in a World of Conflict*, New York: Rowman and Littlefield.

Seiter, Ellen (1993) *Sold Separately: Children and Parents in Consumer Culture*, New Brunswick, NJ: Rutgers University Press.

Segal, Lynn (ed.) (1983) *What is to be Done about the Family?*, Harmondsworth: Penguin.

Serra, Sonia (2000) 'The Killing of Brazilian Street Children and the Rise of the International Public Sphere,' in James Curran (ed.) *Media Organisations in Society*, London: Edward Arnold, 151–72.

Shanahan, James and Morgan, Michael (1999) *Television and its Viewers: Cultivation Theory and Research*, Cambridge: Cambridge University Press.

Sharrett, Christopher (2002) 'End of Story: The Collapse of Myth in Postmodern Narrative Film,' in Jon Lewis (ed.) *The End of Cinema as We Know It*, London: Pluto, 319–31.

Shelley, Percy Bysshe (1991) *A Defence of Poetry*, in Charles Kaplan and William Anderson (eds) *Criticism: Major Statements*, 3rd edn, New York: St. Martin's, 309–35.

Shklovsky, Victor (1965) 'Art as Technique', trans. Lee T. Lemon and Marion J. Reis, in Lemon and Reis (eds) *Russian Formalist Criticism: Four Essays*, Lincoln, NE: University of Nebraska Press, 3–24.

Signorielli, Nancy and Morgan, Michael (eds) (1990) *Cultivation Analysis: New Directions in Media Effects Research*, Newbury Park, CA: Sage.

Silverstone, Roger (1994) *Television and Everyday Life*, London: Routledge.

—— (1999) *Why Study the Media?*, London: Sage.

Skoble, Aeon J. (2001) 'Lisa and American Anti-Intellectualism,' in William Irwin, Mark T. Conard, and Skoble (eds) *The Simpsons and Philosophy: The D'Oh! of Homer*, Chicago: Open Court, 25–34.

Sloterdijk, Peter (1987) *Critique of Cynical Reason*, trans. Michael Eldred, Minneapolis, MN: University of Minnesota Press.

Smythe, Dallas W. (1981) *Dependency Road: Communications, Capitalism, Consciousness, and Canada*, Norwood, NJ: Ablex.

Sperber, Dan (1991) *On Anthropological Knowledge*, Cambridge: Cambridge University Press.

Spigel, Lynn (1992) *Make Room for TV: Television and the Family Ideal in Postwar America*, London: University of California Press.

—— (1995) 'From the Dark Ages to the Golden Age: Women's Memories and Television Reruns,' *Screen* 36.1, 16–33.

Stabile, Carol A. and Harrison, Mark (eds) (2003) *Prime Time Animation: Television Animation and American Culture*, London: Routledge.

Staiger, Janet (1992) *Interpreting Films: Studies in the Historical Reception of American Cinema*, Chichester: Princeton University Press.

—— (2000) *Blockbuster TV: Must-See Sitcoms in the Network Era*, London: New York University Press.

Stallybrass, Peter and White, Allon (1986) *The Politics and Poetics of Transgression*, London: Methuen.

Stam, Robert (1989) *Subversive Pleasures: Bakhtin, Cultural Criticism, and Film*, London: Johns Hopkins University Press.

Stephens, Mitchell (1998) *The Rise of the Image the Fall of the Word*, Oxford: Oxford University Press.

Stewart, Susan (1979) *Nonsense: Aspects of Intertextuality in Folklore and Literature*, London: Johns Hopkins University Press.

Stivers, Richard (1994) *The Culture of Cynicism: American Morality in Decline*, Oxford: Blackwell.

Street, Sarah (1997) *British National Cinema*, London: Routledge.

Taylor, Ella (1989) *Prime-Time Families: Television and Culture in Postwar America*, London: University of California Press.

Taylor, Paul (1988) 'Scriptwriters and Producers: A Dimension of Control in Television Situation Comedies,' in Chris Powell and George E. C. Paton (eds) *Humour in Society: Resistance and Control*, New York: St. Martins, 179–205.

Thompson, John O. (1982) *Monty Python: Complete and Utter Theory of the Grotesque*, London: BFI.

Thornton, Sarah (1995) *Club Culture: Music, Media and Subcultural Capital*, Cambridge: Polity.

Turner, Chris (2004) *Planet Simpson: How a Cartoon Masterpiece Defined a Generation*, Cambridge, MA: Da Capo.

Tushnet, Rebecca (1997) 'Legal Fictions: Copyright, Fan Fiction, and a New Common Law,' *Loyola of Los Angeles Entertainment Law Journal* 17.

Van Wolde, Ellen (1989) 'Trendy Intertextuality,' in Sipke Draisma (ed.) *Intertextuality in Biblical Writings: Essays in Honour of Bas Van Iersel*, Kampen: Uitgeversmaatschappij J.H. Kok, 43–9.

Volosinov, Valentin Nikolaevic (1973) *Marxism and the Philosophy of Language*, trans. Ladislav Metejka and I. R. Titunik, London: Seminar.

Wallace, James M. (2001) 'A (Karl, not Groucho) Marxist in Springfield,' in William Irwin, Mark T. Conard, and Aeon J. Skoble (eds) *The Simpsons and Philosophy: The D'Oh! of Homer*, Chicago: Open Court, 235–51.

Weinstein, David (1998) 'Of Mice and Bart: *The Simpsons* and the Postmodern,' in Cristina Degli-Esposti (ed.) *Postmodernism in the Cinema*, Oxford: Berghahn, 60–72.

Weispfenning, John (2003) 'Cultural Functions of Reruns: Time, Memory, and Television,' *Journal of Communication* 53.1, 165–76.

Wells, Paul (1998) *Understanding Animation*, London: Routledge.

Welsford, Enid (1935) *The Fool*, London: Faber and Faber.

White, Mimi (2003) 'Flows and Other Close Encounters with Television,' in Lisa Parks and Shanti Kumar (eds) *Planet TV: A Global Television Reader*, London: New York University Press, 94–110.

Wilcox, Rhonda V. and Lavery, David (eds) (2002) *Fighting the Forces: What's at Stake in Buffy the Vampire Slayer*, Lanham, MD: Rowman and Littlefield.

Willeford, William (1969) *The Fool and his Sceptre: A Study in Clowns and Jesters and their Audience*, London: Edward Arnold.

Williams, Raymond (1974) *Television: Technology and Cultural Form*, London: Fontana/Collins.

Williamson, Judith (1978) *Decoding Advertisements: Ideology and Meaning*, London: Marion Boyars.

Willis, Paul (1977) *Learning to Labour: How Working Class Kids Get Working Class Jobs*, Westmead, UK: Saxon House.

—— (1990) *Common Culture: Symbolic Work at Play in the Everyday Cultures of the Young*, Milton Keynes: Open University Press.

Winnicott, D. W. (1974) *Playing and Reality*, Harmondsworth: Penguin.

—— (1975) *Through Paediatrics to Psycho-analysis*, London: Hogarth.

Wordsworth, William (1991) 'Preface to *Lyrical Ballads*,' in Charles Kaplan and William Anderson (eds) *Criticism: Major Statements*, 3rd edn, New York: St. Martin's, 256–75.

INDEX

INDEX

Related titles from Routledge

Cultural Studies: A Critical Introduction
Simon During

Cultural Studies: A Critical Introduction is a wide-ranging and stimulating introduction to the history and theory of Cultural Studies from Leavisism, through the era of the Centre for Contemporary Cultural Studies, to the global nature of contemporary Cultural Studies. *Cultural Studies: A Critical Introduction* begins with an introduction to the field and its theoretical history and then presents a series of short essays on key areas of Cultural Studies, designed to provoke discussion and raise questions. Each thematic section examines and explains a key topic within Cultural Studies.

Hb: 0-415-24656-3
Pb: 0-415-24657-1

Available at all good bookshops
For ordering and further information please visit:
www.routledge.com

Related titles from Routledge

The Everyday Life Reader
Edited by Ben Highmore

The Everyday Life Reader brings together thinkers ranging from Freud to Baudrillard with primary sources. It thus provides a complete and comprehensive resource on theories of everyday life.

Ben Highmore's introduction surveys the development of thought about everyday life, setting theories in their social and historical context, and each themed section opens with an essay introducing the debates. Sections include:

- Situating the Everyday
- Everyday Life and 'National Culture'
- Ethnography Near and Far
- Reclamation Work
- Everyday Things

Contributors: Roland Barthes, Jean Baudrillard, Walter Benjamin, Pierre Bourdieu, Fernand Braudel, Michel de Certeau, Steven Connor, Guy Debord, Sigmund Freud, Betty Friedan, Luce Giard, Jean-Luc Godard, Erving Goffman, Stuart Hall, Harry Harootunian, Alice Kaplan, Mary Kelly, Siegfried Kracauer, Henri Lefebvre, Bronislaw Malinowski, Karal Ann Marling, Anne-Marie Mi'eville, Daniel Miller, Trinh T. Minh-ha, Georges Perec, Jacques Ranciere, Kristin Ross, Georg Simmel, Dorothy Smith, Lynn Spigel, Caroline Steedman, Xiaobing Tang, Leon Trotsky, Raymond Williams, Paul Willis.

Hb: 0-415-23024-1
Pb: 0-415-23025-X

Available at all good bookshops
For ordering and further information please visit:
www.routledge.com

Related titles from Routledge

The Subcultures Reader, Second Edition
Edited by Ken Gelder

Subcultures are groups of people which are represented – or who represent themselves – as distinct from normative social values or 'mainstream' culture through their particular interests and practices, through what they are, what they do and where they do it. They come in many different forms, from teds and skinheads to skateboarders, clubbers, New Age travellers, graffiti artists and comic book fans.

The Subcultures Reader brings together key writings on subcultures, beginning with the early work of the Chicago School on 'deviant' social groups such as gangs and taxi-dancers, and research from the Centre for Contemporary Cultural Studies at the University of Birmingham during the 1970s on working-class youth cultures and punks. In this fully revised and updated second edition, these classic texts are combined with essential contemporary writings on a variety of subcultural formations defined through their social position, their styles and language, their bodies and their sexuality, their music and their media. Subcultures can be local and face-to-face; but they can also be global, mediated and 'virtual'. This new edition gives expression to the rich diversity of subcultural locations, from underworlds, bohemias and micro-communities to scenes, 'tribes' and the 'global underground'.

The chapters in this Reader are grouped into thematic sections, each with a comprehensive introduction by Ken Gelder. There is also a new general introduction that traces the historical development and key concerns of subcultural studies.

First edition (1997) edited by Ken Gelder and Sarah Thornton

Hb: 0-415-34415-8
Pb: 0-415-34416-6

Available at all good bookshops
For ordering and further information please visit:
www.routledge.com